797,885 Books
are available to read at

www.ForgottenBooks.com

Forgotten Books' App
Available for mobile, tablet & eReader

ISBN 978-1-331-88912-0
PIBN 10250206

This book is a reproduction of an important historical work. Forgotten Books uses state-of-the-art technology to digitally reconstruct the work, preserving the original format whilst repairing imperfections present in the aged copy. In rare cases, an imperfection in the original, such as a blemish or missing page, may be replicated in our edition. We do, however, repair the vast majority of imperfections successfully; any imperfections that remain are intentionally left to preserve the state of such historical works.

Forgotten Books is a registered trademark of FB &c Ltd.
Copyright © 2017 FB &c Ltd.
FB &c Ltd, Dalton House, 60 Windsor Avenue, London, SW19 2RR.
Company number 08720141. Registered in England and Wales.

For support please visit www.forgottenbooks.com

1 MONTH OF FREE READING

at
www.ForgottenBooks.com

By purchasing this book you are eligible for one month membership to ForgottenBooks.com, giving you unlimited access to our entire collection of over 700,000 titles via our web site and mobile apps.

To claim your free month visit:
www.forgottenbooks.com/free250206

* Offer is valid for 45 days from date of purchase. Terms and conditions apply.

English
Français
Deutsche
Italiano
Español
Português

www.forgottenbooks.com

Mythology Photography **Fiction** Fishing Christianity **Art** Cooking Essays Buddhism Freemasonry Medicine **Biology** Music **Ancient Egypt** Evolution Carpentry Physics Dance Geology **Mathematics** Fitness Shakespeare **Folklore** Yoga Marketing **Confidence** Immortality Biographies Poetry **Psychology** Witchcraft Electronics Chemistry History **Law** Accounting **Philosophy** Anthropology Alchemy Drama Quantum Mechanics Atheism Sexual Health **Ancient History Entrepreneurship** Languages Sport Paleontology Needlework Islam **Metaphysics** Investment Archaeology Parenting Statistics Criminology **Motivational**

Camden Society. n.s. 31.

THE CAMDEN MISCELLANY,

VOLUME THE EIGHTH:

CONTAINING

FOUR LETTERS OF LORD WENTWORTH, AFTERWARDS EARL OF STRAFFORD, WITH A POEM ON HIS ILLNESS.

MEMOIR BY MADAME DE MOTTEVILLE ON THE LIFE OF HENRIETTA MARIA.

PAPERS RELATING TO THE DELINQUENCY OF LORD SAVILE, 1642-1646.

A SECRET NEGOCIATION WITH CHARLES THE FIRST, 1643-1644.

A LETTER FROM THE EARL OF MANCHESTER ON THE CONDUCT OF CROMWELL.

LETTERS ADDRESSED TO THE EARL OF LAUDERDALE.

ORIGINAL LETTERS OF THE DUKE OF MONMOUTH.

CORRESPONDENCE OF THE FAMILY OF HADDOCK 1657-1719.

LETTERS OF RICHARD THOMPSON TO HENRY THOMPSON, OF ESCRICK, CO. YORK.

PRINTED FOR THE CAMDEN SOCIETY.

WESTMINSTER:
PRINTED BY NICHOLS AND SONS,
25, PARLIAMENT STREET.

[NEW SERIES XXXI.]

COUNCIL OF THE CAMDEN SOCIETY

FOR THE YEAR 1882-3.

President,

THE RIGHT HON. THE EARL OF VERULAM, F.R.G.S.

J. J. CARTWRIGHT, ESQ., M.A., *Treasurer.*
WILLIAM CHAPPELL, ESQ., F S.A.
F. W. COSENS, ESQ., F.S.A.
JAMES E. DOYLE, ESQ.
REV. J. WOODFALL EBSWORTH, M.A., F.S.A.
JAMES GAIRDNER, ESQ.
SAMUEL RAWSON GARDINER, ESQ., *Director.*
J. W. HALES, ESQ., M.A.
ALFRED KINGSTON, ESQ., *Secretary.*
CHARLES A. J. MASON, ESQ.
THE EARL OF POWIS, LL.D.
EVELYN PHILIP SHIRLEY, ESQ., M.A. (*the late*)
REV. W. SPARROW SIMPSON, D.D., F.S.A.
WILLIAM JOHN THOMS, ESQ., F.S.A.
J. R. DANIELL-TYSSEN, ESQ., F.S.A. (*the late*).

The COUNCIL of the CAMDEN SOCIETY desire it to be understood that they are not answerable for any opinions or observations that may appear in the Society's publications; the Editors of the several Works being alone responsible for the same.

FOUR LETTERS

OF

LORD WENTWORTH,

AFTERWARDS EARL OF STRAFFORD,

WITH

A POEM ON HIS ILLNESS.

EDITED BY

SAMUEL RAWSON GARDINER, LL.D.,

DIRECTOR OF THE CAMDEN SOCIETY.

PRINTED FOR THE CAMDEN SOCIETY.

M.DCCC.LXXXIII.

PREFACE.

For the four letters now published the Society is indebted to Mr. G. F. Warner, who met with them in arranging a collection of the correspondence of the Earl of Carlisle which has recently been purchased by the British Museum. The first of them is valuable as embodying Wentworth's opinion on Gustavus Adolphus at a critical point in his career, whilst the last gives us his opinion of the Irish officials soon after his arrival in Ireland. All four of them have an interest as showing intimacy between Wentworth and the husband of Lady Carlisle.

The poem, which must have been written in the end of May or the beginning of June 1640, was pointed out to me some years ago by Mr. R. Laing of C. C. C. It has since been copied for me by Mr. A. Plummer, the Librarian of the College, who has been good enough to collate it as printed here with the original MS. There is nothing except internal evidence to bear on the question of authorship, but Professor Hales and Mr. Gosse agree in selecting Cartwright as the probable writer. At the time when the collected edition of his poems was published there was every reason to omit a panegyric of Strafford.

FOUR LETTERS

FROM

LORD WENTWORTH TO THE EARL OF CARLISLE.

[EGERTON MSS. 2597.]

---

g. 12,
632,
l. 76.

MY MUCH HONORED LORD,

Thorowe the favoure of yours of the nine and twentithe of the last moneth methinks I see the affaires of the house of Austria a little to quicken againe, for the intrenchmentt of the Swede[a] showes the others to be maisters of the feilde; and that soe many peeces of importance have declared themselves for Monsieur[b] asseures me France will not be in case to hurtt Spaine abrode having soe much to doe for himself att home, being a solitary Prince and a heire apparantt the heade of a Party aganst him. Soe it seemes Fiat[c] was a righteous man and taken from the evill to cum, which methinks the Cardinall should hardly escape. But, if I may prie into the Arke, I beseeche your Lordship, whie doe not wee sum way or other declare ourselves roundly and put ourselves in sum posture, at least in sum hope of regaining the Palatinate. That Prince seems to me on all sides to be in the lande wheare all things are forgotten. Oh my Lord, the house of Austria hath a roote, will up againe; the King of Swede can have noe time to make more then one faulte, and that proves irremedilesse, if it should

---

[a] At Nüremberg, where Gustavus Adolphus was facing Wallenstein.

[b] Gaston Duke of Orleans was at this time in Languedoc taking part in an insurrection with the Duke of Montmorency.

[c] The Marquess of Effiat, who had been ambassador in England in 1624-25. He had been superintendent of the Finances, and had done much to bring about the insurrection by his demands upon the estates of Languedoc. He died July $\frac{17}{27}$.

chance to befalle him, therfore me thinks still it weare well we be not all togeither swallowed up in the contemplation of his last battell at Lipssick; besides that in his successfull progresse hetherto he hath not presented himself soe lovely to us, as that we have cause to dote on him. And now, my Lord, give me leave to tell you how sore it presseth upon the zeale I have to serve you that my condition in this place affords me noe meanes to performe it, as I infinitly desire it might. In good faithe, one pleasure I have when I thinke of Irelande, and therin judge that imploymentt to have much the better of this, it is that I hope ther to finde sum pathes open for my thankfullnesse to walke in, and to meete with sum of your interests in my passadge. Beleeve me, my Lorde, I will with all diligence and perseverance treade the stepps which may leade me to sum happy issue, which may becum in sum degree acceptable unto you and soe hartely apprehende your commaundes your honoure or benifitt. that he must be a bold man at armes that setts them and me asunder. Till I manifest unto your Lordship this constantt truthe, be pleased to oblige me by your beleefe (whearin you shall never be deceaved) of my remaining

Your Lordship's
Most humble and most faithfull servantt,
WENTWORTH.

Yorke, this 12th of August, 1632.

---

c. 20, 632. . 108.

MY VERY GOOD LORD,

Ther is upon the way towards your Lordship a whole kennall of houndes; five cople of them are for me, nor was I ever maister of soe many before in all my life. I wishe they prove for your liking; thus much in therbyhalfe, according to the dialecte of a Northeren Cracker. Ther ancestors weare of thos famouse Heroes that in the feildes of Hanworth[a] and Wettwange[b] weare of the cheefe in sentte and vewe, and, if it came to a blacke hare, run doggs,

---

[a] In Middlesex. [b] In the East Riding of Yorkshire.

horse, and men cleare out of sighte, and the silly beaste was sure to die for it before she gott to the tow miles end. Your Lordship is left free to your beleafe, but thus much shall be sworne, if you desire an oathe for it; what thes thar oxpring may performe upon the Alpes I cannot be resolved by our huntsmen, but it is strongly supposed they will not prove *Pejores avis,* and then the day is ours sure. The subjectt I am upon is ritche and noble, and losse it weare to give it over soe quickly; but truly, my Lord, if I end not quickly I shall not see to write, soe as I must intirely assigne them over to ther good fortune and myself to your favoure, wishing sum better occasion by which I may expresse unto you how sincerely and hartely I am

    Your Lordship's
      Most faithfull and most humble servante,
        WENTWORTH.

Yorke, this 20th of December, 1632.

My humble service to my Ladye I beseeche you; for such is the speede and dullnesse of my sight as both conspire to give me noe leisure or meanes to write any more.

MY VERY GOOD LORDE,

  This place administers little matter whearupon to exercise the service I finde my hartte inclined to expresse unto your Lordship everywheare, which misfortune I trust my industrye and desire shall free me from the burthen of long labouring under and sett me in sum nearer and better posture to your affaires in Irelande, whear with extreame much comforte I flatter myself att least not to continue thus still uselesse and fruitlesse in thos lardge returnes towe your noble freindshippe.

I have written to my Lord Mountnorris to pay over to Mr. Heye for your Lordship's use the surplusadge of your wine customes in Irelande, your rentt to his M^{tie}_a deducted; but I am not a little troubled with the apprehension that he will not take itt for a sufficient warrantte for him to issue the m . . . . upon, as indeed itt is not, and soe your Lordship be disappointed. To helpe this the best I can till I can thether myself, I still call upon such of your servants as I conceave are intrusted with your businesse to hasten to your Lordship your warrantt from Mr. Atturney, which may be returned backe heare and see the booke ready drawen accordingly aganst his Maties cumming hether, when your Lordship willbe pleased to see it perfected, and past under the great seale. What they doe in it I heare not, but I will by God's helpe goe to the Atturney myself, and, if they have slacked, I will not, nor suffer him to be in quiet till I procure itt and send it after you. Good my Lord, let it not be any longer neglected, for it is of greate value, and willbe worthe your paines to have it finally and authentically settled in good forme of lawe.

The Counsell goe every Sunday to waite upon the Queen.[a] Her Ma^{ty} useth them with great grace and civility; but methinks is sumthing sadde and lookes very much paler than she useth to doe.

For myself, I am using all the diligence I possibly can to gett away, and shall, God willing, be in a readinesse to begin my jurney soe soon as I heare Captaine Plumley is gott aboute to Beaumorris with the shipp that is to transporte me. He is allready out of the river, soe as the next post that cums from Chester I trust to have the newes of his safe arrivall, and till then it weare to very little purpose for me to stirre from hence.

Wee heare ther is greate curtesyes passe betwixt your Lordship and my Lord of Hollande, and heare all his freinds make mighty addresses to my Ladye, but weather out of true respectts to you tow singly, or complicated with sum secrett designe to fortifie themselves the better to make themselves more able to ballance to doe the Treasorour[b] a shrewde turne, I conceave may in good judgmente be doubted; for I am one of thos that beleeve noe miracles, but that freindshipps which are to be trusted grow up *per media* upon sum noble precedent existent matter, wheare thos

---

[a] The King was on his way to Scotland.   [b] Richard Weston, Earl of Portland.

which are skiped into thus *per saltum* are for the most partte only to serve turnes and deceatfully temporary, and therfore ever to be suspected. It must be time and your owne wisdome which must discover this mistery, and therunto as unto lights much abler to discerne and judge I submitt itt, having myself noe other interest then to desire that all may succeede to the honoure and happinesse of your Lordship and my Ladye; and then in good faithe I am well pleased (that granted) which way soever itt be convayed unto you. I am sorry this day proves soe ill as will of necessitye keep his M^{ty} within doores,[a] and by that meanes I feare hinder him from seaing the parke at Yorke, which I have taken soe much care to reserve out of the Forest, rather for the honoure and conveniency of the place I ther held than for any private benefitt of my owne; for in good faith, my Lord, money is not the price with me of anything, but the kindnesse and love to my freinds, particularly to your Lordship, I confesse must not be denied whatever can be required, and in the power of

       Your Lordship's
         Most faithfull humble servante,
           WENTWORTH.

Westminster.
Indorsed: 1633, June 25.

MY VERY GOOD LORD,

  Whatever my occasions or hast be, it must not deprive me the happiness of still putting your Lordship in remembrance of this servante of yours, who will ever be the readiest to receave and the most carefull to fullfill your commaundes in the whole world. Hear I am the whilst in excessive labourre to gett a little before hande with my businesse, if possibly I may be soe happy, being to deale with a generation that have the pointes of ther weapon turned

---

[a] On his passage through York on his way to Scotland.

wholly to ther owne privates, but noe edge att alle for the publike; heare they are as dull as sharpe and eager to cut out for themselves in the other. I see itt is a maxime amongst them to keepe the Deputye as ignorantt as possibly they can, that soe allbeit not in peace yet he may be subordinate to them in knowledge, which I take to be the true reason that not any of them hethertoo hath made me any proposition att all for the bettering of his Ma^{tyes} service. I am purposed on the other side to open my eyes as wide as I can and dispaire not in time to be able to sounde the depthe they covett soe much to reserve from me. I finde all the revenew hear reduced to fee farmes and noe possible meanes consequently to advance it, and in the meane time greate matters expected, indeed impossibilities, from me in Englande, which is a wofull condition of a servant to dwell under the pressure of exspectation and be left or afforded noe meanes to dischardge himself from under the burthen of itt. I beseech your Lordship lett me in this, as I have dun in many things els, finde your favour, and be pleased to take me soe farre into your care as to weede out this growing inconvenience forth out of our maister's minde, in case you at any time finde itt to shoote up with him. There is not many that have the meanes to doe it for me, nor many the particulars wherein you may oblige me more than in this. I shall be sure to doe the uttermost that lies in me, for I have a hartte can willingly sacrifice all that ever I have for his Ma^{ty} (if I doo not deceave myself) with a chearfullnesse and faithe extraordinary; only I am fearefull, that whilst impossibilities are exspected at my hands, the best I can doe should not be accepted, nay, imputed unto me as a crime. My Lord, I will detaine you noe longer, further then to beseeche you to be confidentt I must ever inviolatly approve myself

    Your Lordship's

      Most humble and most faithfull servantt,

        WENTWORTH.

Dublin, this 27th of August, 1633.

POEM

ON THE EARL OF STRAFFORD'S ILLNESS.

[MSS. OF CORPUS CHRISTI COLLEGE, OXFORD. No. 316.]

To my Lord Lieftenant of Ireland.

How much you may oblige, how much delight
The wise and noble, would you dye to-night?
Or would you, like some noble victo^r, dye
Just when the Triumphs for the victory
Are setting forth; would you dye now, to eschew
Our wreaths, for what yor wisedome did subdue,
And though they'r bravely fitted to yor head
Bravely disdaine to weare them till you'r dead.
Such Cynnicke Glory would outshine the light
Of Grætian greatnes, or of Roman height.
Not that the wise and noble can desire
To loose the objects they soe much admire.
But Heroes and Saints must shift away
Their flesh, ere they can gett a holy day.
Then like to time, or book-fam'd Registers,
Victo^{r}s and Saints renown'd in Calenders,
You must depart to make yor valew knowne,
You may be lik'd, but not ador'd till gone.
Soe curs'd a Fate hath humane Excellence,
That absence still must raise it to our sence,
Great vertue may be dangerous whilst 'tis here;
It winnes to love but it subdues to feare.

The mighty Julius who soe long did strive
At more then man, was hated whilst alive,
Even for that vertue which was rais'd so high ;
When dead it made him straight a Deitye.
Embassadors that carry in their Breasts
Secrets of Kings, and Kingdomes Interests
Have not their callings full preeminence
Till they grow greater by removing hence.
Like Subiects here they but attend the Throne
But swell like King's Companions when they'r gone.
My Lord, in a dull Calme the Pilott growes
To noe esteeme for what he acts or knowes ;
But still neglected, as he useles were,
Or con'd his Card like a young Passenger:
Yet when the silent wind [*sic*] receave their breath
And stormes grow lowde enough to awaken death,
Then, were he absent, every Traffacker
Would with rich wishes beg his being there.
Soe in a Kingdomes Calme you beare noe rate,
But rise to valew in a storme of State,
Yet I recant, I beg yo^w would forgive,
That in such times I must perswade yo^w live
For with a storme wee all are overcast
And Northerne stormes are dangerous at last.
Should yo^w dye now that onely knowes to steere
The windes would lesse afflict us then our feare.
For each small Statesman then would lay his hand
Upon the healme, and struggle for Comand,
Till the disorders that above doe grow
Provoke our Curses whilst we sinke below.

INDEX.

Carlisle, Earl of, his payments from the Irish wine customs, 3

Gustavus Adolphus, Wentworth's opinion of, 1

Portland, Earl of, parties at Court against, 4

Leipsic, Battle of, 2

Wentworth, his opinions on foreign affairs, 1; praises his dogs, 2; prepares to go to Ireland, 4; his opinion on the character of the Irish officials, 6; poem on the illness of, 7

MEMOIR

BY

MADAME DE MOTTEVILLE

ON THE

LIFE OF HENRIETTA MARIA.

EDITED BY

M. G. HANOTAUX.

PRINTED FOR THE CAMDEN SOCIETY.
M.DCCC.LXXX.

NOTE BY THE DIRECTOR.

The document which M. Hanotaux has kindly consented to edit for the Society is one of considerable literary interest. Being prepared for the use of Bossuet in the preparation of his funeral sermon upon Queen Henrietta Maria, it enables us to trace the changes made by a great orator in the simple language of the material from which he drew his information.

As a contribution to history the paper is of less importance. Henrietta Maria's own story has already been told in the *Memoirs of Madame de Motteville;* and, though that story will help us to understand the position of the Queen in Charles's Court, it has to be confronted with many other documents before any part of it can be accepted as history. One part, for instance, which reappears here—that, namely, in which the Queen describes her interviews with members of Parliament during Strafford's trial—is so obviously absurd, that we are apt to pass over its real significance. She talks of secret meetings with rebels, who showed their confidence in her by coming to her, though they had to fear lest they should be arrested for their own crimes. The persons in question were, no doubt, men like Savile and Digby, who had taken part against the Government, but who were in no sense rebels, unless, indeed, Savile's part in the invitation of the Scots was to be counted as rebellion. Yet there is strong reason to believe that the words, incorrect as they are, convey a true impression of the Queen's feeling. It is quite a mistake to look on the attempted arrest of the five members as a sudden and isolated action. From the very first weeks of the Long Parliament Henrietta Maria was planning schemes of attack upon the Parliament; and, though the parliamentary leaders may have imported imaginary elements into the plot the mysteries of which they strove to unravel, they were perfectly right in their sense of danger, and in fixing upon the Queen as their most active enemy. Another point on which this document is clear is the feeling of the Queen towards Strafford. Writers have sometimes supposed that the Queen disliked her husband's great minister. Though this is true of earlier years, when Strafford felt himself called on by duty to object to various jobs on behalf of the Queen's favourites, it was certainly untrue in 1640 and 1641. In a lately-recovered fragment of the Earl of Manchester's Memoirs we are told that until the last days of danger the Queen was on Strafford's side, and on this, therefore, the assertion of the present document may be taken as correct.

That the House of Commons should be roused to special enmity against the foreign woman whose hand was to be seen in all violent plots against its independence was intelligible enough. It is also intelligible that a later generation should have felt kindly drawn to one who suffered much. The modern historian will be inclined to temper his condemnation with pity. If Henrietta Maria's conduct was disastrous to herself and to her husband, it could hardly have been expected to be otherwise. It is hard for us now to conceive what were the difficulties of a foreign Queen in the seventeenth century. At present a continental Princess who marries into the English Royal family brings with her a certain difference in thought and feeling from that which would be brought by a lady of English birth. But that difference is not great. The resemblances between the nations of Western Europe are far stronger than they were even fifty years ago, and they are growing stronger every day. In the seventeenth century a Frenchwoman differed from an Englishwoman on almost every conceivable point on which governmental difficulties were likely to arise. It was absolutely impossible that a Frenchwoman could enter into the ecclesiastical or parliamentary constitution of England, or that her advice should be otherwise than bad. To blame Henrietta Maria for leading her husband astray is simply to blame her for being his wife ; and, as she was only fifteen years old at the time of her marriage, this is only to transfer the blame to the politicians who overlooked the real objections to the arrangement which they regarded with satisfaction.

INTRODUCTION.

Pour un orateur sacré il n'y avait point d'épreuve plus délicate que de prononcer l'oraison funèbre de quelqu'un des " grands de la terre." Dans ce genre littéraire, sorte de compromis entre le libre langage de la religion et les ménagements des cours, Bossuet surpassa tous ses émules. Ce n'était point seulement par l'élévation de la pensée, la pompe de la phrase, l'étonnante opposition des grandeurs et des misères humaines, et le majestueux balancement de l'idée divine planant sur toute son œuvre, qu'il emportait les suffrages; c'était aussi par le sentiment exquis des convenances, par la finesse des allusions à peine indiquées, et saisies de tous, par le tact avec lequel il savait renfermer dans un sous-entendu habile les endroits les plus scabreux de son sujet, et se réserver les bénéfices d'une franchise prudente et d'un silence éloquent. C'était dans ces passages surtout que ses contemporains l'admiraient. Tout pleins encore du souvenir du mort; conservant le plus souvent à son sujet l'inévitable impression des infirmités humaines, ils ne ménageaient pas leur enthousiasme pour un art qui les enlevait en quelque sorte hors d'eux-mèmes et qui savait dérouler sur le fonds étroit et quelquefois misérable d'une vie à peine éteinte, le riche et somptueux voile des nobles pensées et des paroles sonores. Une génération si polie, si précieuse, si juste appréciatrice du talent de bien dire et de dire ce qui convient, devait trouver au régal d'une oraison funèbre bien faite la saveur la plus exquise.

Tandis que Bourdaloue frappait "comme un sourd," au grand émoi de Mme. de Sèvigné, et " qu'il se jetait à corps perdu dans ces endroits que font trembler, que tout le monde évite, qui font qu'on tire les rideaux, qu'on passe les éponges," Bossuet, plus homme de cour, trouvait de ces mots appaisés qui n'évoquent la faute que pour rappeler le pardon, et ne laissent plus du péché que le souvenir pieux du remords et de la pénitence.

Certes la vérité des oraisons funèbres n'est par la vérité de l'histoire. L'histoire cependant ne doit pas dédaigner les renseignements qu'elle peut rencontrer en les lisant. Sans compter que le jugement des hommes considérables qui les ont composées mérite souvent d'échapper un soupçon que la nécessité de la louange peut faire jeter sur elles, il est des faits qu'un homme et qu'un prêtre ne peut taire ni faire semblant d'ignorer. Il y a une opinion générale qui s'impose à l'orateur parcequ'elle est celle de l'auditoire. Ce serait mal connaître le grand Condé que de ne savoir pas comment on le louait de son temps, et dans quels termes un Bossuet pouvait le louer.

Cependant, si à la lecture d'un de ces panégyriques on pouvait joindre la connaissance des renseignements exacts sur lesquels l'orateur sacré a fondé son opinion; si l'on pouvait connaître la mine d'où il a tiré tant de nobles endroits que brillent dans son discours; si l'on pouvait compter ceux qu'il a dédaignés et laissés dans l'ombre; si l'on pouvait assister en quelque sorte a ce travail intime qui du bloc informe a su tirer l'admirable statue du héros, certes l'intérêt historique, comme l'intérêt littéraire, se trouverait singulièrement accru.

De pareilles fortunes littéraires sont rares. C'en est une de cette sorte que nous offrons au lecteur. Nous publions aujourd'hui pour la première fois le Mémoire que Madame de Motteville rédigea sur l'ordre de Henriette d'Angleterre pour servir à l'oraison funèbre

INTRODUCTION.

de la mére de celle-ci, Henriette-Marie de France, femme de Charles Ier. Cette oraison funèbre fut prononcée par Bossuet le 16 Novembre 1669, en l'Eglise des rèligieuses de Ste. Marie de Chaillot, où le cœur de la reine d'Angleterre avait été déposé.

Madame de Motteville[a] était la niéce d'un poëte.[b] Ses contemporains n'ignoraient pas " qu'elle avait autant d'esprit que lui et qu'elle écrivait aussi bien en prose qu'il avait fait en vers."[c] Madame de Motteville, amie et confidente de la reine Anne d'Autriche, était plus que personne au courant des faits particuliers qui s'étaient passés dans la cour de la Reine Régente. Il est inutile d'insister sur ce point. Ses *Mémoires*, publiés au XVIII[e] siécle, nous apprennent assez ce que son esprit avait gardé de remarques curieuses et de souvenirs exacts. Elle avait connu également la veuve de Charles Ier et, comme elle le dit elle-même, " avait approché familièrement de cette Reine malheureuse." Il est donc naturel qu'au moment où l'on songeait à glorifier dans la chaire chrétienne les malheurs et les vertus de la princesse défunte, on se soit adressé de préférence, pour obtenir des renseignements précis sur elle, à Madame de Motteville.

Le Mémoire qu'elle rédigea à la demande de Madame Henriette

---

[a] Née en 1621, morte en 1689. Fille de Pierre Bertaud et niéce de Jean Bertaud, évêque de Séez. Elle fut dès l'age de 7 ans placée près d'Anne d'Autriche, et devint plus tard sa confidente intime. Elle épousa, en 1639, Langlois de Motteville, premier président de la cour des Comptes de Normandie.

[b] Jean Bertaud fut l'un des plus célèbres adeptes de l'école de Ronsard. Il fut premier aumônier de Marie de Médicis, évêque de Séez, et mourut en 1611. Boileau l'a ménagé plus que son maitre Ronsard :—

" Ce poëte orgueilleux trébuché de si haut
Rendit plus retenu Desportes et Bertaud."
Art Poët. ch. I. ii.

[c] Voir la note du temps ajoutée au Portrait de la Reine-Mère fait par Madame de Motteville, dans Galerie des Portraits de Mdlle. de Montpensier, édit de Barthélemy, 1860, p. 180.

ne doit pas se confondre avec le récit des Révolutions d'Angleterre, qui a trouvé place dans ses Mémoires. Les faits et les appréciations générales émanant d'une mème personne et s'appliquant à un même objet ne diffèrent pas certainement d'une façon considérable. Mais les détails et la rédaction n'out rien de commun.

Il n'y a pas lieu de douter qu'en écrivant ces lignes qui devaient passer sous les yeux de M. de Condom, Madame de Motteville ait fait le possible pour s'élever en quelque sorte au dessus d'elle-même. Le ton de l'oraison funèbre l'a gagné, autant qu'il était compatible avec la liberté d'allure et la naïveté d'impression qui fait le fonds même de son talent. Il y a quelques faits qu'elle même connaissait et qu'elle a voulu taire. Il en est d'autres sur lesquels elle a insisté. Si l'on compare ce chapitre avec celui qu'elle a inséré dans ses *Mémoires*, on remarquera qu'elle a su mettre dans le portrait de la Reine quelquechose de plus grave, dans le récit de ses malheurs quelquechose de plus ému; mais qu'elle a fondu en les adoucissant d'avantage les traits du caractère et les nuances particulières de la personnalité qu'elle avait mieux burinés dans son autre ouvrage.

Il y aura profit à voir ainsi, sous ces deux faces diverses, le portrait d'une Reine que l'Histoire de France et l'Histoire d'Angleterre peuvent revendiquer toutes deux avec honneur.

Mais ce qui donne au document que nous publions un intérêt de premier ordre, c'est, comme nous l'indiquions en débutant, la comparaison qu'il permet de faire désormais entre l'oraison funèbre de Bossuet et les renseignements qu'on lui avait mis entre les mains.

Le grand orateur a souvent suivi pied à pied le récit de la dame de compagnie. C'est d'une de ces remarques naïves, d'une de ces phrases sans prétention qu'il part en quelque sorte, à chaque instant, et prend son vol vers les plus hauts sommets de l'éloquence et de la poësie. Il a tiré parti de bien des traits que Madame de

Motteville avec une sagacité remarquable indiquait et soulignait même.[a] Mais lui, de quelle aile il emporte leur élan, jusque dans les cieux.

La littérature ne saurait fournir de plus curieux sujet d'étude. Bossuet apparait surtout ici comme grand écrivain. La mystérieuse grandeur que son style jette sur tout ce qu'il touche montre combien cet homme avait *le don;* et de quelle sorte d'émotion intime, personnelle, et subjective était fait son génie.

On voit, à la lecture de ces deux pièces, que par la méditation et l'étude l'orateur finissait par s'abstraire pour ainsi dire de son sujet, et qu'il ne conservait plus du sentiment de la réalité que ce qui était nécessaire pour que ses leçons restassent encore frappantes pour l'esprit de ses auditeurs.

C'était une autre Henriette, une autre Marie Thérèse, même un autre Condé, qui se levait peu à peu dans son âme. C'était la gloire et les malheurs des Rois, les divers succés de la fortune, les alternatives des splendeurs et des misères humaines, sortes d'abstractions morales et religieuses, qui devenaient son véritable sujet, et qu'il ennoblissait de toute la pourpre de son style, qu'il caressait, qu'il faisait belles, pour les jeter enfin, toutes parées, au pied de la miséricorde et de la justice divine.

La nécessité des convenances sociales conspirait avec l'imagination de l'orateur pour opérer ces métamorphoses. Sans compter la louange obligée du défunt, il y avait dans la composition de l'auditoire et dans l'assistance invisible ou présente du Roi Soleil des motifs de gêne pour l'orateur. Il ne pouvait satisfaire à ces exigences diverses qu'en se tenant le plus souvent au dessus de son sujet,—au dessus et en dehors.

Sans qu'il fut absolument contraint, comme le Simonide de la

[a] V. la note de la p. 26.

fable, de parler de Castor et de Pollux, il ne pouvait cependant se servir que de certaines formules dans la louange de son héros.

C'est encore ce travail et ces transformations que l'on pourra suivre dans le rapprochement que nos notes rendront plus facile. On y verra que l'un des plus beaux moments de la vie de Henriette-Marie, un de ceux qui devaient lui faire le plus d'honneur, a disparu dans l'oraison funèbre, probablement parcequ'on craignait de souligner dans la brave conduite de la Reine une sorte d'oubli momentané de ses devoirs de Chrétienne.[a] On y verra les traits d'un catholicisme trop fervent et funeste à l'Etat, exaltés au détriment de ceux qui faisaient plus d'honneur à son caractère et à son cœur.[b] On y verra enfin une personnalité trés vive, très remuante, très tranchée, dans le portrait de Madame de Motteville, éteinte dans le panégyrique sous une magnifique enveloppe de généralités pompeuses et d'éloges parfois peu mérités. On y verra enfin—détail plus curieux encore—les défauts que Madame de Motteville avait crude voir indiquer avec une franchise touchante et respectueuse. non pas seulement laissés dans l'ombre, mais transformés chez l'orateur chrétien de manière à motiver l'image et la louange des qualités absolument contraires.[c]

Il ne conviendrait pas de reprocher trop vivement à Bossuet cette manière d'arranger en quelque chose ses récits et ses jugements. Son esprit ne pouvait se défaire des idées de son temps, idées dont il fut peut-être d'ailleurs le plus éclatant interprète. Homme de cour il devait suivre les usages de la cour. Tout ce qu'il pouvait faire c'était de se souvenir qu'il était évêque aussi. Et certes il s'en souvenait, multipliant les occasions d'humilier au pied de la divinité les grandeurs humaines qu'il exaltait lui-même d'une maniére que nous trouvons trop pompeuse.

[a] V. la note [e], p. 27.   [b] V. la note, p. 23.   [c] V. la note [b]. p. 28.

Le Récit de Madame de Motteville dans ses *Mémoires,* les pages que nous publions ici, l'oraison funèbre de Bossuet, sont les trois, points d'une situation historique et littéraire qui fera pénétrer vivement le lecteur dans la connaissance du véritable esprit de la Cour et de l'Eglise en France au XVIIe siècle.

MEMOIRE

DE

MADAME DE MOTTEVILLE.

AVERTISSEMENT

Il nous reste maintenant à donner quelques détails sur l'original même du document que nous publions. Ce document est conservé aux *Archives Nationales de France* (Musée, Vitrine 58). C'est un autographe écrit tout entier de la main de Madame de Motteville. Les corrections, assez nombreuses et dont nous avons citées les variantes les plus importantes, sont bien de son écriture, quoique d'une encre différente. L'ensemble de la piéce forme un petit cahier de neuf feuilles de papier in-folio, du XVIIe siécle. Ce cahier porte en tête la note suivante: " *De Madame de Motteville. Mémoires que j'ai donnés par l'ordre de Madame pour faire l'Oraison funèbre de la Reyne d'Engleterre. 1669.*" L'intérêt exceptionnel de ce document, qui a été entre les mains de Bossuet, a motivé son exposition dans les salles du Musée des Archives. Nous n'avons pu obtenir aucun renseignement sur la façon dont il est entré au Dépôt National.

Il n'est point d'ailleurs absolument inconnu du public. M. de Laborde lui a consacré un courte notice dans son *Catalogue du Musée des Archives*. M. A. Floquet l'a également indiqué dans ses *Etudes sur Bossuet* (t. iii. 357). M. l'Abbé Houssaye en a publié les premiéres lignes dans un article de la *Revue des Questions Historiques* (Janvier 1878, p. 176), article consacré à *l'Ambassade de M. de Blainville en Angleterre*, et où la vérité des assertions de Madame de Motteville est, selon nous, vainement mise en doute.

Nous avons nous-mêmes manifesté le regret que M. de Baillon n'eut point fait usage de ce *Mémoire* pour son Histoire de Henriette-

Marie. C'est cette dernière indication qui a donné lieu à la publication actuelle, entreprise par le bienveillant intermédiaire et avec l'appui de M. Gardiner. C'est à lui qu'en revient tout l'honneur.

Nous avons cru devoir suivre l'orthographe du manuscrit, si bizarre qu'elle paraisse, parceque c'est l'original méme de Madame de Motteville. On remarquera que pour un grand nombre de mots cette orthographe figure assez bien la prononciation du xviie siècle.

Les rapprochements faits avec le texte de Bossuet sont empruntés à l'édition de Didot, in-4°, 1860, t. ii. pp. 1-13. Les citations des Mémoires de Madame de Motteville sont faites d'après l'édition de Charpentier en 4 volumes in-12°. Paris, 1869.

DE MADAME DE MOTTEVILLE.

Mémoires que j'ai donnés par l'ordre de Madame pour faire l'Oraison funèbre de la Reyne d'Engleterre.
1669.

La Reyne d'Engleterre aussy tost après son mariage eust a soufrir quelques chagrins quy luy arivèrent par imprudence des personnes quy avoient eu l'honneur de la suivre quy l'empeschèrent d'abord de cognoistre les bonnes intentions du Roy son mary et l'amour qu'il avoit pour elle, mais leur esloignement l'ayant mise en estat de se servir de ses lumières naturelles qui estoient grandes, elle jugea bien viste qu'il faloit faire son plesir de son devoir.[a]

Comme elle cognut les louables calitès du Roy son mary quy estoit honeste homme et quy l'aymoit, elle se dona entièrement à luy, et leur amitié a esté sy grande qu'elle a esté admirée de toutte l'Heuroppe.

Une sy cordialle union entre des personnes Royalles, une grande paix dens ce Royaume, et de grandes richesses, rendirent la Reyne d'Engleterre pendant dix ou douze ans la plus heureuse princesse du monde. Elle estoit belle, aymable, spirituelle, famillière, bonne, jénéreuse et liberalle; elle estoit honorée de tous ses sujets et tendrement aymée de ses serviteurs particuliers. Cette grande princesse

---

[a] Ce premier paragraphe a trait, à des luttes et à des imprudences vainement niées par des historiens modernes. Malgré ce que la matière avait de délicat, Bossuet n'a pu s'empécher d'y faire allusion, du moins en passant :—" Comme elle possédait son affection, dit-il en parlant du Roi (car les nuages qui avaient paru au commencement furent bientôt dissipés), ... " &c.—V. l'Etude de l'Abbé Houssaye dans la *Rev. des Quest. Histor.* Janvier 1878, p. 176.

a esté dens ces temps là le secours des exilés de France,[a] et il i an a présentement encore à la cour quy se souviennent de ces bontés avec beaucoup de recognoissance. Elle a esté la consolation de ceux quy en Engleterre ont soufert pour la Religion ; elle les a protégés par sa puissance et soulagés par ses Royalles osmones. Je luy hé ouy dire qu'ayant alors de grands trésors qu'elle guardoit elle mesme sous la clef, toutte sa joye estoit d'en faire part à ceux qu'elle vouloit gratifier, à ceux qui en avoient besoin et à ses serviteurs qu'elle vouloit bien dire ses amis. Un jour, voulant secourir une personne de calité quy luy avoit fait cognoistre sa necessité, elle prist elle mesme un sy grand nombre de jacobus que, ne les pouvant pas portter, elle s'avisa d'atacher un cordon au sac où elle les avoit mis et le trena jusques à ce qu'elle l'eust conduit derrère une tapisserie, puis avertit la personne à quy elle vouloit faire ce bien de l'aler querir sens que ces femmes mesmes peussent le sçavoir. Elle estoit sure dens l'amitié, segrette et fidelle à ceux quy se confioient en elle. Je luy hé ouy dire qu'il faloit que les Roys fussent comme des confesseurs quy doivent tout sçavoir et ne rien dire; que ceux quy les aprochent leur disent leurs nécessités et leur montrent souvent leurs passions, leurs haines, leur malice et leur injustice par les mauvais offices qu'ils se font les uns aux autres, et qu'il faut, tant par charité que pour ne brouller personne, ne redire jamais rien de toutes ces choses.[b]

Ceste princesse a vescu avec le Roy son mary avec une douceur et une defferance admirable ; elle m'a fait l'honneur de me dire

---

[a] Ces exilés de France auxquels il est ici fait allusion étaient les ennemis du Cardinal de Richelieu, et en particulier Madame de Chevreuse.

[b] On reconnaîtra facilement dans les lignes du portrait tracé par l'orateur celles qui ont été empruntées à ce passage :—"Elle eut une magnificence royale et l'on eut dit qu'elle perdoit ce qu'elle ne donnoit pas. Ses autres vertus n'ont pas été moins admirables. Fidèle dépositaire des plaintes et des secrets, elle disoit que les princes devoient garder le même silence que les confesseurs et avoir la même discrétion. Dans la plus grande fureur des guerres civiles jamais on n'a douté de sa parole ni désespéré de sa clémence. . . . Douce, familière, agréable autant que ferme et vigoureuse."

qu'elle pouvoit se vanter de ne l'avoir jamais desobey en la moindre de ses volontés. Elle a partagé avec luy et ces biens et ces maux, mais les derniers ont esté beaucoup plus grands que les autres. Elle a jouy de beaucoup de bonheur, elle a soufert ensuitte les plus funestes disgraces, les plus grandes infortunnes et les plus grands maux qui puissent ariver à une personne de cette naissance, et on peut dire de cette grande princesse qu'elle a senty les deux extremités du bien et du mal.

Quent les peuples d'Engleterre se revoltèrent contre leur Roy, la Reyne d'Engleterre entra dens les chagrins du Roy son mary, elle fut la confidente de ces desplesirs, et sa consolation dens ces maux. Elle n'espargna ny ses veilles, ny ses soins, ny ses peinnes pour le secourir. Quent le vice roy d'Irlande fut injustement ataqué par le parlement, la Reyne gagnea au Roy plusieurs de ceux quy se trouvèrent engagés à la faction contrère. Je luy hé ouy dire[a] qu'elle aloit seulle les soirs avec un flambeau à sa main, parler aux rebelles qu'elle fesoit venir dens une chambre d'une de ces dames, proche de la sienne, et ceux quy y venoient, quoy qu'ils eussent à redoutter leur propre crime quy les devoit faire craindre d'estre arrestés, ils avoient tant de confiance en sa parolle qu'ils n'en fesoient nulle dificultté. En plusieurs rencontres, cette grande Reyne obtenoit d'eux ce qu'elle desiroit, mais enfin ces misérables, par le déréglement de leur esprit, perdirent leur Roy et leur propre bonheur.

Après la mort du vice roy d'Irlande que ces babares firent mourir injustement, le Roy, pour apaiser les troubles d'Escosse, fut conseillé d'aler dens ce Royaume pour y tenir les estats. Il partit et envoya la Reyne proche de Londres, à Otland, l'une de ses maisons, avec les princes ces enfens. Pendant son sejour en ce lieu, les parlementaires mendèrent à cette princesse qu'il seroit bon dens l'apcence du Roy qu'elle leur mit les princes entre les mains, et qu'ils cregnoient qu'elle ne les fist papistes. La Reyne leur respondit qu'ils

---

Bossuet dit :—" On sait que la Reine a souvent exposé sa personne dans ces conférences secrettes." Tout le passage environnant est inspiré du récit de Madame de Motteville.—Cfr. *Mémoires de Madame de Motteville*, p. 196.

se trompoient, que le prince avoit ses maistres et qu'elle ne le feroit point papiste puisqu'elle sçavoit bien que ce n'estoit pas la volonté du Roy. En suitte de cela, pour la forcer par la peur à sortir hors du Royaume, ils firent semblant qu'ils avoient dessein de l'enlever.[a] Pour la persuader de leur dessein, ils envoyèrent un ordre de leur part à un gentilhomme quy comendoit dens le vilage où estoit la Reyne, de se tenir prest avec certain nombre de peïsans armés en estat de servir le Roy à leur comendement, et de les atandre jusques à minuit à la portte du parc d'Otland où il devoit trouver de la cavalerie à quy il luy estoit comendé d'obeir. Ce gentilhomme vint aussy tost trouver la Reyne, luy montra son ordre et luy demande ce qu'il luy plesoit qu'il fist. La Reyne sens s'estonner, luy comende de n'y point obeir et de se tenir en repos. Ces principaux oficiers ce jour là estoient alés à Londres pour leurs afaires particulières; elle envoye aussytôt les avertir de la venir trouver avec diligence et d'amener avec eux le plus de leurs amis quy leur seroit possible et de se rendre oprès d'elle avant minuit, puis fist armer tous ses petis oficiers et sens montrer nulle peur ala se promener dens le parc. Ces oficiers vindrent la trouver. La nuit se passa fort tranquillement et on ne vit de ce dessein que quelque vint cavaliers quy parurent roder autour du parc. Pendant le sejour de la Reyne dens cette maison, ells s'ocuppa à gagner des creatures au Roy et particulièrement le maire[b] de Londres quy d'ordinaire a grand credit dens Londres et parmy le peuple. Le Roy, à son retour d'Escosse, profitea de ces soins et de ces aplications; il fut receu en triomphe à Londres avec de grandes marques de joye et d'amour. Le prince suivyt a cheval et la Reyne dens son caroce, quy prist part à sa gloire comme elle en avoit pris à ses pennes. Mais cette tranquilité ne dura guerres, parceque les esprits des factieux estoient trop opiniastres dens leur infidélité.

[a] Cfr. *Mémoires*, p. 203-205. C'est ici le point sur lequel le document se rapproche le plus du texte des *Mémoires*.
[b] "Elle avoit encore gagné un maire de Londres, dont le crédit étoit grand, et plusieurs autres chefs de la faction."—Bossuet.

Quent cette princesse vit que ces soins n'enpeschoient point le progrès de la révolte, elle crut qu'il estoit à propos d'aler chercher du secours en Holande d'où elle en devoit atandre, car despuis peu leurs magestés britaniques avoient marié leur fille aynée, agée seulement de dix ans, au fils du prince d'Orange. Elle quitta le Roy avec une doulleur bien sensible, acompagnée de courage et de ce grand ceur quy ne l'a jamais abandonnée dens tous les malheurs de la vie. Elle fut une année toutte entiére en Holande, où elle estoit allée en aparance pour mener la jeune princesse à son mary, mais en effet pour trouver les moyens de secourir le Roy son mary; ce qu'elle fit en plusieurs manières. Elle mit touttes ses pièreries en gage, et de cet argent joint à celuy qu'elle obtint du prince d'Orange, elle en envoya au Roy de quoy armer quarante mille hommes, ce qui luy servit à lever des trouppes dens l'Ecosse. Ensuitte de cela cette généreuse Reyne voulant tout de nouveau aler en Engleterre partager les infortunes du Roy son mary, elle se mit en mer pour l'aler trouver avec onze vesseaux remplis d'argent et de munitions de guerre; mais il plut à Dieu quy régne sur la mer et sur la terre et quy ordonne de la destinée des Roys comme il luy plest, que son dessein fut traverssé par une tempeste[a] de neuf jours, la plus forte et la plus terible quy se soit jamais veue. La Reyne pendent ces jours-là, souffrit les frayeurs d'une mort continuelle et casy certaine, liée dens un petit lit, ses femmes oprès d'elle, liées de la mesme manière, avec quelques uns de ses oficiers et des prestres et des capucins qu'elle avoit avec elle. La Reyne et tous les catoliques en cet estat se confessérent tout haut, et l'horreur de la mort leur fesoit

[a] Bossuet a tiré un grand parti de ce récit du voyage de Henriette Marie, et de la tempête qu'elle essuya lors de son retour. Il y a ajouté quelques traits que la tradition probablement lui avait apprise. Il en a retranché d'autres qui eussent pu altérer l'image qu'il voulait donner d'une reine catholique par excellence :—" Elle se met en mer au mois de février, malgré l'hiver et les tempêtes, et, sous prétexte de conduire en Hollande la princesse royale, sa fille ainée, qui avait été mariée à Guillaume Prince d'Orange, elle va pour engager les Etats dans les intérêts du Roi, lui gagner des officiers, lui amener des munitions. L'hiver ne l'avoit pas effrayée quand elle partit d'Angleterre ; l'hiver ne l'arrête pas onze mois après, quand il faut retourner

oublier la honte de publier leurs péchéz, dont ils recevoient l'absolution à chaque moment, croyant que celuy là devoit estre le dernier de leur vie.

J'ey ouy faire à la Reyne une estrange description de cette tempeste. Elle m'a fait l'honneur de me dire, parlant de cela, qu'on s'acoutume à la mort de mesme qu'aux autres avantures fâcheuses quy arrivent aux hommes.[a] Elle revint enfin à La Haye où le vent la forcea de descendre, ayant perdu deux de ces vesseaux, et celuy où elle estoit estant casy tout brizé et en estat de perir, sy elle n'eut esté jetée dens les ports de Holande, c'est-a-dire à La Haye. Elle fut quelques jours en fort mauvais estat et sens pouvoir marcher, mais cela n'empescha pas cette courageuse princesse de se remetre en mer avec les vesseaux quy luy restoient, et alors elle aborda heureusement en Engleterre.

Elle descendit à un petit vilage avec dessein d'atandre en ce lieu des trouppes que le Roy luy devoit envoyer. L'armèe du parlement l'avoit suivie de prés assès longtemps, pour la prandre. Elle vint border le vilage où la Reyne estoit, comme elle dormoit dens son lit, et luy tirèrent une sy grande cantité de coups de canon[b] que la petite maison où elle logeoit en fut toutte percée. Il falut que la Reyne se levast de son lit et qu'elle alast se cacher dens ces rochers quy estoient un peu plus loing que le vilage et hors de la portée du canon.

Après que les parlementaires, lassés de batre ce petit vilage se

[a] Cfr. *Mémoires*, p. 210.
[b] "Après s'être sauvée des flots, une autre tempête lui fut presque aussi fatale; cent pièces de canon tonnèrent sur elle à son arrivée et la maison où elle entra fut percée de leurs coups."—Bossuet.

auprès du Roi. Mais le succès n'en fut pas semblable. Je tremble au seul récit de la tempête furieuse dont sa flotte fut battue durant dix jours. Les matelots furent alarmés jusqu'à perdre l'esprit et quelques uns d'entre eux se précipitèrent dans les ondes. Elle, toujours intrépide autant que les vagues étoient émues, rassuroit tout le monde par sa fermeté. Elle excitoit ceux qui l'accompagnoient à espérer en Dieu qui faisoit toute sa confiance, et, pour éloigner de leur esprit les funestes idées de la mort qui se présentoit de tous côtés, elle disoit avec un air de sérénité qui sembloit déja ramener le calme, que les reines de se noyoient pas."

furent retirés et que les trouppes du Roy furent arivées, la Reyne se mit à leur teste et comenda l'armée. Elle y vescut comme un jénéral,[a] sens ancune delicatesse; elle mengeoit a descouvert et trettoit ces soldats comme ses fréres. En alant trouver le Roy elle assiégea et prist une ville quy estoit assez considerable et utille à son party.

Leurs Magestés britaniques se revirent avec une grande joye, et ce fut avec quelque espoir que leurs armées et leur argent les feroient surmonter leur malheur; mais touttes ses forces se dissippèrent et ne servirent casy de rien. Ils furent environ une année ensemble,[b] puis il furent contrains de se séparer, parceque la Reyne devint grosse et tomba par son chagrin et sa doulleur dens une maladie lenguissante quy ne luy permit pas de pouvoir demeurer avec le Roy son mary.[c] Elle vint à Oxfort, accablée de maux et de tristesse, elle y acoucha[d] de sa dernière fille, de Madame, que nous possedons à cetheure en France. Les parlementaires la suivirent en ce lieu et parurent vouloir l'assiéger, si bien qu'elle fut forcée de se metre sur mer et de se sauver en France, quoy qu'il y eust peu de jours qu'elle fust acouchée et dens un estat pitoyable. La Reyne Regente luy avoit desja envoyé à Oxfort, par Me Peronne, sa sage femme, vint mille pistolles avec toutes les choses necessaires dont elle crut qu'elle oroit besoin.[e] La Reyne d'Engleterre envoya l'argent au Roy son mary et nostre Reyne luy en redona d'autre

---

[a] Elle marche comme un général à la tête d'une armée royale, pour traverser des provinces que les rebelles tenoient presque toutes; elle assiège et prend d'assaut en passant une place considérable qui s'opposoit à sa marche."—Bossuet.

[b] Cfr. *Mémoires*, p. 212.

[c] "La Reine, qui se trouva grosse et qui ne put, par tout son crédit, faire abandonner ces deux sièges (de Hull et de Glocester), qu'on vit enfin si mal finir, tomba en langueur et tout l'état languit avec elle."—Bossuet.

[d] Il y a ici une erreur que Madame de Motteville n'a pas laissée dans ses *Mémoires* (v. pp. 184 et 212), et que Bossuet corrigea dans son Oraison funèbre. En réalité Henriette d'Angleterre naquit à Exeter et non à Oxford.

[e] Cfr. *Mémoires*, t. i. p. 184.

et receut cette princesse afligée avec toutte la bonté qu'elle meritoit qu'on eust pour elle.[a]

La Reyne d'Engleterre, en passant de son peis en France fust poursuivie de ses ennemis, et dens la créance qu'elle aloit estre prise par eux, estant à font de calle pour se guarantir des coups de canon, elle fit venir le pilotte; elle lui comenda de ne point tirer, d'avancer toujours chemin, et de metre le feu aux poudres s'il voyoit qu'elle ne peut eschapper.[b] Souvent elle m'a fait l'honneur de me dire qu'alors, se souvenant d'estre crestienne, elle s'en repentit, et qu'elle ne l'oroit pas fait; mais elle m'a avoué qu'en ce rencontre elle ne sentit rien de plus violent dens son âme que l'horreur que luy fit la pencée de se voir soumise à ses ennemis. Mais enfin elle aborda heureusement en un port de Bretagne.

Les premiéres années que cette princesse fut en France, elle receut toujours de grands secours de nostre Reyne, et cette princesse malheureuse en envoyoit au Roy son mary la plus grande partie, ne retenant pour elle que ce quy luy paroissoit entièrement nécessaire à sa subcistance. La guerre civile quy survint en France quelque

---

[a] Madame de Motteville a écrit en face de ce passage, dans la marge :—" Il ne faut pas oublier de marquer cet endroit à l'avantage de la feu Reyne mère, et louer l'union de ses deux grandes Reynes."

Madame de Motteville remarque dans ses *Mémoires* (p. 185) que le conduite de la Reine Anne fut d'autant plus méritoire qu'elle-même n'avait pas été bien traitée par Henriette Marie, dans les premiers temps de son mariage :—" Car cette princesse étant soutenue par la Reine sa mère (Marie de Médécis) lui faisoit de ces petites malices qui sont de grands maux à ceux qui les reçoivent."

Bossuet a mis à profit et ce passage et l'avertissement que Madame de Motteville elle-même avait mis en marge :—" Ce n'est pas que la France ait manqué à la fille de Henri le Grand. Anne la magnanime, la pieuse, que nous ne nommerons jamais sans regret, la reçut d'une manière convenable à la Majesté des deux reines ; mais les affaires du Roi ne permettant pas que cette sage princesse put proportionner le remède au mal, jugez de l'état de ces deux princesses: Henriette d'un si grand cœur est contrainte de demander du secours ; Anne d'un si grand cœur ne peut en donner assez."

[b] Cfr. *Mémoires*, p. 213. Cet épisode, tout a l'honneur du courage et de l'énergie de Henriette Marie, ne pouvait convenir à l'éloge qu'en voulait faire l'orateur chrétien. Il l'a passé sous silence.

temps après priva la Reyne d'Engleterre de ce soulagement; si bien qu'elle tomba dens une extreme misère, ce qu'elle a soufert avec constance et force d'esprit. Nous luy avons veu vendre touttes ses hardes l'une après l'autre, ces meubles et le reste de ces pièreries, et engager jusques aux moindres choses pour pouvoir subsister quelques jours de plus. Elle nous fit l'honneur de nous dire un jour, estant dens les grandes Carmelites, qu'elle n'avoit plus ny or ny argent à elle qu'une petite tasse dens quoy elle buvoit.[a]

Quent elle perdit le Roy son mary, elle soufrit une violente doulleur[b] et pleurant amèrement elle me fit l'honneur de me dire, comme j'estois oprès d'elle, que le Roy son mary avoit perdu son Royaume et sa vie pour avoir ignoré la vérité, et que ce malheur estoit la cause de touttes les infortunnes des Roys.[c]

Estant à Ste Marie à Chaliot[d] où elle a pratiqué beaucoup de verttus, nous l'avons veue prendre sens repugnance et sens chagrin le soin de sa despence quy a esté en certains temps fort petite, elle

---

[a] Ces mêmes faits ont donné lieu à un récit plus détaillé dans les *Mémoires* de Madame de Motteville. C'est le passage souvent cité qui commence par ces mots. "L'étoile était alors terrible contre les Rois."—T. ii. p. 104. Retz aussi nous a peint cette misère de la Reine d'Angleterre. C'est lui qui dit que ses enfants "ne pouvaient se lever faute de feu."

[b] Sur la façon dont la Reine apprit et reçut la nouvelle de la mort du Roi, il faut voir le récit des *Mémoires*, t. ii. p. 352-5.

[c] La réflexion que Madame de Motteville met ici dans la bouche de la Reine, a été reprise pleusieurs fois par Bossuet dans le cours de l'oraison funèbre. C'est aussi à ce qu'il nomme l'impiété des Rois d'Angleterre qu'il attribue les malheurs qui frappèrent ce pays :—" Que si cet esprit d'indocilité et d'indépendance s'est montré tout entier à l'Angleterre et si sa malignité s'y est déclarée sans réserve, les Rois en ont souffert ; mais aussi les Rois en ont été la cause. Ils ont trop fait sentir aux peuples que l'ancienne religion se pouvoit changer. . . . " et plus loin : " La Reine avoit bien raison de juger qu'il n'y avoit point de moyen d'ôter les causes des guerres civiles qu'en retournant à l'unité catholique. "

[d] Il y a quelques détails sur le séjour de la Reine d'Angleterre à Chaillot dans les *Mémoires*, t. iii. p. 387. Mais ils sont beaucoup moins complets que ceux qui sont ici. On y verra seulement que la sœur de Madame de Motteville dont il est question dans notre texte, celle que dès son enfance on nommait Socratine, était religieuse dans ce couvent de Carmélites et que Madame de Motteville en était la bienfaitrice.

en fesoit les contes, et s'ocupoit à cela dens un esprit de pènitence et d'humilité, avec intention sens doute de l'offrir à Dieu en réparation de l'orgeul humain quy acompagne toujours les testes couronnées. On luy a ouy dire souvent à Chaliot qu'elle remercioit Dieu tous les jours de deux choses ; la première de l'avoir faite crestienne, la segonde de l'avoir fait Reyne malheureuse.[a] Despuis plusieurs années elle lisoit chaque jour un chapitre de l'Imitation de Jésus, et quent ce livre estoit fini, elle recomensoit, disant que c'estoit sa noriturre journaliére et qu'elle ne s'en lassoit jamais.[b] Je scay qu'elle fit à Chaliot, il i a quelques années, une confession géneralle à une personne d'une grande reputation de piété, et que ce fut avec de grandes aplications et de très-solides desseins de s'apliquer au soin de son salut.

Cette princesse avoit beaucoup d'esprit. Il estoit vif, agréable et pénétrant. Sa converssation estoit libre et gaye, elle railloit de bonne grace, et pour l'ordinaire il estoit difficille, malgré l'inocence de son intention, quele prochain n'y fut un peu blessé.[c] Mais nous

[a] " Combien de fois a-t-elle en ce lieu (au couvent de Chaillot) remercié Dieu humblement de deux grandes graces ; l'une de l'avoir faite chrétienne, l'autre, messieurs, qu'attendez-vous ? Peut-être d'avoir rétabli les affaires du Roi son fils ? Non ; c'est de l'avoir faite Reine malheureuse."—Bossuet.

[b] " Aussi rappeloit-elle souvent ce précieux souvenir (de la Majesté divine) par l'oraison et par la lecture du livre de l'Imitation de Jésus, où elle apprenoit à se conformer au véritable modèle des chrétiens."—Bossuet.

[c] Il y a ici, dans les paroles de Madame de Motteville une légère intention de blâme qui n'échappera pas au lecteur. Il est curieux de voir que Bossuet a pris exactement, dans l'éloge funèbre, le contre-pied d'une critique formulée si délicatement: "Rappelez en votre mémoire, s'écrie-t-il, avec quelle circonspection elle ménageait le prochain et combien elle avoit d'aversion pour les discours empoisonnés de la médisance. Elle savoit de quel poids est non-seulement la moindre parole, mais le silence même des princes, et combien la médisance se donne d'empire quand elle a osé seulement paroître en leur auguste présence." Je m'imagine qu'à cette apostrophe, il y eut un léger sentiment de surprise dans un auditoire qui devait connaître le défaut souligné par Madame de Motteville, et celle-ci put sourire discrètement, malgré la gravité des paroles et la solennité de la circonstance."

Nous ne croyons pas inutile de mettre ici le portrait que Madame de Motteville a tracé de Henriette Marie dans ses *Mémoires :*—"Il faut avouer qu'elle avait infini-

avons remarqué qu'à mesure qu'elle avansoit dens la piété, à mesure aussy elle se retenoit de parller casy sur touttes choses. Les dernières années de sa vie elle estoit devenue scrupuleuse la dessus, elle examinoit ces parolles et paroissoit fort destachée de la vie.

Sens faire la dévotte, elle l'estoit beaucoup. Soit ches elle ou dens le couvent, elle vivoit toujours avec la mesme règle. Quent elle estoit à Chaliot, outre ses priéres du matin, elle ne menquoit jamais à l'oraison du soir et à complie. Une religieuse de cette S^{te} maison quy avoit l'honneur d'estre oprès d'elle et de la servir m'a dit que dens le dernier voyage qu'elle y fit elle leur avoit dit un jour qu'il estoit vray que despuis quelque temps elle se sentoit toutte à Dieu. Elle est morte dens un grand desir de vouloir mourir dens ce couvent.[a] Elle cregnoit la mort, mais je ne doutte pas que devant Dieu et avec son confesseur elle n'y pensast souvent, car despuis cet iver qu'elle a eu une grande maladie, elle nous a dit souvent qu'elle voyoit bien qu'il faloit pencer à partir.

Voila ce que je scay de cette grand princesse, et je puis dire de plus que dens les longues converssations que j'ey eu l'honneur de faire avec elle sur touttes sortes de chapîtres, j'ey toujours recognu en elle des sentimens plains d'honneur et de bonté envers tous et particulièrement envers ses domestiques. J'ey veu en elle non-

ment d'esprit, de cet esprit brillant que plait aux spectateurs. Elle étoit agréable dans la société, honnête, douce et facile; vivant avec ceux qui avoient l'honneur de l'approcher, sans nulle façon. Son tempérament étoit tourné du côté de la gaieté; et parmi les larmes s'il arrivoit de dire quelque chose de plaisant elle les arrêtoit en quelque façon pour divertir la compagnie. La douleur quasi-continuelle qui lui donnoit alors beaucoup de sérieux et de mépris pour la vie la rendoit à mon gré plus solide, plus sérieuse, et plus estimable qu'elle ne l'auroit peut-être été si elle avoit toujours eu du bonheur. Elle étoit naturellement libérale," &c.—P. 223.

[a] Il convient de rétablir ici une phrase que Madame de Motteville a effacée :

" Il faut demander au père Lambert les dispositions de son âme sur la mort, qu'elle crégnoit beaucoup."

Je ne sais quel est ce père Lambert. M. de Baillon dans son *Henriette Marie* a donné des fragments très curieux d'un Récit du Père Cyprien de Gamaches, aumônier de la Reine d'Angleterre.

seulement qu'elle avoit esté fort fidelle à l'amitiè conjugalle, mais que se souvenir occupoit toujours son esprit. Il m'a semblé recognoistre en elle[a] une grande pureté de ceur, ce quy se pourroit juger par ses parolles et par beaucoup d'honeteté naturelle quy paroissoit dens ses sentimens. Elle estoit cincère, parloit librement à ceux qu'elle estimoit, se familliarisoit beaucoup avec eux, mais sens perdre l'air de la Magesté. Elle aymoit la verité, aymoit à la dire et à l'entendre. Je n'orois jamais fait sy je voulois dire tout ce quy pouroit remplir l'estime que je conserve pour cette princesse. Je prie Dieu qu'il luy donne la recompence de ses vertus et qu'il luy pardonne ses péchés et luy face misericorde.

Ma seur m'a dit avoir eu avec la Reyne d'Engleterre de profondes converssations sur des matières de conscience; qu'en toutes elle a recognu qu'elle avoit une grande droiture d'intention avec des sentimens très honestes. Que son ceur estoit peur et quelle avoit lieu de croire d'elle que Dieu l'avoit sauvée des feblesses ordinaires de la jeunesse, que l'amour propre et la vanité ont acoustumé de produire dens le ceur des femmes. Elle m'a dit de plus qu'elle avoit remarqué que cette princesse avoit eu cette destinée d'avoir esté toujours servie par des personnes d'une humeur fort opposée à la sienne: Elle estoit vive et prompte, et celles quy ont eu l'honneur d'estre a elle avoient naturellement de la paresse et de la lenteur; que la Reyne avoit sur cela une patience admirable, et quoy qu'elle en soufrist beaucoup, elle n'en a jamais tesmoigné nul chagrin, du moins à leur esguard. Qu'elle avoit un grand soin de ses domes-

---

[a] Madame de Motteville avait écrit d'abord " une grande chasteté d'esprit et de corps." Elle a effacé ces mots. A propos de ces corrections, il n'est pas inutile de dire qu'il y en a plusieurs moins importantes sur le manuscrit original. Je suis porté a croire qu'elles ont été faites sur les observations de la sœur de Madame de Motteville. Ce qui tend à le prouver, c'est que l'appendice ajouté après coup, que nous publions ci-après et qui commence par ces mots, " Ma sœur m'a dit," est écrit de la même encre plus noire dont sont faites les corrections.

tiques et de les peyer fort ponctuelement des gages et apointemens qu'elle leur donnoit. Elle avoit le mesme soin des autres à quy elle devoit, et ma seur et moy avons remarqué touttes deux que cette princesse après tant de grandeur, vivoit en France contante et satisfaitte dens sa solitude, qu'elle estimoit beaucoup plus que l'esclat où elle s'estoit veue autrefois, car elle estoit destrompée du monde et cognoissoit parfaitement le néant des grandeurs de la terre. La derniére fois que j'ey eu l'honneur de la voir, elle nous dit à Mlle Testu et à moy qu'elle aloit s'establir à Chaliot pour y mourir, et qu'elle ne vouloit plus pencer ny aux medecins ny aux medecinnes,[a] mais seulement à son salut.

---

[a] Cette remarque a d'autant plus d'importance, qu'on sait que dans ce temps on accusoit les médecins d'étre la cause de la mort de la Princesse.

PAPERS RELATING

TO THE

DELINQUENCY OF LORD SAVILE.

1642—1646.

EDITED BY

JAMES J. CARTWRIGHT, M.A., F S.A.,

TREASURER OF THE SOCIETY.

PRINTED FOR THE CAMDEN SOCIETY.

M.DCCC.LXXXIII.

INTRODUCTION.

Thomas, Viscount Savile, was the son of Sir John Savile, of Howley, Member for Yorkshire, who was one of the earliest opponents of Wentworth, afterwards Earl of Strafford, both in that county and in Parliament. Sir John was created Baron Savile, of Pontefract, on the same day, viz. 21 July, 1628, that Wentworth obtained his first step in the peerage; his death occurred on 31 August, 1630. His son and heir, Thomas, became attached to the court of Charles, first as Controller and afterwards as Treasurer of the Household. Lord Clarendon described him as a man of an ambitious and restless nature; of parts and wit enough; but, in his disposition and inclination, so false, that he could never be believed or depended upon. Thomas Savile inherited his father's hatred of Wentworth and lost no chance of doing him a mischief. With this object he is said to have been the chief means of inducing the Scots to march an army into England in 1640; and the grave charge was brought against him of having forged a letter from some of the English nobility to the Scots Commissioners inviting them to enter the kingdom. His private confession of this plot to Charles gained him much favour; but on the King's coming to York, writes Clarendon, the county in which Savile's fortune and interest lay, his reputation was so low that none of the gentlemen of position there would hold any communication with him. His subsequent proceedings are best gathered from the papers here printed, the originals of which are preserved in the Public Record Office, London, and the Bodleian Library, Oxford. In May, 1644, the King created

INTRODUCTION.

him Earl of Sussex, but the Parliament does not appear to have recognised the title, which ultimately descended to his son James and became extinct in 1671. The family estates went through female descendants into the hands of the Earls of Cardigan. Lord Savile's seat at Howley, near Morley, in Yorkshire, so frequently referred to in these papers, is now a ruin, having been demolished in 1731 by Lord Cardigan to save, it is said, the great cost of maintaining it. Burke, in his Extinct Peerage, puts down Lord Savile's death as having occurred in 1646; and this date has been accepted without question by later writers. It is, however, clearly a mistake. In a paper here printed, dated in August, 1646, he speaks of himself as childless, his second marriage having taken place about 1641; at the time of his death there is no doubt he had both a son and daughter living. Local evidence also exists that in 1650 he granted a lease of the Old Chapel in Morley to the Presbyterians. The Journals of the House of Commons contain references to him as a living person of a much later date than 1646; and among the Royalist Composition Papers is a petition from him not thought necessary to give in this collection, which is undated, but is distinctly referred to in another document as having been presented by Lord Savile on 31 January, 1652-3. Scatcherd, the historian of Morley, sets down his death as having probably occurred in 1661, but no positive evidence of the date has hitherto been brought to light.

The statement at page 2 is valuable as giving direct evidence of the authorship of the Petition of the Peers, which has hitherto been believed to have been the work of Pym alone, but which is here shown to have been drawn up by Pym and St. John.

J. J. C.

PAPERS RELATING

TO THE

DELINQUENCY OF LORD SAVILE.

LORD SAVILE TO LADY TEMPLE.[a]

[Royalist Composition Papers, Second Series, vol. vi.]

MY LADIE TEMPLE, [November, 1642.]

I was verie much troubled at a report I had y^t yor house was visited wth ye plague, but am exceeding glad to heare so well of it now, as my Cosen Bland[b] assures me, by a letter from yo^rselfe, in wch letter shee saith you write y^t you are sorie to heare y^t I have absolutelie declared my self ag^t the pliam^t, wch I wonder at this time to heare, when all the gentlemen of this countie complaine of me to the King for being to affectionate to the pliam^t. And I am confident y^t Sr John Hotham himselfe will say otherwaies of me then you are enformed.

But it hath beene my fortune still, ever to receive worst usage where I thought y^t I had best deserved, and never more aparent then in the dealing w^{ch} (by misenformation I hope) the parliament hath done to me. To you I may wthout vaunting say, that if this

---

[a] Sir Peter Temple, of Stowe, married for his second wife, Christian, daughter of Sir John Leveson, of Trentham. Whitelocke, in his *Memorials*, describes this Lady Temple as a busy woman, and a great politician, who had acted as the agent and messenger of Lord Savile.

[b] The writer's sister, Katherine, married Sir Thomas Bland, of Kippax Park.

parliam^t have done anie greate matters for ye publique, ore are in a condition more free then other parliam^{ts}, God wch governes all things, and knowes all secretts, knowes this, that if I were not at first the onelie, yet I was (though unworthie) his chiefest, instrum^t to bring it to pass. I never so much as differd from them in anie thing whilst there was a syllable of the petition ungranted wch wee delivered at Yorke, and was drawne, as you know, by Mr. Pymm himselfe and Mr. Sollicitor. And so farr onelie wee were obliged by covenant amongst oureselfes. For there alterations wch they now desire in the Church, let my Lo. Say and Brooke witnes for me, if ever I was for it in my life; and therefore in a free pliam^t why it was not lawfull for me to vote freelie, according to my conscience, wthout to be made of ye malignant partie, I could not imagine. Was there ever anie good message wch they ever had from ye King but something I contributed to it? Was there ever anie violent one but I oposed it? The message at Windsor, where ye K. granted the militia, I drew (which I have often hard of). When my Lo. Howard and Sir Philipp Stapleton was at Yorke, let them report of me what my part was; what I did wth the King at Bev^{r}ley, when my Lord of Holland and Sir Ph. Stapleton brought the overture of peace, let them and all the courte report. The message at Nottingham, where the King offered to take downe his standard, dismiss his forces, and recall his pclamations, all the lordes know y^t I both persuaded it, and wth my owne bandes, by the King's pmission, drew it up. My Lord of Cumberlande's Comission I protested against, made my name be putt out of it, and where there was a clause to enable him to levie money uppon the countie, in the open assemblie of the gentlemen I declamed against it as being ag^t the law and subiectes libertie, for w^{ch}, as my Lord of Dorsit and others know, I was complained of to the King. Now I would faine know for wch of these actes I am forbidden to sitt in parliam^t and declared an enemie to the publique. Was I found guiltie of bringing up the armie ag^t the parliam^t, or privie to the Kings going into the Howse of Commons? Was I so much as privie much less psuading to his leaving ye parliam^t, and going to Yorke? Was I not against both his going ag^t Hull, Coventrie, and Warwick? Have I taken anie commaund in the armie in this unnaturall warr? Did I not retire to my owne howse (when the King broke up his house, so as my attendance and oath tied me no longer) in peace and quiett, and when I could do no further good, yet would not contribute to anie of the fatall evills wch must follow? Do I not at this time heere protect all ministers and others y^t pfess religion from ye violence of the times, so farr as to render me suspected to all my frendes? Now, my Ladie Temple, iudge y^t when men y^t have done the contrarie to all ye good y^t I have done, have done as much ag^t the meeting of this pliat as I have done for it, as much ag^t peace as I have done for it, have taken armes, commandes, ag^t the parliam^t, and still continew so; have given publique and violent counsells when I gave peaceable ones ; yet not a man but myself, that I know this day in England (without any impeachm^t or calling to answer), is forbidden the pliament howse, and stigmatized wth the name of enemie to the publique. I never yet could learne y^t ever they had anie thing ag^t me to balance all the good offices wch I have done, but these 2 thinges onelie: the comminge downe to Yorke w^thout leave, and contrarie to there order, and for what I did at Heworth Moore, in Yorkeshire, when the countie was assembled there by the King's commaund; to both wch thus much. The oath which I tooke as Tresorer of ye King's howse is flatt and plaine, to serve his Matie in y^t office in his howse and not to departe w^thout his espetiall licence had and obteigned first. As long as I could by anie mediation prvaile wth the King to let me stay at ye parliam^t I did stay when he pemptorilie under his owne hand, both uppon paine of my allegiance, and my oathe taken, charged me to come downe and do my s^rvice in his howse. I durst not forsweare my selfe, but came accordinglie and staied wth him whilst his household continued, and then went home; for I was shutt out of the pliam^t by a vote before, my offence being that I durst not forsweare my selfe positivelie to obey an order, though manie went contrarie to there order (no oath compelling them neither), wch for all that have no such sentence. For y^t of Heworth Moore, wch they declared me an enemie to the publique for doing, thus in breife:—Before my coming to Yorke the King had apoynted y^t meeting; and y^t morning I, finding that the devided people entended to have pressed 2 petitions contrarie one to another uppon the King, wch in such a mightie concourse of people might have ended in violence, and knowing that those who they terme the good partie, and who came fearefullie under my assurance and ptection, were farr ye lesser number, I called to me John Reyner, Mr. Farer, Mr. Todd, Mr. Rigeley, and all the heades of that partie, and told them y^t if they would assure me that there side would deliver no petition, I would take such order that the other should not. They repaired to there partie, and assured me there should be none delivered by them; and so wee went to the field, and finding Sr John Bourchier reading, as they said, a petition (though it was none), I, conceving he did it in ignorance of oure agreem^t, and contrarie to the will of the honest men of his side, tooke it from him. And now behold ye act y^t makes me an enemie of ye Commonwealth. I have beene long in these expressions, because I desire you would let them be knowne, though not openlie publish my letter. To the truth of all in it God is witnes, and men allso. Madam, I am

Yo^r faithfull freind,
SAVILE.

Commend my service to my Ladie Carli[sle and ?] Bedford, and all my frendes, and particularlie to my poore Cozen Carr and his wife, whose busines I am afraide may miscarie by reason of my absence from the courte, which greives me much.

The Same to the Same.

Ma.

I shall ever augnowledge you have done me the office of a frend, and in that way wherin I most valew frendshipp, that is in good offices to the parliam^t, towards whome, though I know my owne harte, how it is and ever hath beene sett, yet it is now a greate office of frendshipp to make one to be understood as he is. Comend my service to my Lord Sey and to noble Sir Ph. Stapleton, and assure them that I will never forgett ye publique nor these pticuler favoures (if it please God to leave me anie power). Tell my Lo. Sey y^t peradventure he may be as falselie represented where I am at the courte, as I may be where he is at the parliam^t. I desire but the same iustice from him there as he shall be sure to find from me heere, and to believe thus of me, that either I will see such an acomodation as I may live in court in the fellowshipp of noble, vertuous, and deserving persons, or at least not at all wth such persons (whome he may imagine) y^t shall beare sway. For anie honor to be done to the howse by anie augnowledgm^t of mine I shall never grudge, nor thinke I took anie honor y^t the howse gaines by me. My hart should second my wishes in comming to you, but y^t this bearer can tell you how strictlie wee are beseiged heere, so as not so much as a serving man, much less my selfe, can yet stirr one mile out of towne. And wch is most miserable, oure deliverance in probabilitie must come by my Lord of Newcastle's forces, manie of which are Papists as his declaration (wch I presume you have seene) will let you understand: all which doth leade me into the consideration of those unspeakable miseries which this once flourishing contrie doth now grone under. First Sr John Hotham's and ye Lincolnshire forces called to his assistance under the pretence of setling the militia and seazing of delinquents, this countie (I will speake faithfullie) hath been robbed of and impoverished above a hundred thowsand pound wthin this little space, and manie licentious plunderings and villanies committed as are incredible, and wch I am loth to name, because done under the sacred name of parliament; and to say truth according to there power, much after the same manner done by oures. And to remedie all this and to make the mesure of there suffrings full the loosing side is glad to call in my Lord of Newcastle wth 6,000 men qualified as aforesaid; and padventure my Lord of Derbie allso, if t'other be not sufficient, will be called in allso, to do as much for the one part as hath allreadie been don to the other, and so leave no one pson between them that shall not be made miserable, ruined, and undone, besides an occasion given the Romanistes to assemble in a bodie together. For preventing of this miserie I am now as active as I can; and if I can prevaile and y^t anie reason will satisfie the parliam^t forces, wee will endure it rather than admitt this cure, wch being effected or attempted to my power, if I can gett by anie meanes away, you shall see me shortlie after; and in the meane space I will be preparing and shall ever rest

Your faithfull frend and servant.

The Same to the Same.

Madam, [December, 1642.]

I did receive youre letter, which was dated the 29 of Octob. uppon the 10 of November, so it had a verie slow passage. All letters are now opened, so I am glad to disguise my hand neither with superscription nor subscription; the bearer will know who to deliver it unto, and you will then easilie guess from whome it comes. You desire to know what my aimes and intentions are, that my frendes may do me service. I answer, the same they ever was; since you let in my Lord Lowden, I would not have the K. trample on ye pliam^t nor the pliament lessen him so much as to make a way for the people to rule us all. I hate papists so much as I would not have the King necessetated to use them for his defence, nor owe anie obligation unto them. I love religion so well as I would not have it putt to the hazard of a battle. I love libertie so much that I would not trust it in the handes of a conqueror. For as much as I love the King, I should not be glad he beate the pliam^t, though they were in the wrong. I would do all good offices I could for the parliam^t, and me thinkes I could do manie wthout loosing either my conscience or my master. If they would give me leave and if I might uppon those faire and Christian termes, I would be glad to come to my house at London, where I should be able to enlarge myselfe further then now I dare where nothing can pass wthout search. Madam, you see, as I ever did, that I speake freelie, and not as biased nor enclined by the pliam^{ts} success; for wee heere are assured the K. is prosperous at this time neere London. The Q.^{a} wee heare, last night landed at Newcastle with great supplies from Denmarke. My Lo. of Newcastle and wee heere have almost ten thousand men together; and yet my desires are still the same to have no conquests of either side, nor shall ever desire to live to see the ruine of an English parliam^t. I will say it once againe, if I may safelie and honorablie come to London, I doupt not but they shall find there worst frend is not com.

Since I writt first unto you Mr. Hotham (when I litle expected such a comand) by a command from ye parliam^t, as he saith, hath seased on my howse, and all I have, to the valew of som 1,300l. in money and goodes, and yet threatens to deface the carcase of Howley. Whether I have deserved this usage God will determine one day, and how iust it is the aughters will feele.

I am infinitelie glad, for all this that my Cleopatra is recovered, that all youres are well, and would be mightie glad to see both my cozen Carrs.

[Cover addressed: " For La. Te. Lincolne Ins feildes."]

---

^{a} The Queen landed from Holland at Bridlington at the end of Feb. 1643.

The King to the Earl of Newcastle.

[Draft in the handwriting of Sir Edward Nicholas. Clarendon MSS. 1682.]

Rt. Trusty,

Having receav[ed] and perused the charge against our right trusty, the Lo[rd] V[iscount] Savile, and being resolved ourselfe in person to hear him answer to the same: our w[ill] and command is that you forthwith give order to the Governor of Newark for his present release, and because the wayes are full of souldiers we will that you cause the said governor to allow such a convoye to conduct him hither as he shall desire to prevent him being intercepted by any forces of the rebells, for which.

Given Oxon.
13° Maii, 1643.

E. Newcastle.

Informations against the Lord Viscount Savile.

[Clarendon MSS. 1688.]

First it is affirmed by gentlemen of quality and will bee proued that hee before my cominge into the country, and when the enemy had confined them to the city of Yorke, his publique vote and opinion was, that it was best for them and for the peace of their countrey to deliuer upp the citty of Yorke into the Rebells hands, or words to that effect, which I neuer heard of till long after I had conferred the place of Gouernour upon him, which begatt such a generall jealousy in most of the gentry, and besides such a generall feare amongst them at Yorke, that it shold be deliuered upp, that I cold not thincke it safe to continew him in that place.

Secondly there was brought mee part of a letter from my Lord Sauile directed to Mr. John Hotham or Sir John Hotham, in these words:—

I neyther left furniture of use, nor any prouision without doores, besides all my beare in my seller, are by the guards and others druncke of, soe as for the present I am compelled to bee here at the mannour of Yorke, and shall presume of your noble curtesy for the convoy of my wife hether, and protection from feare when shee is here as you were pleased to offer mee before. And I doe desire also you wilbee pleased giue mee a passe to goe to Skipton to her, or my owne howse at Howley, to provide it ready assoone as I can, for if you keepe Yorke soe close about as you doe wee shall haue but short commons here shortly. Sir, I hope you wilbee pleased so[a] worke about, as that it may bee in your power onely to dispose of mee, wherein you shall finde mee, both now and hereafter,

Your faithful friend and seruant,
SAUILE.

Thirdly, I send a letter dated the 24th of December from Grayes Inne from Wm. Risley to the Lord Viscount Sauile exprest in mistical tearmes which I leave to interpretation.

Fourthly, there was a letter writt from a gent. of quallity beinge at Leedes to Sir Marmaduke Langdale, being then att Pontifract, which amongst other things had this exposition: about a weeke agoe I receaued from his Excellence a command to send 30^{ty} muskitiers to Howley to my Lord Sauile's howse to bee commanded by some of his servants, which I did acordingly, and this day at dinner they came hether and said Sir Thomas Fairfax hath sent word that the howse and parke shold bee safe, and soe my Lord Sauile had given order to send them to their quarters, I pray you acquaint his Excellence therewith. *These ires h turned to gi enemy' place.*

Fifthly, I have received a letter from a gent. of quality from Leedes, which amongst other things is conteined as followeth· My Lord, I have received your Excellence his letter, and doe

[a] *Sic.*

conceive you doe expect from mee what I know concerning my Lord Sauile's howse, by any command from the enemie; the trueth is, it came not to mee as a secrett. If your Excellence send to Mr. Copley at Doncaster, my Lord Sauile's nephew, or M^r. Bonnicar at Howley, they can tell you that my Lord Sauile is assured from the enemy that neyther his howse nor partie shalbee troubled. And I heare that the enemy hath sent to see whether it was not fitt for them to putt some men into the howse, it lyinge upon a convenient passage from Bradford, etc.

Sixthly, I saw a letter from a gent of quality to the Maior-Generall Sir Francis Mackworth, as followeth: In this night, betwixt sonne sett and day breake, Bradforde men sent sixty musketiers, and put them into my Lord Sauile's house at Howley; they was brought thether by the Lord Sauile's steward, and it is thought with my Lord Sauile's consent. This howse is foure myles distant from this towne (meaninge Wakefeild), and in the way to Bradford. Three troopes of horse came with them. I sent to Howley to bee certainely informed, and they brought mee answer that it was thought the troopes were retourned backe.

Seauenthly, I received and have a letter from a gent of quality of the 17th of January, 1642, directed to myselfe, as followes, amongst other things: This morneinge one Elizabeth Cade, of Woodchurch, giveth this information to mee, that the last night about twylight some 250 foote and horse came to Howley, my Lord Sauile's howse, and so soone as they came, William Birkby and Michaell Midleborrow, my lord's cheife servants, did with all the kindness possible enterteine them, and the principall men that came with them where three of the Greatheades. And they that went to fetch them were Richard Burnely, William Sparlinge, and Richard Scott, all being my Lord Sauile's tennants, and Nicholas Greathead said to one Rose, an old servant to the howse, that my lord was now tourned to their side.

Eighthly, I saw a letter to Sir Edward Osborne and Sir Marmaduke Langdale from a gent of quality, as follows: That hee was informed the Lord Sauile's howse was taken, and 60^{ty} musketiers of the enemies put into itt; whereupon hee sent three gent thether to bring him certaine knowledge thereof, and they retourned it so, and that the Lord Sauile's steward did come thether with them, and it is thought with the Lord Sauile's consent.

Ninthly, it is confessed, if not will bee proued, that my Lord Sauile gave Mr. Hotham 200^{li}.

And if it bee objected that displaceing of him had beene sufficient to satisfy the peoples jealousy, I answere as these tymes are, wee had not need to give those that are likely to bee against his Majestie's seruice liberty to excercise their power, which would bee made worse by being displeased.

Answer to the Informations against the Lord Viscount Savile.

[Clarendon MSS. 1690.]

To the first, where it is sayd to be affirmed, and wilbe proued, that before the Earle of Newcastle's comming into Yorkshire he did publiquely vote to deliuer the citty of Yorke into the Rebell's hands: Its answerd that there was neuer any such thing put to the vote to his remembrance, neither did he ever deliuer any such opinion: but doth appeale to my L^d of Cumberland, and the gentlemen of that countie, for his justification herein, and 'tis to be presumed that my L^d of Cumberland is a man of such honor and trust that he would not have heard any such opinion from a person of the Ld Sauil's qualitie without acquainting his Mat^y with it, at least, if he did noe more, and he is verie sure that whosomeuer was earnest for my Ld Newcastle's comming in, could not be of that opinion.

For the E. of Newcastle's conferring the gouvernment of Yorke uppon the Ld Sauile, it was doen iust at his Lor^{pps} parting from Yorke to Tadcaster, and not known to the Ld Sauile untill the instant of his goeing; and when my Ld Sauile heard from his L^{spp} of this letter and other iealousies he did humbly desir, at Pomfret, that this gouvernment might be disposed of into some other hand, protesting that he should take it no way unkindlie: but my L^d of Newcastle seemed then soe well satisfied concerning the letter, and all other things, that he was pleased to say that he would offer my Ld Sauile soe much violence (as he term'd it) to continue him ther, whether he would or noe; and so he did retourne him to that charge with greater trust then he had before, and doth a little wonder that what then was not thought worthy any reproofe, should since cause his imprizonment: but my Ld Sauile complaines not of it, since this hath given him the opportunitie to cleere himselfe to his Ma^{ty}.

To the second, he confesses he did write a letter to Hotham: but it was with the privitic of my Lord of Cumberland for a conuoye for his lady and her servants, who was then at his Lordshipps house at Skipton, wherein he might say, to devert the ennymie from rifling his house, which was in ther power, that ther was at that tyme in it neither furniture of vallewe, nor provisions of beare, or victualls, which might inuite soldiers thether. And for the clawse in the letter, that they should have short commons in Yorke shortlie, he appeals to the gent. in Yorke, whether it was not ther designe to make the ennymie belieue they were in danger of famine, which they feared not, to avoyd an assault, which they feared; and then were directed on purpose, as can be proued, to brute the necessities of victuall, which is notoriously knowne they abounded in, to the end the ennymie might set quiet in that expectation, untill they were relieued, which was then assured to be souddainly, etc.; besides the Ld Sauile did acquaint some gent. publiquely at an ordinarie with that particular clawse of his letter and the reasons of it. For that other clawse, when the Ld Sauile desires Hotham soe to worke about, as that it might bee in his power only to dispose of him, it was uppon this occasion Hotham denyed the Ld Sauils sister, the

Lady Bland, to give any quarter to his house, because he was a man proscribed by the parliam{t}, and only excepted in his commission which he had from the parlm{t}. But told her, if my Lord would take the courtesie from him and not be beholding to my Ld Fairfax, nor any other for it, he would send to the parlm{t} for power to spare the house, all which wilbe made appeere by Hotham's owne letters, that there agreement was only for the saueguard of the house at Howley, and nothing else besides.

To the third, concerning Rislye's letter, he was a man sent to Mr. Sec{re} Nicholas to Oxford about my Ld Sauil's goeing to London with instructions, that if he could by his reasons make it appeere to Mr. Sec{re} that the Ld Sauil's goeing thether could be for his Maties seruice, and he might haue his Maties approbation, then he would goe, and not otherwise, and the token that the Ld Sauile was to know it by was this, either affirmative in putting in a chancerie bill, if 'twere consented to, or negatiuely if 'twere denyed; and of the truth of this appeale is made to Sec{rie} Nicholas he write[a] negatiuely. Soe the Ld Sauile understood his Maties mind and went not. Diuers of these letters the Ld Sauile receau'd, for he wrot manie least some might miscarry.

To the fowrth 'tis answerd that the Ld Sauile haueing 10,000{li} worth of plate, iewles, and goods in his house at Howley, he desired of the E. of Newcastle a guard of 30 musquetiers to secure the house, which was granted; but after that by a conuoye of horsse sent by Generall Goring, all the vallewable goods were brought to Yorke. Captaine Copley came to my Ld Sauile and informed him that Sir Wm Sauile (then gouernour of Leeds) wanted these men, and that the neighbors therabouts (who were molested by these soldiers) would rather take uppon them the defence of the house and parke then suffer soe much as they did by these soldiers; wher uppon my Ld Sauile wrot to Sir Wm Sauile that he might remoue them if he pleased. What the musquetiers sayd at ther retourn the Ld Sauile knows not, neither it is[a] much materiall that being no

[a] *Sic.*

profe; but sure it is the Ld Sauile know not of any such engagement of Sir Thom. Fairfax as is spoken of, and the euent shewes the contrary; for since they have both taken and defaced the house, consumed corne, hay, and all the stock, destroy'd both parkes about it, receaued his rent and reuenues, and this without any late offence of my Ld Sauile, who hath bine euer since a prisoner; soe as either Sir Thom. Fairfax kept his word ill (if he made any such promise) or the Ld Sauile, who was then a prisoner in Newarke Castle (and knew not that his house was taken untill long after), had a verie ill bargaine of itt, who euer made it.

To the 5th, 6th, 7th, and 8th, all which are onlie relations of certaine letters of unknown persons concerneing the takeing of the house at Howley and ther opinions, that it was done with the Sauil's[a] consent, 'tis answerd as before, being done after he was prizoner, and that he was so far from being consenting to it as that he did not soe much as know it untill long after it was done, and then receaved it as the saddest news he ever had in his life, loosing by it the bewtie of his house, parkes, and possession of his goods and reuenewes, which was to mentaine him and his. With what kindnesse any of the Ld Sauil's tennants entertained the ennymies, either for loue or feare, is nothing material at all to him, it being well known to all Yorkshire that many of his tennants and of other men's are fauorers of that cause, and doe pay euen his rents to the ennymies, which surely none will belieue to be done with his consent; but, to say the truth, ther are few in the West Riding (my L^d of Cumberland's tennants not excepted) who doe not in this case play the knaues. What he was that told old Rose that my Ld Sauile was turned to ther side matters not much, since 'tis likely when he was a prisoner many might iudge it was for fauoring ther party; but the Ld Sauile doth challenge any profe whatsomever that either in letters, treatie, or any other way, he did euer soe much as intimate a thought to desert the King's cause, for supporting which he hath lost all the estate he had.

[a] *Sic.*

For the 9th 'tis answerd after he had defended his house from Lowinger's assault, wounded him and diuers with him, he was commanded by the E. of Cumberland to assist him at Yorke, and his house was left in the custody of his sister, the Lady Bland, with these instructions, that the men in it should defend it untill cannon were brought against it, and then according to his ^{Maties} permission (given at Nottingham to the Ld Savile, Sir Edward Osborne, and Sir Francis Muncton) to compound the best she could. Our men being forced out of Leedes, they marched with their army towards Howley, a house that cost 30,000^{li} the building, and hauing at that tyme in it to the vallewe of 10,000^{li} in goods, plate, &c. The Lady Bland with much a doe obtained of Mr. Hotham (by promising a some of mony to the soldiers that were hurt before it) respit that it should not be plundred at that tyme; though, as Hotham said, it was beyond his commission so to do, yet he promised to send up to the parliam^{t} for power to doe it. This mony, 'tis belieued, the Lady Bland did pay uppon this extremity, and the L$_{\text{d}}$ Sauile will not denye, but he was glad of it, when he knew it, to haue his house and goods saued soe, rather then to be ruined by the ennymie; and this was a thing generally known or familiarlie debated at Pomfret, long before my Ld Sauil's restraint, betweene the E. of Newcastle and him, and in the presence of many gentlemen of the countrie, and neuer obiected as a fault untill now.

Lastlie, if the displacing of the Ld Sauile would haue quenched jealousies, the E. of Newcastle knowes how earnestly his Lo^{pp} was desired by the Ld Sauile at Pomfret to doe it for that cause, that gouvernement in his hands, if it were not for his M$_{\text{a}}^{\text{ties}}$ seruice being but soe much unnecessarie care and trouble to himselfe; but it seemes it was thought better in this manner to remoue him then at his own request. But my Ld Sauile is farr from belieueing this to be the act of the E. of Newcastle, and doth assure himselfe it proceeded from the wrongful information of some other personnes, he having receiued such assurances of the E. of Newcastle's good affection as that he can not in honor doubt of them.

Sir Edward Nicholas to the Earl of Newcastle.

[Clarendon MSS. 1695.]

As wee found in the charge against the Ld Sauile very good cause of suspicion *and ground for what you did*, so have wee receaved from him soe full and cleere an aunsweare as wee have not whereto to reply; but yet wee thought not fitt to accept his aunsweare as satisfactory till wee had sent the same to you and receaved from you your opinion of it, or what may be further said to it, which when wee shall understand from you wee shall then soone make our determinate iudgment upon it ; and therefore wee desire to heere from yow in this particular with as much diligence as conveniently you may.

Given att Oxen 5° Junii, 1643.

E. Newcastle.

Reply of the Earl of Sussex to the Charges brought against him by the King.

[Clarendon MSS. 1820.]

[January, 1645.]

It is most true that in my peticion I doe urge the breach of the liberties of parliament, notwithstanding his M^{aties} promise engaged to the contrary. But I add that I assuredly beleeue it was unknowne to his Mat^y, by which I meant that his M^{atie} conceived, that without acquainting the House of Peeres before, and desyring that upon such reasons such persons might be secured, hee might by his owne speciall command have done it without breach of priviledges of parliament. I did humbly conceive otherwaies, and that although his Ma^{ty} did not knowe soe much, yett it was against the essentiall priviledges of the House.

1. That I am very sory that his Ma^ty hath been so misinformed as that I should att any tymes deny the proteccion or vilify the power and jurisdiccion of the Lords heere assembled, which I both doe and shall euer honour and study to preserue. But, peraduenture, I may have sayd (though I doe not remember) somthing concerning their jurisdiccion as the House of Peeres untill themselves should please to declare themselues so, but never doubted they had now as much priviledge as if they were so, in regard his Ma^ty hath been so gracious as to have granted it unto them.

2. 'Tis true that whilst I was in the North the Marques of Newcastle, hauing by some malicious persons beene informed that I had a designe to sease on the Quecnes Maties person when shee should land, did sease on my person at night and hurried me to Newarke Castle, where I remained close prisoner 26 weekes. How many tymes I pressed his Ma^ty to haue a tryall, by many letters to my Lord of Falkland, I knowe his Ma^ty well remembers. How assuredly he was made belieue that I had such a designe against the Queenes Ma^ty doth well appeare by his Ma^ts owne writing to the Queene (which shee hath since told me) how great a danger shee escaped in not comming when shee intended to doe. At last my tryall was granted, and I sent for to Oxford to answer the Marques of Newcastle's charge, in which was not one syllable of that great crime I was committed for, but some (as I may modestly say) other fragments collected to make a charge against mee, which I answered in halfe an howers space to the full satisfaccion of his Matie, as in his letter to my Lord Newcastle hee expressed, unto whome my answere was sent to see if hee could reply unto it; who returned his Ma^ty a letter that he had nothing to reply against that answere, but should be heartily glad of any grace or favour his Ma^ty should doe my Lord Sauile; and hath most nobly and ingenuously since in a great assembly asked mee pardon for that commitment, saying he was ashamed to looke mee in the face, that he would with his life and fortune giue mee any satisfaccion he could, and named unto mee the particular persons that was the cause of doing me that

violence and the suggesters of that groundles crime. And I am confident I am, in the opinion of that noble Lord, at this instant as cleere from any suspition of disloyalty or disaffection as any person living, and therefore doe wonder that this which hath been soe fully allready answered, and, if there were any error committed, is since, by his M^{aties} sealed pardon as well as his verball, remitted, should nowe be questioned. But I doe not mencion the sayd pardon as to thinke that action deserved any, but am ready againe either to produce my old answere or to make another as his M^{atie} shall thinke fitt. I knowe very assuredly noe dishonour can touch me in that busines, which is so well knowne to many. And for the wordes that Sir John Hotham should say, I doe beleeve to be sayd because his M^{atie} avowes it; but that any man that knowes how infamous, how inconstant, how detestable a traytor that man was, I hope his words will bee of no value or esteeme. When he returned to his allegeance 1 knowe not, but I have assuredly heard that at his death hee tooke it, that all the pretences hee made to the King was but further to serve the parliament by him.

3. I doe say, upon my honor, that since my comming to Oxford, I doe not knowe whether Sir Peter Temple or my Lady bee living, and that excepting to my wife and for money, cloathes, and accommodacions for her, I haue neither written letter, nor received any, sent message nor received any from them nor any person living of the enimies party, which I beleeue fewe in this Towne can say besydes my selfe. But it was my resolucion to keepe my selfe soe cleere, as doubting how many evill eyes I had upon mee. But if this correspondence be meant by my Lady Temple when I was at York, with which I did acquaint his Ma^{ty} and Secretary Nicholas, withall, and which was lykewise charged by my Lord of Newcastle but upon his Ma^{ts} owne knowledge of the thinge, and Mr. Secretary Nicholas discharged, if yett his Ma^{ty} shall require a newe answere unto it, he shall be glad of the occasion, as well knowing that as often as that busines shall bee layd open, so often shall my integritie, sinceritie, and loyalty be manifested. And concerning

what he hath done by his agents he doth lykewise protest upon his honour, that he never gave direction to any person living, to give any such intelligence as in the charge is mencioned, neither did nor doth know of any that ever did.

4. Hee understands this to be that old peece of letter written to Captaine Hotham, mencioned before in my Lord of Newcastle's charge, and therefore does refer it to that answere. But how I may have been represented to the Close Committee, to bee theyr friend, and for what reasons I stay heere, I doe not know. But I am sure I gave no cause for it, for I protest before God I doe not so much as know who they are which bee of that committee; never received, never sent the least message, letter, or had any intelligence whatsomever with them; and upon this issue will he venture his life.

5. If the persons were named that I should goe about to corrupt in theyr affections to his Ma^{ty}, or the speeches which I should say were used by his Ma^{ty} against them, I should gine a more particular answere to this charge. Now only in the generall I must say this, that I have euer endeavoured to increase his Maties partye (as God knowes), never to diminish it; that it was neuer in my heart to doe so false and meane a thing as this, nor euer in my toung. I am ashamed to utter it.

6. There is no person hath been more bound to his sacred Ma^{ty} then himselfe, which both hee and his posterity after him, hee hopes, will ever with gratitude remember. All which is so notorious to the whole world, as that person must needes laugh at him, that should heare him say, his Ma^{ty} hath done nothing for him. And that he should speake of his Ma^{ts} person with contempt is the most foule untsults that can be uttered; for there are many noble persons, which I can produce, who in my private and most solemne communication with them have heard mee often and lately admire his Ma^{ts} great personall abilities, and particularly have heard mee say these very wordes, I protest, and before God,

I thincke and know the King himselfe to be a wiser man, and of greater judgment then any he advises withall. I can say no more but this, that my heart is and ever shall bee full of gratitude, for so many great obligations, which I owe to his sacred Matie; and that there is no man lining that is more thoroughly perswaded of his great and personall partes then my selfe.

7. Hee never did goe about to vilify the actions of this Assembly, nor to perswade any not to giue obedience unto them, nor did euer lessen theyr power, unlesse it were in the sense formerly expressed concerning the full jurisdiction, as if they were the two entyre Houses of Parliament. Concerning which I may have sayd somthing, which I cannot remember.

That concerning the perswading men to teare out and embezill the Actes of that counsell, hee remembers that in jeast one morning in the House, in the presence of the Lord Keeper and many other Lords, hee did upon occasion say, that how could they aboue know who voted them traytors if the names in our clerkes booke were not to be seene? Upon which by approbacion of the laughter of all present, my Lord of Douer swore he would take order for it. This was a mere jeast openly done, and noe more concernes mee then any other present.

8. That many things which wee of late, especially in his Ma^{ts} absence, have had at the Counsell Table, were of such a publique nature, as concerning the mais^{r}, the workes, the towne and such other things as all men both know, before and after all the matter; and such things peraduenture I might speake of out of the Counsell, as everybody did. But that euer I did reveale any counsell of importance to any disaffected persons, I utterly deny.

9. To the last, I doe soe utterly deny every syllable in it, as I will loose my life if any one bee proved. I never so much affected to be of this treaty as ever to open my mouth to any man living, or use any meanes to bee. I hope it is in better and wiser hands, and I shall have the fruit of theyr laboures.

Indorsed: Copy of A Reply of the Earle of Sussex, written in his owne hand upon sight of the Reasons given by his Ma^{ty} to the Lords for his confinement, shewen him this 28th of January, by his Ma^{ts} command by mee,

EDW. WALKER.

PETITION OF VISCOUNT SAVILE.[a]

To the hon^{ble} ye Com^{ttee} for Compositions.
The petition of the Lord Viscount Savile.

SHEWETH,

Whereas ye pet^{rs} estate hath bin long sequestred, and all his personall estate, goods, and houshold stuffe amounting to a great value seized and sold, and his house at Howley in ye County of York demolished, and his pson also imprisoned 26 weeks in Newark Castle by ye Earle of Newcastle, and afterwards sent to Oxford, and there imprisoned by his Matie, and now since his voluntary coming in to ye parliament comitted to ye Tower, where hee hath bin a prisoner for many moneths, and of late hath bin and still is by reason of ye incurable disease of the stone in ye bladder in imınent danger of death.

Hee therfore praieth (being exceedingly desirous to leave his poore estate unincombred with this sequestracõn) you would bee pleased to admit him to composicõn, and to take into yor inst consideration ye paps annexed, being most willing to submit to any thing the most Honble House of Comons and this Com^{ttee} shall determyne concerning him.

And hee shall pray, &c.

SAVILE.

rec^d M'ch 26, 1626 (*sic*. ? 1646).

---

[a] This petition and all the documents which follow are taken from the Royalist Composition Papers in the Public Record Office, Second Series, volume vi.

Michael Middlebrooke.

I humblie certifie whome it may concerne that in October 1642, at Captain Hotham's comminge up from Caw-wood Castle into our partes of Yorkeshire, hee seized upon a trunke of my Lord Savile's, wherin (to my owne knowledge) there was three hundred and twentie poundes in monie besides divers suites of rich apparell, and other things of great vallew, which trunke he found at the house of Mr. Abraham Hinchcliffe, a tenant to my Lord Savile.

Within a few daies after I received order from my Lord to [pay] to the said Captaine Hotham fower hundred and twentie poundes more, which accordingly I pformed, takeing two men more with me, and carried the fower hundred and twentie poundes in money and plaite and paid it to the said Capt. Hotham in Caw-wood Castle, according to an agreement betwixt himselfe and my Ladie Bland in my Lords behalfe. Upon the receipt of which somes Capt. Hotham did ingage himselfe to procure from ye parliam^t a protection and freedome for his Lo^{ps} pson and estate.

All which I am able to prove, and shall be readie (God willing) to depose the same, if I shall be thereunto called.

Witnes my hand,
Michaell Middlebrooke.

Kerkstall Iron-workes,
this 4 of Aprill, 1646.

Katherine Bland.

That in the behalfe of my Lord Savile I did treate withe Captayne Hotham and agreed withe him for the preservacon of his estate and protection of his person payeing him the some of a thousan poundes, wch was accordinglye payed and received by him. For Captayne Hotham himselfe att Leedes, in October 1642, confessed to me that he hadd received the some of 320*l*. in money besides apparell and other thinges of greate vallew, in a truncke of my Lord Saviles att the house of Mr. Abraham Hinchcliffe at Kerstall Abbey—the rest of the money wee agreed upon (Captayne Hotham being content to take that in the trunck in pte). I gave order to one Michaell Midlebrooke, a serv^t of my Lords, to carrye to Cawood to Captayne Hotham, which he did accordinglye; for not onlye by word of mouthe but under his hand he did acknowledge the receipt of it, and did ingage himselfe to procure a protection from the parle^{mt} or Close Comittee for his Lordshippes person and estate, which the said Captayne Hotham tould me he had power to doe. This agreem^t betwixt Captayne Hotham and my selfe was in Sept^{mbr}, 1642. All which I shall be readye to depose if I be theareunto lawfullye called.

Witnesse my hand this 8th of Aprill, 1646.

Ka: Blande.

Henry Anderson.

That being at Oxford, a prisoner, I hard the Lord Savile had beene accused for making a composition and paying certaine sommes of money to Captaine Hotham my sonne in law, whereuppon being afterwardes a prisoner in the tower wth Captaine Hotham I did demaund of him before his execution the truth of the said business, who then told me that he had made such an one wth the Ladie Bland in behalfe of the Lo. Savile, and had received therefore a certaine somme of money (what the particuler somme was he doth not now remember), and did allso declare unto him how he had disbursed some of the said moneyes to some particular officers of his armie.

Witnes my hand,

Hen: Anderson.

Statement of William Risley.

May it please you, att the earnest importunity of Sir Peter Temple, Knt., and his worthie and most virtuous Lady, I was overruled to take an ill journey in a dirty season in the latter end of a Michaelmas Tearme, about 3 years and odd moneths since, to Yorke, to the Lord Savill, haveing noble Sr Phillip Stapleton's letter to the younger Hotham to lett me passe (if pchance his forces mett me), whither when I came I was, with the postboy of Tadcaster, carried before the Earle of Cumberland and others for our examinacon. The postboy being first and apart strictly examined (as I understood after) whether I had any conference with the Lord Fairfax or any of his privately att Tadcaster (where then the said Lord Fairfax kept garrison), which, when nothing by him appeareing, I was for that night and p^{r}sent slenderly examined by them concerninge my buisnes, and occasion of my tedious journey to my Lord to Yorke ; and was dismissed with a small guard, but with many watchfull ieyes over mee, to the posthouse, my lodging, without any admission to my Lord Savill that night. And to my greate amazem^t was rushed upon about one or two of the clocke att night, my cloathes, bootes, and sadle, and my selfe searched to the skinn for paps and instruccons; but findeing nothing but a letter of the Lady Temple to the Lord Savill concerninge law buisnes formerly shewed them they left me for that p^{r}sent. I was, as soone as I stirred in the morninge, carried againe before the Lord of Cumberland and others for further examinacon, which held long, soe that I was not admitted to the speech of my Lord Savill till two or three of the clocke in the after noone, whom after some passages and enterchange of discourses betweene us found him most desireous to come here to the parliam^t (as I conceaved) with his severall attempts to breake from them att Yorke, but was hindred and p^{r}vented by their ielous ieyes over him in the towne, some attending him aloofe of with horses after him, when as we went out to take the aire. The Lord of Newcastle's horses alsoe being quartered in places in about Yorke, the day after I came into Yorke (as we had intelligence in the towne), which sumerie of my now weake and obsoleete remembrance (by reason it is soe long agoe) I humbly then acquainted the right hono^{ble} the Lord Say with all att my returne and the very same to the best of my now remembrance att th'earnest request of my Lord Savill, I most humbly rep^{r}sent now againe.

WILLIAM RISLEY.

Thomas Lord Viscount Savill maketh Oath.

That hee did not desert the parliament at that tyme when his Matie comanded all the members to attend him, which might shew like a designe to disolve the two houses, but long before when none but his Ma^{ts} houshold servants did attend him, amongst which hee was a sworne servant and bound by oath to that attendance, and at y^t tyme when there was noe outward visible appearance of a warre on either side.

But hee saith that on the 6th of June, 1642, hee was voted a delinquent for a supposed misdemeanor committed in May before upon an informacon to the House of Comons out of Yorkshire, to which hee was never called to answere, neither was it true as it was prsented, as hee is able to prove by good testimony.

That at his being with his Matie at Yorke, when hee had pvided himselfe of armed guards, hee did, at the desire of some of ye Com^{ttee} of both Howses then resident at York, as an acceptable service to ye parliam^t as they alleadged pswade the King to dismisse them as looking to like a semblance of warre, wherein hee p^{r}vailed wth his Matie, for which act hee was represented to ye parliam^t as two hon^{ble} psons then Com^{rs} from ye parliam^t did expresse unto him, and wch hee is confident they will upon occasion testifie. And when afterwards his Matie was at Beverley, intending to beseige

Hull, hee did at ye desire of another com^{ttee} of both Houses use all his power to diswade his Matie from y^t resolucõn though not with the like successe as before.

That when his Matie went to Nottingham to set up his standard this dep^t refused to goe wth him, but returned to his owne house, p^rsuminge for his good service aforesaid hee might have continued there in ye good opinion of the parliament.

But afterwards hee understanding from Capt. Hotham, then intrusted with ye parliam^{ts} forces, that hee was under the parliam^{ts} displeasure for ye misdemeanor aforesaid, unlesse hee would pay a some of money for a composıcon hee must proceed against him as a delinquent, the said Capt. Hotham assuring him that hee had an absolute power to compound wth him and all other delinquents in those pts, even with my Lo. of Cumberland himselfe, wherupon hee treated with him, and at last concluded and agreed to give him 1,000*l*. to ye use of the State, the which he paid and satisfied accordingly, and therupon Capt. Hotham pmised to discharge him of his delinquency and pcure ye parliam^{ts} protection for him also.

That p^rsently afterwards the Earle of Newcastle came with his forces into Yorkshire and therupon Capt. Hotham retired into Hull, and by that means hee could not pforme his pmise in pcuring this deponent's discharge from ye parliam^t; and not long after the said Earle, having notice of the said composıcon, caused him to bee app^rhended in the night with 200 horse, or thereabouts, under the comand of Sir Thomas Glemham and Colonel Causfeild, a Romish Catholique, and p^rsently carryed in ye night towards Newark, and there comitted a close prisoner.

That during the tyme of this dep^{ts} imprisonem^t the Earle of New Castle did goe in pson unto his house at Howley, in Yorkshire, and there upon a councell of warre, which hee then called, did seize and dispose of his goods as the goods of an enemye, and further did ın a sort demolishe his house, to his damage above 10,000*l*.

That upon payment of his said composıcõn this dep^t did send up to ye Lady Temple to desire her to acquaynt some of ye parliam^t

wth his resolucon to come to London, wherupon one Mr. Risley was sent downe unto him to invite him to repaire thether, the wch hee attempted to doe, but could not effect by reason of ye great jealously [a] that was upon him.

That after 26 weeks imprisonem^t at Newark hee was sent a prisoner to Oxford together wth his accusacon, the two principall articles whereof were for his said composicon with Capt. Hotham and for voting against his [b] comming into Yorkshire, all wch was shewed unto this dep^t from his Matie with intimacon that if his Matie should pceed vigorously against him it was not to bee answered.

That his Matie engaged him not to dep^t thence without lycence, in hope that at ye meeting of ye Assembly then shortly after being appoynted to come together, hee would deserve ye passing by of ye said offences and further merit such other favors as his Matie had pmised and intended to conferre upon him.

That the said Assembly being met, in wch this dep^t not answering his Maties expectacon, nor deserving (as his Matie was pleased to say) his favor and lenity extended towards him, hee was againe comitted close prisoner at Oxford for about 3 moneths and impeached againe by his Matie himselfe for the composicon made with Capt. Hotham, and for contemptuously speaking against and villifying ye acts of that Assembly; and thereupon an impeachm^t of treason was p^rferred against him by ye Lo. Digby in ye King's name, and a letter produced by his Matie under this dept^s owne hand to Capt. Hotham intimating his said composicon and his desire to have his discharge and proteccon of Parliam^t according to his pmise; upon w^{ch}, the judges being consulted withall and their opinion declared, it was moved in the open Assembly thatt hee might bee tryed by martiall lawe, but the Lords refusing to agree unto such a triall (hee being a peere of the realme), after some tract of tyme hee was released upon condicon hee should dept this kingdome.

That the very day after he was freed from imprisonm^t hee came towards London and voluntaryly (surrendered) himselfe unto y^e

---

[a] *Sic.* [b] *i. e.* the Earl of Newcastle's. *See* p. 31, *post*.

parliam^t, wch was long before Naseby fight, when his M^atie was in an outward probable way of successe.

That besides the composıcon afores^d the parliam^t hath ever since ye battell neere York seized upon all his stock of iron, one peell whereof (as hee is informed by his servants) was valued by the com^ttee at 1450*l*., besides his goods in London solde to their use also.

That his tenants, taking ye opportunity of his misfortune, destroyed his lands, wasted and made havock of his estate, and made it of small value, consisting more of stock then rent by reason of his iron works and tillage that hee managed.

That when ye Earle of Newcastle rifled his house the souldiers seized upon his writings and evidences, wherby hee is disabled to make ye certeynty of his title and estate appeare, but hath delivered in ye substance thereof to his best knowledge and remembrance.

SAVILE.

Jur. 27 die April, 1646.
JOHN PAGE.

LORD LOVELACE.

I John, Lord Lovelace, doth well remember that when I was with the Kinge at Oxford, and that the Lord Viscounte Savil was there, he knewe him to be in the Kinge's displeasure, and was for some times imprisoned, accused for treason, and the treason laid to his charge beinge for vilifyinge and speakinge slightly of that assembly at Oxford, and for compoundinge wth Captaine Hotham, and treatinge wth him about deliveringe upp of Yoarke, or to some such purpose; and for houldinge corespondence wth some heere at London; all W^ch I doe well remember and shall be reddy to verifie uppon occasion. As witnesse my hand this twenty-eight day of April, 1646.

JO: LOVELACE.

Thomas Lord Viscounte Savile maketh oath, that about the year 1634, hee being then violently prosequted in the Starchamber Court by some potent persons ill affected to him, did advice with his Councell Sir Henry Calthrop and Mr. Thorpe, a member of the Honourable House of Commons, to settle his estate in that manner whereby it might bee lesse subiect to those great fines wch did threaten him from them. And that his estate was thereupon setled in the hand of feffees in trust to himselfe for life the remaynder to his brother wch other remaynders over. And hee saith that hee was the rather induced thereunto by reason hee had no childe (neither yet hath any) nor possibility of any by his then wife, or probability of survyving her, shee being then in good health, and himselfe (as hee is now) much afflicted with the stone. And this dep^t further saith, that for more apparant evidence of the truth hereof, a treaty of marriage being with his now Lady (which was performed in the beginning of this parliam^t, and before theis warrs began), and hee being desired and desirous to make her a convenient joynture after his decease, did to that end submit his writings by which his estate was settled to the pusall of Mr. Beniamin Weston, Esqr (Father in law to this dep^{ts} now wife) and his councell, who upon his examinaçon thereof told this dep^t that they found that hee had then no power to settle the joynture desired after his death. Whereupon hee gave assurance and satisfacçon by collaterall security, wch was accepted. And lastly this dep^t saith, that his writings concerning his estate were lost, when his house at Howley in Yorkshire was plundred by the Earle of Newcastle since the beginning of theis warrs, as is sufficiently knowne to Sr John Savile and many others who kept his said House for the parliam^{ts} use.

SAVILE.

Attestat sup honore et spontanee jurat, 4 Augusti, 1646.

ROBT. AYLETT.

Statement of the Delinquency of Thomas Lord Viscount Savile.

That beinge his Ma^{ts} sworne servant, and long before there was any visible appearance of a warre, his absence from the parliam^{te} was occasioned by his personall attendance upon his Ma^{tye}, and when afterwards at Yorke his Matie provided himselfe of armed guards at a request of a com^{tee} of both howses then attendinge there, his Lo^{pe} did perswade the Kinge to have dismissed them, as havinge too like a semblance of warre, and afterwards again at Beverly did the like, and when his Ma^{tye} went to Nottingham to set up his standard he refused to goe along and retired to his owne howse, yet the 6^t of June, 1642, he was voted a delinquent by the Howse of Commons upon an informaĉon from Yorkeshire of a misdemeanor supposed to have been comitted the May before, and doth nowe depose upon his oath that that informacon was not true, as it was represented ; that afterwards he was notwithstandinge inforced by Captaine Hotham then in armes for the parliam^{te} to compound with him for that delinquency, who assured his Lo^{pe} that he had a full power from the parliament soe to doe, and not onely to compound with him, but with the Earle of Cumberland alsoe, and all others in those parts, to whom his Lo^{pe} paid 1,000*l.*, and was thereupon promised by him to have a dischardge from the howses for that offence; and then his Lo^{pe} was resolved to come for London, and for that purpose sent hither and laboured his freinds heere to make way for his returne, who had such incouradgem^{te} therein that he made two severall attempts to have left the country and come upp, but was both tymes prevented. And shortly after the Earle of Newcastle tooke the field and enforced Captain Hotham to retire into Hull, and sent a party of 200 horse under the comaund of Sr Thomas Glemham and one Collonell Causfeild, a papist, who surprized him in his howse, and in the night tyme caryed him to Newarke, where he was comitted close prisoner, and lay 26 weeks restraynd, his onely offence being his composiĉon made with Captaine Hotham, and for votinge against the Earle of Newcastle's comeinge into Yorkshire. And after this tyme of imprisonmente he was sent in custody to Oxford to the Kinge, and his l̃res intercepted that passed betweene Captaine Hotham and him concerneinge it, obiected against him by his Ma^{tye} at his comeinge thither, and the same produced that after some reprehension his Ma^{tye} gave him the liberty of the towne upon an ingadgem^{te} that he should not depart thence without his licence; and shortly after that Assembly mett in which he noe waies answeringe his Ma^{ts} expectation nor deserveinge (as his Ma^{tye} was pleased to say) his highnes favors, he was againe comitted a close prisoner there at Oxford; and after a quarter of a year's tyme of imprisonm^{te} he was impeached by his Ma^{tye} himselfe of high treason for makeinge the said composıcon and for speakeinge against and vilifyinge the Acts of the Assembly, and was indicted for the same, but upon a consultation thereof had with the iudges they determined that the said crimes obiected were rather tryable by martiall lawe, to which the lords there would not agree; and then after some further tyme lyinge in prison he was againe released upon his undertakeinge that he should leave the kingdome, and then took an opportunity and came to London, where he lyes now restrayned. All this matter doe appeare by his Lo^{pps} affidavit, and by severall other certificates and testimonialls subscribed under the hands of many noble parsonadges and others, testifyinge the same, and heereupon doth pray that this matter may be specially reported togither with his fine, hopeinge as his cause is to finde the favor of the howse therein.

He hath taken the nationall covenant and negative oath before the Com^{rs} of the Greate Seale and before Samuell Gibson, minister of Margaretts, Westm̃, the 28th of Aprill, 1646.

That he compounds upon a perticuler delivered in under his hand, by which he doth submit to such fine, &c., and by which it doth appeare:—

That his Lo^{pe} is seized of a francktent^{te} for life in possession, the remainder to his first sonne in taile . . . &c. of and in the manno^r of Howley, lyinge and beinge in the county of Yorke, and of divers demeasnes, lands, and ten$\tilde{t}$s in Howley and Woolchurch, and of the rectory of Morley and of other lands and ten$\tilde{t}$s lyinge in East and West Ardislawe, and of the manno^r and lands in Clynt, and of other lands and ten$\tilde{t}$s in Christall, Hedingly, Burley, Haighall, Lowe Cutles, and of the manno^r and lands of Moreley, and the manno^r and lands of Stapleton, all perticulerly mentioned in the perticuler given in of his Lo^{ps} estate, and doe amount togither in the whole unto 1,674l. 0s. 2d., for which his fine at a third comeinge in before the first of December is 8,370l. 0s. 10d.

That heeretofore his Lo^{pe} purchased from Sr William Savile, of Castle barre, knight, the manno^r and lo^{pp} of Darrington, in the said countye, and divers lands and tenements to the same, belongeinge, lyinge, and beinge in the townes and feilds of Darrington, Wentbriggs, and Smeaton, of the yeerely value before theis troubles 200l. That for securinge of 4,160l. the purchase money, he hath by his deed indented of the 21 Februarii, 17 Caroli, graunted, bargained, sold, and demised unto the said Sr William Savile all the said lands to hold for 99 yeeres under a pepper corne rent reserved, upon condi$\tilde{c}$on that upon paym^{te} of the said 4,160l upon the first day of May after date of the said deed, then the same to be void, which money he hath not paid at the day, but hath paid 2,400l., or thereabouts thereof, and is truely oweinge about 1,700l., the residue of the purchase money, soe that he hath onely the rever$\tilde{c}$on of this after 99 yeeres and a right in equity to avoid this tearme upon paym^{te} of the money behinde, and is left to consideracon.

His Lordship craves to be allowed an annuitye of 200l., which by his deed indented, dated the 17th of Aprill, 16 Caroli, he graunted unto Robert Hyteh and John Bradly, as feoffees in trust for the use of his Lordship's sister, Mrs Frances Bradly, wife of Mr Thomas Bradly, to hold duringe the tearme of his Lo^{ps} life, and was graunted in consideration of a 1,000l. that was her portion given by her father and in his Lo^{ps} hands; it is issueinge out of his manno^{rs} and lands of Morely, as by the deed thereof, which wee have perused, and doe thereupon finde the same to be settled accordingly, and for which he is to be allowed 500*l.*

Alsoe he prayes an allowance of another annuitye of 40*l.* graunted unto Edmund Savile, his brother, by the last will and testam^{te} of his father, as by the same will, dated the 23th of August, 1630, doth appeare, which wee have perused and doe finde the same to be soe, and for which he is to be allowed 100*l.*

Alsoe he prayes an allowance of 400*l.* with which his said lands are further chardged by his father's will to be paid unto Mrs. Anne Leigh, his sole executrix, towards the paym^{te} of his debts, which doth alsoe appeare to be soe upon perusall of the will, and for which he is to be allowed 100*l.*

His Lo^{pe} deposed that the grauntees of the said annuityes are liveinge, and that the same annuityes doe nowe contynue payable, and that the said some of 1,700*l.* or thereabouts is remayneinge due and yet unpaid unto Sir William Savile, and that he is still oweinge and indebted unto the said Mrs Ann Leigh the said somme of 400*l.*

JERO^{m} ALEXANDER.   D. WATKINS.

Fine 8,000*l.*

Concluding Note.—The fine of 8,000*l.* however was not fully enforced. The losses which Savile had previously sustained from the damage done to his house at Howley, and from the seizures made upon his goods there and at other places, were taken into consideration by the Commissioners, and the amount was reduced to 4,000*l.* Of this sum the 1,000*l.* paid to Captain Hotham " in a very needfull tyme to pay his forces " was reckoned a part. The sum of 2,000*l.* out of the 3,000*l.* to which the fine was thus reduced was soon paid. A report of the Committee of the House of Commons three years later, namely, under date 11th June, 1649, shows the balance to be still owing. The Committee then recommend to the House that Lord Savile should be discharged of his delinquency and of all further payments. No heed was paid to this recommendation, for so late as March, 1654, a list was issued of those delinquents who had not yet paid their compositions, and Savile appears in it.

INDEX.

Anderson, Henry, deposition by, 23
Ardsley, East, 32
Ardsley, West, or Woodkirk; *see* Woodchurch

Beverley, 2, 25, 30
Birkby, William, 10
Bland, Lady, Katherine, 1, 13, 15, 22; deposition by, 22
Bonnicar, Mr. 10
Bourchier, Sir John, 4
Bradford, 10
Bradly, John and Thomas, 32
Brooke, Lord, 2
Burley, near Leeds, 32
Burneley, Richard, 10

Cade, Elizabeth, 10
Calthrop, Sir Henry, 29
Carlisle, Lady, 4
Causfield, Colonel, 26, 30
Cawood Castle, 22, 23
Charles I. at York and Beverley, 2, 25, 30; at Nottingham, 2, 26, 30; his charges against Lord Savile, 16, 27, 31
Copley, Mr. or Captain, 10, 13
Coventry, 3
Cumberland, Lord, 2, 11, 12, 14, 15, 24, 26, 30

Darrington, 32
Derby, Lord, 6
Digby, Lord, 27
Doncaster, 10
Dorset, Lord, 2
Dover, Lord, 20

Fairfax, Lord, 13, 24
Fairfax, Sir Thomas, 9, 14
Falkland, Lord, 17
Farer, Mr. 4

Gibson, Samuel, minister, 31
Glemham, Sir Thomas, 26, 30
Goring, General, 13
Gray's Inn, 9
Greathead, Nicholas, 10

Headingley, 32
Henrietta Maria, Queen, 7
Heworth Moor, meeting on, 3, 4
Hinchcliffe, Abraham, 22, 23
Holland, Lord, 2
Hotham, Sir John, 1, 5, 12, 18
Hotham, Mr. or Captain, 7, 11, 15, 19, 22, 26, 30
Howard, Lord, 2
Howley, Yorkshire, 7, 9, 10, 13, 14, 15, 21, 26, 29, 32
Hull, 3, 26, 30
Hyteh, Robert, 32

Kirkstall iron works, 22; abbey, 23

Langdale, Sir Marmaduke, 9, 10
Leeds, 9, 13, 15, 22
Leigh, Anne, 33
Loudoun, Lord, 6
Lovelace, Lord, deposition by, 28

Mackworth, Sir Francis, 10
Midleborrow or Middlebrooke, Michael, 10, 23; deposition by, 22
Monckton, Sir Francis, 15
Morley rectory, 32; manor and lands, 32, 33

Naseby fight, 28
Newark, 8, 14, 17, 21, 26, 30
Newcastle, Earl of, 5, 6, 7, 11, 13, 15, 17, 26, 28, 30, 31; letter to, 16
Nicholas, Sir Edward, draft by, 8; secretary, 13, 18; letter of, 16
Nottingham, 2, 26, 30

Osborne, Sir Edward, 10, 15
Oxford, 13, 17, 21, 23, 27, 31; documents dated at, 8, 16

Pontefract or Pomfret, 9, 12, 15
Pym, John, petition drawn by, 2

Reyner, John, 4
Rigeley, Mr. 4
Risley, William, 9, 13; statement by, 24

Savile, Lord, letters of, 1, 5, 6, 9; at Newark, 8, 14, 17, 21, 26, 30; informations against, 8; answer to, 11; the king's charges against, 16, 27, 31; his petition to compound, 21; his defence, 25; his delinquency and fine, 30
Savile, Sir John, 29
Savile, Sir William, 13, 32, 33
Saye and Sele, Lord, 2, 5, 25
Scott, Richard, 10
Skipton, 9, 12
Smeaton, 32

Sparlinge, William, 10
Stapleton, Sir Philip, 2, 5, 24
Stapleton manor, 32

Tadcaster, 12, 24
Temple, Lady, letters to, 1, 5, 6, 18
Temple, Sir Peter and Lady, 1n, 18, 24, 26
Thorpe, Mr. 29
Todd, Mr. 4

Westminster, St. Margaret's, 31
Wakefield, 10
Walker, Sir Edward, document signed by, 21
Warwick, 3
Wentbridge, 32
Weston, Benjamin, 29
Woodchurch, Yorkshire, 10, 32

York, 2, 4, 8, 11, 15, 24, 25, 30; the battle near, 28

A SECRET NEGOCIATION

WITH

CHARLES THE FIRST.

1643—1644.

EDITED,

FROM THE TANNER MSS. IN THE BODLEIAN LIBRARY,

BY

BERTHA MERITON GARDINER.

PRINTED FOR THE CAMDEN SOCIETY.

M.DCCC.LXXXIII.

PREFACE.

The following documents, from the Tanner Collection of MSS. in the Bodleian Library, are especially interesting; in the first place, because so far as we know they contain the first overtures ever made to Charles in which the practice of religious toleration was proposed as means of effecting a settlement able to satisfy the bulk of the nation; in the second, because they help to explain how it was that the Independents, who at the beginning of the Civil war were few in number and unpopular, had become in 1645 a numerous and powerful party. Their proposal for the re-establishment of Episcopacy with a new set of bishops and toleration for those who wished to remain outside the Established Church, had the support of large numbers of persons, who had been converted into enemies of bishops by ceremonial innovations and the system of Church government upheld by Laud, but who had no theoretic or theological objections either to the service of the English Church or to Episcopacy, and to whom the idea of submission to the galling yoke of the Presbyterian Church was as distasteful as to the Independents themselves.

The outline of the story of the negociation is as follows:—A certain Captain or, as he is sometimes called in these papers, Major Thomas Ogle, a prisoner in Winchester House, conceived the idea that those whom he terms " moderate zealous Protestants" and Independents might be induced to combine together and defend the royal cause, in order to prevent the establishment of a Presbyterian Church in

England, which appeared to be imminent, in consequence of the recent acceptance of the Solemn League and Covenant. He wrote a letter (No. 1) to the Earl of Bristol, who had at that time great influence with Charles, urging his views at length, and at the same time inclosed a paper containing six propositions (No. 2), representing the terms on which both Independents and moderate Protestants would be ready to support the King. Ogle wrote this letter on Oct. 17, 1643, but it did not leave London till the 24th of the following month: it was then sent to Oxford through Lieutenant-Colonel Mosely, one of the officers of the garrison of Aylesbury, and delivered into Bristol's hands on Dec. 2. Ogle says in this letter that as proof of good faith Aylesbury should be delivered up to the King's forces; and it seems probable that it was through him that Mosely was engaged to enter into the transaction. Ogle also informed Bristol that if the King would send a warrant ordering the keeper of Winchester House prison, Thomas Devenish, to set him at liberty, the order would be complied with. The exact time at which Ogle's plans were betrayed does not appear, but it is certain that Mosely and Devenish were prepared to give information before Ogle's letter to Bristol left London. Copies were made both of it and the Propositions, and were exhibited to some members of Parliament in all probability before Nov. 24. Mosely at some previous date, or when he forwarded Ogle's letter and the propositions, must have written to Bristol, for the first letter of his to Bristol which is in our possession (No. 3), dated Dec. 6, is clearly not the first communication that he had had with the Earl. Bristol had no knowledge of Ogle, but complied with his requests, forwarding a warrant to Devenish to set him at liberty, also a safe conduct with a blank left for the insertion of names, and further, a bill of exchange for 100*l*. to enable him to pay his expenses and make his way to Oxford. These documents were all forwarded to Mosely at Aylesbury, and taken by him to London, where they were examined by Lord Wharton, Gerard, and Clotworthy on Dec. 11. Ogle was afterwards suffered to escape [a] and go to Oxford, where he arrived on Jan. 3, and received an encouraging reception both from Bristol and the King. From Oxford, besides writing to Devenish, Ogle wrote to the Independent ministers, Goodwyn and Nye, who were members of the Assembly of Divines, then sitting in London, urging on them to come to Oxford, and informing Nye that the King was prepared to make him his chaplain.

Unfortunately the whole of the correspondence relating to this affair is not in the Tanner Collection. It appears, however, from the entries in the Journals, that Devenish wrote to Bristol offering to betray Windsor Castle, and that the Earl replied, approving of the design and sending to him a royal warrant to raise 200 men under his son's command to put into that garrison.[b] Charles also wrote a letter to Mosely, shortly before the royal forces marched against Aylesbury, in which he instructed him, in case the plan of surrender failed, to blow up the powder magazine.[c] On Sunday night, Jan. 21, in spite of a heavy fall of snow, the royalists approached the town, but only to find that they were deceived, and to withdraw again to Oxford with the loss of many lives in consequence of the inclement weather. Those who had cognizance of the negociation doubtless had allowed it to continue so long with the object of getting the better of the King, but it was not possible that Charles

[a] Ogle was son-in-law to Peter Smart, former prebendary of Durham Cathedral (see No. 13, note). On Dec. 28 Smart petitioned the House of Lords that his son Ogle might be at liberty to go abroad with a keeper, as in consequence of his imprisonment he cannot prosecute or prepare for the hearing of his cause.—L. J. vol. vi. p. 355. On Jan. 6 is the further entry :—" That whereas this House ordered that Captain Ogle should have liberty to go abroad with a keeper to solicit for Mr. Smart in his business, the said Ogle is ran away."—L. J. vol. vi. p. 367.

[b] C. J. vol. iii. p. 378. The King also wrote a letter to Devenish, dated Jan. 12. —L. J. vol. vi. p. 394.

[c] L. J. vol. vi. p. 394. C. J. vol. iii. p. 378.

should be longer hoodwinked, and on Jan. 26 Lord Wharton brought the affair before the notice of the House of Lords.

Like most conspirators, Ogle immensely overrated his own importance and underrated the difficulties in the way of the execution of his plans. But it is none the less probable that the propositions which he forwarded really represented the views of those whose spokesman he declared himself to be. He informed Bristol that they were drawn up by the advice of some of the principal men on each side, and there is no reason for doubting his word on this point. It is evident from his letters to Goodwyn and Nye that he was personally acquainted with both of them, and it is of course possible that men too honourable and too far-sighted to enter into treasonable plots for the betrayal of garrison towns may yet have been willing in the first instance to take advantage of Ogle's overtures in order to discover whether there was hope that Charles would ever be ready to make peace on terms acceptable to them. There is besides reason for concluding that the Parliament felt more uneasiness than it cared to confess, since in opposition to the usual practice in such cases as little publicity as possible was given to the details of the negociation. No advantage whatever could be gained by spreading abroad such intelligence as that the Independents and Brownists had drawn up a very high and daring petition, threatening if the Scots covenant were forced upon them to lay down their arms;[a] a fact hitherto so well concealed that no notice of it had appeared in any of the numerous papers and pamphlets published on either side.

At the same time that Charles through the Earl of Bristol was negociating with Ogle, through Lord Digby, Bristol's son, he was carrying on a second negociation with other persons in London.[b] This negociation was discovered and made public (Jan. 6) about three weeks before information concerning Ogle's plans was laid

[a] See p. 5. [b] Referred to by Ogle, No. 23.

PREFACE.

before Parliament; and the different course pursued on the two occasions reveals how differently the Parliament felt itself affected by the two transactions. Two Roman Catholics, Sir Basil Brooke and Colonel Read,[a] endeavoured to prevail on various influential men in the city to enter into a plan of engaging the Corporation of London to present peace propositions to Charles. The desire for peace that existed in London as well as the national jealousy of the Scots were the levers by aid of which the contrivers hoped to effect their design. Thomas Violet, a goldsmith, who had been imprisoned for refusing to pay a tax imposed by the Parliament, and Theophilus Riley, the scout-master of the city, both took part in the business, and Violet, as well as an under-agent Wood, conveyed letters from Digby and Read[b] at Oxford to Riley and Brooke in London. Hints of the design were made to various persons known to be desirous of speedily bringing the war to an end,—Alderman Gibbes, Sir David Watkins, and others. Sir David Watkins appears at once to have given information to certain members of the House of Commons. Both Violet and Riley, when examined, denied that it had been their intention to engage the city to act independently of the Parliament; but from the evidence brought before it the Parliament was perfectly justified in concluding that the King's object was to inveigle the Corporation to

[a] Read, a Scotchman by birth, was a Roman Catholic, and had held the charge of lieutenant-general in Strafford's army in Ireland. The revolted Irish had employed him to negociate for them with the Lords Justices, but on his arrival at Dublin he was seized and racked. He was afterwards sent to London along with Lord Maguire and MacMahon (see No. 3, note).—*History of the Irish Confederation and War in Ireland* 1641-1643, edited by John T. Gilbert, vol. i. pp. 77, 78.

[b] Riley made use of his influence as scout-master of the city to obtain Read's release, representing him to have been a Captain Read, made prisoner in England, and getting him exchanged for a Parliamentarian prisoner at Oxford. Riley also effected the release of Violet.—" *A Cunning Plot to Divide and Destroy the Parliament and the City of London,*" *King's Pamphlets*, E.23.

enter into a negociation with himself at Oxford, and to recognize the Assembly which was to meet at that town on Jan. 22 as the lawful Parliament of England. A letter, of which the first draft had been made in London by Violet, Brooke, and Riley, was written by the King, and addressed " To our trusty and well beloved our Lord Mayor[a] and Aldermen of our city of London, and all other our well-affected subjects of that city." This was committed to the care of Brooke, with instructions to cause its presentation or not, accordingly as he should think fit.

After a preamble the letter ran:—

Being informed that there is a desire in some principall persons of that city to present a petition to us, which may tend to the procuring a good understanding between us and that our city, whereby the peace of the whole kingdom may be procured, we have thought fit to let you know that we are ready to receive any such petition, and the persons who shall be appointed to present the same to us shall have a safe conduct. And you shall assure all our good subjects of that city whose hearts are touched with any sense of duty to us, or of love to the religion and laws established . . . . that we have neither passed any act, nor made any profession or protestation for the maintenance and defence of the true Protestant religion and the liberties of the subject, which we will not most strictly and religiously observe, and for the which we will not be alwaies ready to give them any security can be desired. And of these our gracious letters we expect a speedy answer from you. And so we bid you farewell. Given at our Court at Oxford, in the 19 year of our raign, 26 Dec. 1643.

Propositions were agreed on between Read, Riley, Violet, and Brooke, fit to serve as a basis for negociation. According to Brooke's evidence they were as follows:—

(1.) That the city might be satisfied that the King would settle the Protestant religion, for without that neither the Parliament nor city would admit any treaty.

(2.) That the debts contracted upon the public faith, on either side by King or Parliament, should be satisfied, and the most likeliest way for the doing thereof was to settle the excise for these purposes.

---

[a] Sir John Wollaston, Pennington's successor. Violet, when examined, said that he was directed by Read "to tell my Lord Mayor the King had directed his letter to him, Lord Mayor of London, hearing he was a moderate man in his place."— *A Cunning Plot*, &c., *King's Pamphlets*, E.$\frac{29}{3}$.

PREFACE. vii

(3.) That it was conceived that in respect of the King's declaration that the Parliament was no Parliament, and that therefore the King could not treat with them any more, this treaty was to be immediately between the King and the city, and the city was to be the medium between the King and Parliament.

And this examinat further saith, That the said Wood told the examinat that if any parliament men would joyne with the city in the treaty, they also might come with them to Oxford under the safe conduct granted to the city, though it were not exprest in the King's letter; and that the said Wood received directions at Oxford for this examinat to declare soe much to whom he should think fit.

(4.) That there must be an act of oblivion for all parties and delinquents whatsoever, and a generall pardon. That no cessation should be expected during the treaty, if there had beene any. That no mention was made in all these Propositions either of Scotland or Ireland.

It is characteristic of Charles that he should have carried on negociations at the same time with Roman Catholics and with Independents for the recovery of his power. Most probably indeed when he allowed Ogle to make vague promises to the Independents of toleration and preferment it was not his object to effect a peace, but merely to prevail on the Parliamentary captains to surrender Aylesbury and Windsor. In the same way when he encouraged Read and Brooke in their designs he had probably little expectation of doing more than exciting feelings of ill will and jealousy between the Parliament and the City. His practice however of accepting overtures from whatever side they came had the great disadvantage that it destroyed belief in his sincerity. The readiness of the Independents to treat with him would not be increased by the discovery that he was equally ready to enter into negociations with Roman Catholics, and the Parliament, of course, did not fail to use the opportunity offered by the discovery of Brooke's plot of exciting popular prejudice against the King, and strengthening their own cause. After hearing the report of the committee which had conducted the investigations the Commons resolved:

That the matter of the report contains a seditious and jesuistical practice and design, under the fair and specious pretence of peace (having its rise and fountain from known Jesuits and Papists), to work divisions between the Parliament and the city of London; to raise factions in both, and thereby to render them up to the designs of the enemy, and tending also to the breach of the public faith of this kingdom unto our brethren of Scotland, engaged by the late solemn covenant and treaty entered into by both nations, thereby not only to weaken us in our united forces against our popish and common enemy but also to embroil the two nations in unhappy differences.[a]

The Lords concurred in this vote, and a committee of both Houses was appointed to communicate the business at a common hall, which was held on the following Monday (Jan. 8). The report of this committee was subsequently published, together with the examinations and letters of the various persons concerned, and an intercepted copy of the proclamation lately issued by Charles at Oxford summoning the Parliament to meet at that town on Jan. 22, and offering a free pardon to any member of either House who should within that time return to his duty and allegiance.[b] The occasion was made one for a great manifestation of union. The Corporation invited the Parliament to dinner at Merchant Taylors' Hall. On the appointed day, Jan. 11, the Lords and Commons, the Scottish Commissioners, three ambassadors newly arrived from Holland, the members of the Assembly of Divines, the Lord Mayor and Corporation, Essex, Warwick, Manchester, Cromwell, and other officers of note in London, met together at Christchurch at nine in the morning to hear a thanksgiving sermon from the lips of Stephen Marshall.[c] The preacher prefaced his sermon by a curious address, which shows how eager the Presbyterian party was to prevent the idea getting abroad that division existed in London:—

"You are first met here," he said, "to feast your souls with the fat things of God's house, with a feast of fat things full of marrow, and wine on the lees well refined; and afterwards to feast your bodies with the fat things of the land and the sea, both

---

[a] C. J. vol. iii. p. 358, Jan. 6.

[b] "A cunning plot to divide and destroy the Parliament and the city of London, made known at a common hall," &c. London, Jan. 16, 1643.—*King's Pamphlets*, E. $\frac{29}{3}$.

[c] *The Parliament Scout*, E. $\frac{29}{13}$; *The Kingdom's Weekly Intelligencer*, E. $\frac{29}{7}$.

plenty and dainty. But, if you please, you may first feast your eyes; doe but behold the face of this assembly; I dare say it will be one of the excellentest feasts that ever your eyes were refreshed with. You may first see the *two Houses of Parliament*, the honourable Lords and Commons . preserved from so many treacherous designs, secret treasons, and open violences. . Here you may also see *his Excellency*, the general of all our forces by land, and near him that most noble lord, the commander of our forces by sea; and with them abundance of noble and resolute commanders, all of them with their faces like unto lions. . . . . Here, also, you may behold the *representative body of the city of London*, the Lord Mayor, the Court of Aldermen, the Common Council, the *militia*, and in them the face and affection of this glorious city. *This city* . . after the expense of millions of treasure and thousands of lives, still as faithful and resolute to live and die in the cause of God as ever heretofore. Here you may likewise see a *reverend assembly* of grave and learned *divines*, who daily wait upon the Angel in the Mount to receive from him the lively oracles, and the patterns of God's house to present unto you. All these are of our *owne* nation; and with them you may see the *honourable, reverend, and learned Commissioners of the Church of Scotland.* . .
All these you may behold in one view; and, which is more, you may behold them all of *one heart*. . . . . And, which is yet more, you may see them all met together this day *on purpose*, both to *praise God for this union*, and to rejoice in it, and to hold it out to all the world, and thereby to testify that, as one man, they will live and die together in this common cause of God, of our Lord Jesus Christ his Church, and these three kingdoms," &c.[a]

The sermon over, both entertainers and guests proceeded in procession from the church to Merchant Taylors' Hall, while on the way the London trained bands lined the streets on either side:—

The first that went forth were the Common Councilmen and militia of London in their gowns; after them the Lord Mayor and Court of Aldermen in their scarlet gowns, on horseback, with their officers and attendants; next came the Lord General and Lord Admiral together, with about sixteen earls and lords of the upper House of Parliament, and divers colonels and military commanders, all on foot; and immediately after them came near two hundred of the worthy members of the House of Commons; and then the Commissioners of Scotland; and after all these about eighty divines of the Reverend Assembly: all which did much content and delight the spectators to see these so noble, faithful, religious, and honourable pillars of the truth, and maintainers of their rights and privileges, and patrons of the true religion, appear with so united a concurrence of hearts and spirits.[b]

---

[a] "A sacred Panegyrick, or a sermon of Thanksgiving."—*King's Pamphlets*, E. $\frac{30}{2}$. The italics are as in the original.
[b] *The True Informer, King's Pamphlets*, E. $\frac{29}{15}$.

At Cheapside an entertainment was prepared for the spectators, specially suitable to this celebration of the discovery of a plot in which, happily for the Parliament, Roman Catholics were concerned. At Cheapside, where the cross formerly stood, light scaffoldings of firwood had been raised, "all hung round with pictures and popish trinkets, which caused a very thronged fair.... there was crucifixes, and cunjering boxes, and velvet crosses, and crosses embroidered with gold. There was the Virgin Mary crowned Queen of Heaven ... there was magic spells and jacks in boxes. The bishops' crucifix, Jesus, and the nuns' holy bushes." along with candlesticks, images, beads, trinkets, and similar relics of past times. As the procession passed by these erections were set on fire, and were speedily reduced to ashes. "The smoke of the flames," says one of the papers, "like incense ascended towards heaven, as that which was acceptable to God."

While the crowd amused itself with the bonfire the members of Parliament and other guests dined in the Hall. At the close of the entertainment Dr. Burgess, one of the members of the Assembly of Divines, surprised the company by ascending the gallery, where musicians formerly sat on festive occasions, and proposing that all should join in singing the 85th Psalm. With this testimony of union and thankfulness the proceedings were brought to an end.[a] The following Sunday, Jan. 21, was kept as a day of public thanksgiving, and the vote of the two Houses passed on the discovery of the plot read in the city churches.[b]

The effusions of the weekly papers and the address which Marshall thought necessary to affix to his sermon make the reader incline to exclaim, "Methinks the gentlemen do protest too much." With regard to all that concerned Catholics and Catholicism,

[a] *King's Pamphlets, Mercurius*, &c. E. $\frac{30}{7}$; *The Scottish Dove*, E. $\frac{28}{14}$; *The True Informer*, E. $\frac{29}{18}$.
[b] C. J. vol. iii. p. 370; L. J. vol. vi. p. 384.

the Parliament, the Assembly of Divines, the City, the militia, and the army, might with justice assert that they presented an united front; but the procession in which marched side by side such men as Cromwell and Manchester contained elements which before the year had passed would be unable longer to work together. As yet, however, only the beginnings of division had appeared; and although evidences of ill-feeling between Presbyterians and Independents were not wanting, these took rather a personal than a political form, the Independents remaining stedfastly loyal to the side of the Parliament, expecting when the King was beaten that some solution of the religious question would be arrived at satisfactory to themselves. It is remarkable that, while Ogle was seeking to win Goodwyn and Nye to desert the side of the Parliament, overtures of like character were being made through another source to the younger Sir Henry Vane. Lord Lovelace wrote a letter to Vane from Oxford, in which he desired " to hold correspondence with him, relying upon his true inclination to the public good and knowing him to have a strong party in the House, and he the chiefe of it."[a] Vane showed the letter to the Speaker of the Commons and to the members of the committee appointed to investigate Riley's plot, and it was agreed amongst them that Lovelace's proposal should be accepted. Vane wrote in reply to Lovelace, and sent the chaplain of the Earl of Warwick, Mr. Wall, to have an interview with him at Henley.[b] The matter was first brought before the notice of Parliament in consequence, as it appears, of Essex discovering that communication was being held with the enemy. On Jan. 17 he complained to the House of Lords that letters were passing between Sir Henry Vane and Lord Lovelace, and that unless the correspondence was put a stop to he could not

[a] Whitacre's Diary, *Additional MSS.* 31116, fol. 108b.
[b] Whitacre's Diary, *Additional MSS.* 31116, fol. 109a; C. J. p. 369.

discharge his duty as general.ª The same day the Speaker of the Commons gave information to the House of what had passed. The letter written by Lovelace from Oxford, Vane's reply, and the account given by Wall of his interview with Lovelace, were read and then delivered to the Speaker, " to be kept by him from public view." ᵇ The matter, however, did not rest here. Lovelace, either before or after this date, wrote to Vane from Reading, and Vane again replied.ᶜ The bearer of a letter written by Lovelace was arrested on Jan. 18 as a spy and examined by Dorislaus, the advocate of the army. His answers led to the examination of Wall on the 19th, and the answers of Wall to the examination, on the 20th, of a third man, Mr. Sterry, who was chaplain to Lady Brooke.ᵈ The names of Vane and of other members of Parliament appeared in the examinations, and a report got abroad that Vane was under arrest, and that he and other members of the Commons were, in accordance with an ordinance of Parliament, going to be tried by a court of war for holding correspondence with the enemy.ᵉ Vane complained in the Commons that the privileges of the House had been broken, because witnesses had been examined with regard to the actions of its members without communication having first been made to the House (Jan. 24).ᶠ Essex received an order to send the examinations to the House, with which he complied, at the same time declaring through Strode that he had never thought of causing any members of Parliament to be tried by martial law.ᵍ He also in person presented copies of the examinations to the

ª L. J. p. 381.   ᵇ C. J. vol. iii. p. 369.
ᶜ Whitacre's Diary, *Additional MSS.* 33116, fol. 110b.
ᵈ C. J. vol. iii. p. 376.
ᵉ Whitacre's Diary, *Additional MSS.* 31116, fol. 110b ; *King's Pamphlets, The Kingdom's Weekly Intelligencer*, E. $\frac{10}{19}$.
ᶠ Whitacre's Diary, *Additional MSS.* 31116, fol. 110b.
ᵍ C. J. vol. iii. p. 375.

House of Lords, which ordered the Speaker to give him thanks for his care, and declared that he had done nothing but what was in accordance with his duty as Lord General.[a] The Commons, on their side, proceeded to summon before them and question Dorislaus. After a long debate they appointed a committee to examine the matter further and to report whether in its opinion a breach of privilege had been committed or not.[b]

The letters which passed between Lovelace and Vane are not printed in the Journals of either House; but there is no doubt, with regard to their contents, that offers made to Vane, as chief of a large party in the Commons, would include some general promise of religious toleration.[c] It does not appear whether Lovelace wrote at Bristol's instigation; but, according to Wall's report, he acted with the authority of the King.[d] It was natural that some other agent than Ogle should be employed to approach Vane, in order to preclude danger of the discovery and betrayal of the designs upon Windsor and Aylesbury. Charles by making propositions to Vane, if he did not succeed in much, at least succeeded in nearly involving the two Houses in a quarrel over a question of privilege. The Houses, however, could not afford to quarrel. Two days after Essex delivered up the examinations Parliament was informed of Ogle's conspiracy, and the ill-timed dispute

[a] L. J. vol. vi. p. 391.

[b] L. J. vol. iii. p. 376. Whitacre's Diary, *Additional MSS.* fol. 111a.

[c] The weekly papers only mention the affair slightly. *Anti-Aulicus* gives as follows the contents of Lovelace's letter to Vane :—" That the King having taken notice of him and of others of his judgment, and conceiving them to be reall and hearts in their intentions, did promise unto them liberty of conscience, and that all those laws that have been made by the parliament, and all others, the rights and liberties of the people, should inviolably be preserved : of which hee would give what assurance could be devised ; desiring likewise that either hee or some other by his appointment would upon safe convoy treat further of the business at Henley, or what other place he thought fit."— *King's Pamphlets*, E. $\frac{34}{11}$.

[d] Whitacre's Diary, *Additional MSS.* 31116, fol. 108b.

appears to have been abandoned, since no further notices of it are to be found in the Journals. On Jan. 26 Lord Wharton reported to the House of Lords:—

A discovery of dividing the two kingdoms of England and Scotland, and the design of the betraying of Alsebury, the effect whereof was to this purpose :—That Devenish, the keeper of Winchester House, was dealt with to permit Captain Ogle to make an escape out of his custody, which the said Devenish discovered to some Lords; and the moderate men (as they called them) and the Independents were to join together for suppressing of the Presbyterians, and the Scots to be kept out of the kingdom; and Ogle had an hundred pounds sent him from the Earl of Bristol to bear his charges out of town. And further, the Earl of Bristol dealt with one Mosely to surrender the garrison of Alsebury; and in case the King's forces could not have the town surrendered them, to fire it and the magazine.

Four documents,[a] according to the entry, were then read, after which,

Lieutenant-Colonel Moseley was called into the House and thanked for his fidelity and good service done at Aylesbury for the Parliament: who acquainted the Lords, "That he had been dealt withall from Oxon to have blown up the magazine at Aylesbury and some part of the town, with two engines sent from Oxon, whilst their forces should have surprised the said town."[b]

Upon the further report of Lord Wharton, " that Mr. Nye and

[a] (1) Ogle's letter to Bristol, dated Nov. 24 (No. 1). (2) The King's letter to Lieutenant-Colonel Mosely concerning the surrendering up to him the town of Aylesbury (missing). (3) The King's letter to Thos. Devenish, keeper of Winchester House, dated from Oxford, 12 Jan. 1643 (missing). (4) The Propositions (No. 2).

[b] *The Scottish Dove* (E. $\frac{10}{13}$) gives the following account of Mosely's share in the business: " There having lately been some difference of discontent between Lieutenant-Colonel Mostley and some other commanders, the Lieutenant, coming to London upon his occasions, was closed with by some Oxford factors (for treachery), and, after much sifting, the Lieutenant-Colonell carrying the business smoothly, the bargain came to be confirmed, and 1,000 pound must be the reward to deliver up Alesbury; the place was appointed where and how to agree of the time and way, to which place, according to promise, Lieutenant Mostley sent his man. The time being appointed, he desired money in hand; 100 pound was sent him, a good horse and a sword; and on Monday [1] they came to have possession. But Lieutenant-Collonell Mostley, when he had the 100^{li} had all he looked for, and had made the business known to the governour."[2]

---

[1] They marched Sunday night, Jan. 21-22.

[2] Colonel Aldridge, *The Weekly Account*, E. $\frac{3}{1}$.

Mr. John Goodwin did refuse to meddle in the business," the House—

thought fit that they should have thanks given them from the House for the same; and that Lieutenant-Colonel Mosely and Mr. Devenish should have thanks given and a reward for their faithfulness in the carriage of this business.—(L. J. vol. vi. p. 395.)

The same day, January 26, at the request of the Lords, a conference by committees of both Houses was held in the Painted Chamber. In the report of the conference afterwards made in the Commons the House was informed:

That Ailesbury was much in the King's eye; that Mr. Devenish was very faithful to the Parliament, and in discourse in the whole proceeding of this business; that he got Ogle to pawn his seal unto him; and thereby got a new seal cut, and opened Ogle's letters, and sealed them with the new seal. That Mr. Goodwyn, Mr. Nye, with the privity of my Lord General and some members of this House, had conference with Ogle. That the King's forces came on the Sabbath day [a] last towards Ailesbury; and his forces at Tocester quitted that garrison in hopes of effecting this design. That three hundred fresh foot were sent on that day by his Excellency into the town; of which notice was given by Lieutenant-Colonel Mosely to his Majesty to defer it a few days; but, indeed, to the end, to defer the time, till my Lord General and the Earl of Manchester's forces might march between the enemy and Oxford: yet it so much concerned his Majesty to have that town delivered on that day, in regard of upholding his reputation with his Parliament at Oxford, who were to meet the next day, that he would defer the time no longer; but, in the great storm and snow, marched within two miles of the town; and near four hundred men lost in the march.[b]

---

[a] Jan. 21.

[b] The following is the list of documents entered in the Commons' Journals as being read to the House; several are not in the Tanner Collection, while several in the Tanner Collection are not entered in the Journals. The clerk does not appear to have had regard to order of date:—

(*a*.) A Letter from Captain Ogle, prisoner in Winchester House, to the Earl of Bristol.

(*b*.) Propositions of peace.

(*c*.) A Safe Conduct under the King's hand with a blank of three names.

(*d*.) The Earl of Bristol's letter to Lieutenant-Colonel Mosely.

(*e*.) Lieutenant-Colonel Mosely's Letter to the Earl.

(*f*.) Mr. Devenish's Letter to the Earl of Bristol.

(*g*.) The King's Warrant to Mr. Devenish to set Captain Ogle at liberty.

The Commons, after hearing the report, resolved that thanks should be returned to Mr. Nye, Mr. Goodwin, Lieutenant-Colonel Mosely, and Mr. Devenish, and that the estate of Mr. Samuel Crispe should be forthwith secured. With regard to the main question both Houses dwelt as lightly upon it as possible, and sought to show that the King, when making promises to the Independents, had no other design in view than to foment discord and gain military advantages for himself. The following resolution was adopted by both Houses: " That it doth appear, upon the whole matter, that the King and his council at Oxford do endeavour and embrace all ways to raise and foment divisions betwixt us and our brethren of Scotland, and amongst ourselves, under the fair pretence of easing tender consciences; that during these fair pretences, their immediate design was the ruin of the kingdom by the destroying and burning of the magazines thereof." [a]

What is here quoted from the Journals is all that was ever officially made known. None of the documents were printed or published, and the weekly papers either do not notice the affair at all or pass lightly over it.[b] The Weekly Intelligencer, which has the fullest

(*h.*) Mr. Devenish, his Letter by Captain Ogle to the Earl of Bristol, in figures.

(*i.*) The Earl's Answer to Mr. Devenish.

(*k.*) The King's Warrant to Mr. Devenish to raise two hundred men under his son's command, to be put into the garrison of Windsore.

(*l.*) The Earl of Bristol's letter, in figures, to Mr. Devenish.

(*m.*) Sir George Strode's Letter to Mr. Samuel Crispe to pay one hundred pounds to Captain Ogle.

(*n.*) The Bill of Exchange for the payment of the said hundred pounds.

(*o.*) Mr. Samuel Crispe's Letter to Sir George Strode.

(*p.*) Captain Ogle's Letter to Lieutenant-Colonel Mosely, about the time of delivering up of the town.

(*q.*) His Majesty's Instructions to Lieutenant-Colonel Mosely to blow up the magazine in case of sudden discovery.

The engines or fireworks delivered by his Majesty's own hands for the said service was presented likewise to the House.

[a] C. J. vol. iii. p. 378.

[b] *King's Pamphlets: the Parliament's Scout*, E. $\frac{31}{7}$; *Anti-Aulicus*, E. $\frac{21}{14}$; *The Kingdom's Weekly Intelligencer*, E. $\frac{10}{15}$.

account, dwells entirely on the military side of the negociation. The writer mentions some details which are not in the letters that we possess, and it is likely enough that he drew upon his imagination for some of them.[a] The chief portion of his narrative is as follows:

> After some debate, Ogle could not accomplish his ends unless he might have his liberty. . . Master Devenish did wisely connive at his escape, Lieutenant-Colonel Mosely nobly entertained him at Aylesbury, and concluded on conditions to deliver up the town ; Ogle went to Oxford, kissed his Majesties hand. . . . Hereupon his Majestie writes a letter, and the Earl of Bristol another, to Lieutenant-Colonel Mosely, and also to Mr. Devenish, and thanks them for their affection to his Majesties service. Mr. Devenish writes a letter of compliance to the Earle of Bristol, and also sends him a figure to write by, but yet advises his Lordship that Ogle may not be privy to what he writes, for he loves to be free with solid and reserved men—of either of which Ogle was never guiltie. My Lord Bristol accepted of the figure, answered it in kinde, approved of Mr. Devenish's advice, sent him a letter of indemnity under his Majesties hand and seal for permitting Ogle to escape, intimating unto him that his Majestie had made Ogle a gentleman of his privy chamber, but a badge of greater honour was intended for him. Mr. Devenish finding his addresses so acceptable, writ againe in figures to the Earle of Bristol, and propounded unto him a designe he had to betray Windsor Castle at the same time into his Majesties hands by taking advantage of a feare that would possess them upon the surrender of Aylesbury. His Majesty and the Earl of Bristol well approved of the designe, and both of them in several letters signed with their own hands highly extolled his wisdom, promised great rewards, as by the letters appear.
>
> The plot goes on; Sunday, Jan. 21, at 12 at night, Aylesbury was to be delivered up; to that end his Majesty quits Tocester,[b] and draws all the forces he can also from Oxford and elsewhere to enter Aylesbury: Lieutenant-Col. Mosely sends his Majesty word that there was come in three full companies of foot, fresh supplies, which he expected was sent upon some jealousies, therefore advised his Majesty to forbear to send till a better opportunity: but his Majesty was resolved on the time appointed,

---

[a] See No. 23 and note.

[b] The Royalists had a garrison at Towcester, from whence they made plundering excursions into the surrounding districts. A party of Cavaliers took Sir Alexander Denton's house, Hilsdon, within a few miles of Aylesbury, but were driven away by a body of Parliamentarians coming from Banbury and Newport Pagnell about Jan. 17. On Jan. 18 the Royalist forces abandoned Towcester, after which the place was occupied by the Parliamentarians. *The Kingdom's Weekly Post*, E.$\frac{8\ 1}{1\ 1}$; *Mercurius Civicus*, E.$\frac{2\ 9}{1\ 3}$; *The Scottish Dove*, E.$\frac{2\ 9}{1\ 4}$; *Mercurius Civicus*, E.$\frac{3\ 0}{9}$.

for that the winde had blowne of late much against them, and the great meeting of the Parliament was at Oxford the next day, and some action must suddenly ensue to uphold his reputation at so great a meeting, and therefore sent him, by his own man, some engines to fire the magazine in case he was discovered, that then the towne might be easily taken by storming it: but when they came within two miles of Aylesbury [a] the enemy perceived they were betrayed, so retreated in disorder, and lost neer 400 men and horses in the snow, and lost Tocester besides; and had Lieutenant-Colonel Moseley prevailed to hold off the day of appointment but two days longer, as he endeavoured it, my Lord General's forces had marched between Oxford and the enemy, and cut them off, but unseasonableness of the stormes and wayes were such that they could not march but with much prejudice, though they endeavoured it.[b]

Notice should be drawn to the peculiar use of the word "agitations," on p. 1. which may help to explain the use of the word "agitators" for the agents appointed by the soldiers in 1647.

[a] "The enemy quartered at Ethrop House within two little miles of Alesbury, expecting the prize; but by the next morning by some scout or secret intelligence they had notice that their plot was blasted, so they returned back towards Oxford."—*The Scottish Dove, King's Pamphlets,* E. $\frac{4\,9}{1\,8}$.

[b] *King's Pamphlets: The Kingdom's Weekly Intelligencer,* E. $\frac{4\,9}{1\,8}$. The weather was very inclement, and the operations of the forces on both sides impeded in all parts of the country.

A SECRET NEGOCIATION WITH CHARLES I.

(1) THOMAS OGLE TO THE EARL OF BRISTOL.

[Tanner MSS. vol. lxii. fol. 332.]

MY LORD,

Having by God's great marcy bin soported by his great provydenss (after almost 7 months most myserable close improsinment, aggravated with most exquiset acts of barbarissme and cruelty, in the Lo: Petter's[a] howse, and from thenss 20 days in the hoolr of a ship) obtayned (not through favour but forgetfulnes of these grand refformers) the lyberty of Winchester Howse, where now I am a prisner, som of my freinds and aqueyntans had recorss to me, wherby my former agitations (well known to Sir Nich. Crisp)[b] for

---

[a] Petre's.

[b] Sir Nicholas Crispe, a royalist, a former farmer of the customs, who had fled from London to Oxford in the beginning of the year. On Jan. 18, 1643, several intercepted letters were read in the House of Commons; amongst others, one from Sir Robert Pye, an Exchequer officer, whose son Hampden's daughter had married. In this letter Sir Robert Pye "shewed that hee had paied 3700ˡⁱ due to Sir Nicholas Crispe for secrett service done for his Maᵗⁱᵉ, and would take a course to convey his Maᵗⁱᵉˢ revenue to him."[1] The money lent by Crispe to the King, Whitaker, in his *Diary*, informs us, was part of the money due to the Commonwealth for customs.[2] When questioned, Pye declared that he was entirely ignorant of the service for which the money was paid to Crispe, who was summoned before the House, "and ther answerd, that this 3700ˡⁱ was due to him from his Maᵗⁱᵉ for monies advanced when his Maᵗⁱᵉ went against the Scotts, which afterwards appeared to be a manifest lie by his often

---

[1] D'Ewes' Diary, *Harl. MSS.* 164, fol. 277a.
[2] *Additional MSS.* 31116, fol. 29b.

CAMD. SOC. B

the advansing his Mag^t seuviss did not only revive, but upon the passing the Scots Covynant my former hops and assuranss to add to his Mag^t the most considerable part of the people heere were doubled; who as formerly they boothe insenced and mayntayned the warr against his Mag^t, so now are they censerly^a desyrous to ther utmost to assist his Mag^t for sopresing this Covynant and the mylisha, som humble desyes of thers for ther assuranss of injoying the benyfet of his Mag^t vehement prodistations and gratious declorations, being granted by his Mag^t (as an earnist thereof) for the beter setlement and inabling them with his Mag^t asistans to tourne the streame, to which work they are only led through contiens towards God, devotion to his Mag^t, and compasion to the bleeding state of ther native contry.

To intymate which to his Mag^t they have made use of me, bothe in regard of my former addresses to, and also sopossing that my long and great sufferings for his Mag^t has begot me confydenss and credit at Coort, and lastly in cace of any myscoradg or discovry heerof they know themselvs safe in my hand, wherfore I have made bould to certyfy your honor, being well assured of your fydelity to his Mag^t, our Church and State, and also knowing your wisdom to

uncertaine and almost contradictorie answeares; soe as wee all concluded that this monie had been lent his Matie since his departure from the cittie of London, though the said Sir Nicholas Crispe absolutelie denied, being asked the question by the Speaker; yet awhile after hee slipt away from the doore of the Commons house and went to his Matie to Oxford, which easilie cleared the scruple, when the saied monie had been lent for secrett service."[1] After this the Commons ordered all the goods of the offender to be seized, Jan. 20.[2] The following day Colonel Manwaring, appointed to search the houses of Sir Nicholas Crispe at London and at Hammersmith, to see what money or plate could be found there, made his report, "but of 300^{li} that was found in his house; but he found of gold of his in the Tower, and in other places of the city, to the value of neare about 5000^{li}; all which was seized, because he had slipt away out of the sergeant's custody, and was not to be found."[3]

^{a} Sincerely.

---

[1] D'Ewes' Diary, *Harl. MSS.* 164, fol. 277a, b; C. J. vol. ii. 933.
[2] C. J. vol ii. 936.
[3] Whitacre's Diary, *Additional MSS.* 31116, fol. 21b.

manadg the greatest affayre aright. What the particulore passages betwixt Sir Nich: Crispe and me were I shal not trouble your Lodship with, he being at Oxford, and able to give your honor a full and satisfactory acoumpt thereof, only thus much upon thes proposisions to me. I then tould him it was not possible to setle the comision of array in London untal som reall acts were don by his Mag^t to satisfye the people (who would not be satisfyd with words) of the reality of his Mag$t$ performanss according to his prodestations and declarations, which corrs, if it had bin then taken, I may without bouldnes or vanity afferm to your Lodship that the warr had bin ended, a ferme peace and confydenss of his Mag^t defending the Protestant religion, the laws and libertys of the kingdom, and governing heerafter by the known laws, had bin most assuradly setled in the people. And if it please God this overture be now axeptable to his sackred Mag$t$ and your Lodship it wilbe a notable evydenss that the blessing of God is with us, and that this land is not designed for ruen, which heer is more confydently beleved, because his sackred Mag$t$ having sene the myschefous evels of two extremitys, the goulden meane is to be laboured for, which is obtayned only by moderat not violent corses and counsels.

The only thing desyred for present, is a safe conduct for two or three who on the behalf of many thousands may com to Oxford, and propound ther humble desyrs to his Mag^t, and receve such satisfaction and derections conserning the further prosecution thereof, as to his Mag$t$ and your Lodships wisdom shall seeme meete; for the better effecting heerof I have sent inclosed the effect of what is intended, to be presented to his Mag$t$ at ther comming to Oxford, with the circomstanses, grounds, and reasons of the same, whereby your Lodship may the bettor facilytate the work and guide them and me aright therin.

The party heer that have insenced and mayntaynd this warr consists of 3 sorts of people, the fyrst and greatest are the moderat zelous prodistants, lovers (though desyrous of som amendment) of the Comon Prayer booke. The second and next considorable to this are the rigid Presbyteryans; the third are the Independants and Brownists, among whom doe some few and very inconsiderable anababtists and other fantastick sectuarys myx themselvs. Thes 3 though realy ayming at sevrall ends for ther speritual, yet ther temporall intrests being one and the same, and conseving Episcopasy and the prorogative were the only obsticle to ther desyrs in both, and the way either to remove or abate this were only by this parlament, did joyne together to soport the means against this soposed enemys; evry one cherishing themselvs in ther several hops and wishes for the injoyment of ther freedom in the excrsise of ther devotions; whylst they knew they did unanimosly agree for the security of ther outward estats.

And thus the cunning Presbateryan made a real use of both the others power to effect ther owne ends, which they never aymd at; but now, visably seeing, doe abhor this Scots Covynant, and the rather because thay setle to establish that, they can scarce cal any thing ther owne: hense having recorss to the use of ther reason, they conclud that tis beter for them to live under episcopasy, injoying the benyfyet of his Mag^t frequent prodistations and gratious declarations, than under the terany of the mylisia and malisious Presbyteryan; upon which grounds both thes partys begin to stager, and repent of ther formore actions; and if his Mag$t$ as a gratious father will reseve thes prodygall children, they will not only quyte fall of from thes Covynantors, but visably apere for his Mag^t, which being don, your Lodship easyly sees that the warr will quickly end, the Scots be kept out of the kingdom, and his sackred Mag^t returne home with honor and victory, for what the soule is to the body, so were and are the two to all the actions and opposisons that have bin don and made.

Som of the leading men, both mynisters and others of the fyrst sort, upon passing the Scots Covynant, came to Winchester Howse to me lamenting ther owne and the kingdoms myserys, affirming that the moderat men who at ª asisted the parlament to secure themselves and bring in delinkquents would now most willingly not

---

ª *Sic.* ? had.

only withdraw but assist his Mag^t agst this Presbyteryan warr, if they could be assured of his Mag^t parformanss according to his prodestations and declarations. And the meere dispayre of his Mag^t had drove them and still would inforce them to continew the assistanss contrary to ther desyrs, which were rather for moderated Episcopasy than the Scots Presbitrys, and that the supreme comand of the milisia should continew in the formor antient corss, and not be violently extorted from the crowne.

But in cace ther were, as was affermed, a reall plot to reare Popery and terany upon the ruens of this parlament, then skin for skin, and all that he hath will a man give for his lyfe, how much more for religion, the lyfe of the life, to setle and assure this mene. Thay were assured by Corah and his complyces that popry and terany was both the ends and ayms of al his Mag^t actions, and that ther was no other way to prevent them than a violent alteration of goverment both eclesastycall and civell; for profe heerof ther was a Pops bull found and som victorys [a] sayd to be obtaynd.

The other sort, vid. Independants and Brownists, being more fyry though not more inraged at the Scots Covynant, which wholy blasted ther hops of a toleration or conivanss at the least of the exercys of ther owne disyplyne, mett together, and drue up a very high and daring peticion to the parlament, requyred that the Scots Covynant might not pass, or at least not be pressed upon them, for that thay did not take up arms for the Scots prisbitry, which is as antychristian or more then the Einglish prelacy; if this therfore were not don, they would not fyght themselvs into a worss condision, but the 3 regaments in the army of thes men would lay downe ther arms and the rest withdraw ther assistanss.

The Presbytiryan, seing the mischef and ruen which this petition brought with it, bent all ther indevors to sopress it, and for this end, as thay formerly sent Mr. Nye into Scotland for the cherishing the hops of that faction then, soe now they imploy him agayne to quyet the rage and quensh the fyre of this peticion, giving them

[a] *Sic.* ? miscopied "writings."

assuranss they shall reseve satisfaction and be gratyfyd with what kind of disyplyn ther humors cals for, wherby the peticion was stopt for present.

But yet ther jelosy of the Scots Press[bytery] remayns greater then ther displesur against the Einglish prelat, from whenss coms this ther result of seeking to his Mag^t, from whom if they can obtayne so much favour as the papist eather formorely had or heerafter shal have, thay will realy joyne to the utmost with his Magt to sopress the Scots Covynant and the mylisha. Upon thes reasons and grounds, by the advise of som of the princypall men of both syds, this inclosed paper was drawne up, contayning the substanss of ther humble desyrs to his Mag^t with the grounds therof.

Thus have I, Right hono^{ble}, given your Lodship as breifly as I could an acount of what was intrusted unto me, which if it shall prove effectuall to re-establish his Mag^t just power and athority and the peace of this myserable distraced[a] Church and State, I shall think myself a most hapie man, to have contrybuted any thing to so pious a work for my most gratious sovoragne and contry, and the rather for that your Lodship (whose esteme next to his Magt I am more covytous of then of anys in the world) shall be *opefex*[b] *rerum et meliorum temporum origo*. And that your Lodship may be the more confydent of suckses I have comision to assure your Lordshipp that his Mag., gratiously satisfying those who shall com under safe conduct in this humble desire, Alsbury will be surendred to his Mag^t in earnist of further parformanss as need shall requyre, and that his Mag^t may not be jelos of any trechory as at Poolr,[c] ther wilbe

---

[a] Distressed.
[b] *Sic.*
[c] In September 1643, Captain Francis Sydenham, one of the captains of the garrison of Poole, agreed on a certain night, when he should be captain of the watch, to admit the royalist forces, under the Earl of Crawford, into the town. Crawford arrived at the appointed hour with 500 men, and found the gate, as had been promised, left open; but no sooner had some of his force passed through it than they were attacked by the enemy, who were lying in wait for them, and driven out with loss of many arms, horses, and men.—*Rushworth*, part iii. vol. ii. p. 286.

noe more stranth^a needfull then a comision under the broad seale, whereof that your Lodship may be yet more asured thes letors are safly convayd to your honor, and the answer wilbe as safly returned hither to me, by the countnanss and power by^b one of the chefe offycers in this garyson.^c

And for the further assuranss those who originaly began thes ovorturs and actualy will compleate them, have such power and intrest in the keeper^d of this prison, that upon his reseving a warant from his Mag^t for my discharg I shal com along with those who com to Coort under the safe conduct, to the end I may add my best asistanss for a hapie concluson therin.

I shall therfore feaer further to trouble your Lodship at this tyme, hoping shortly to kiss his Magt hand and wayt upon your honor, only desyring your Lodship to dispach this mesinger spedyly (who knows nothing of the contents heerof) with a safe conduct (leaving a space for 3 nams under his Mag^t riall hand and privy signit, with your Lodship's atestation), and lickwise a warant so signed and sealed, derected to the keeper of Winchester Howse, for my discharg out of prison. The reason why the safe conduct is desyred with a blank is in chanse this letor should myscary, the nams being conseld, noe man can suffer but myself; at our coming his Magisty and your Lodship shall receve a full acount of the stranth^a and state of the army.

Thus agayne humbly and earnisly praying your Lodship spedyly to dispach this mesinger, and not to discover to any person save his or hir Magt (who wilbe humbly peticioned to interpose and medyate with his Magt in thir behalf) in any measure or kynd that cather this or any thing of this nature, or of any great importanss is com from London; for tis known som great ons at Court hould corespondanss heere. With my frequent prayers to Almyghty God

^a Strength.   ^b *Sic.* ? of.
^c Lieutenant-Colonel Mosely. *See* No. 4 and notes.
^d Thomas Devenish, who caused a copy to be made of Ogle's seal, opened his letters, and rescaled them with the new seal.—C. J. vol. ii. p. 398.

for al the blesings of this and beter lyfe upon his and hir Most Sackred Mag*t* and posterity, whom that I may serve in this or any other thing before I com to Coort, I beg your Lodships instroctions, making bould to wryt myself, as I realy am, my Lord,

Y^r Ho: most humble and faythful servant,

TH. OGLE.

Winchester Howse, the 17 of Octo: 1643.

The letter sent was dated 24 Noue. 1643.[a]

Indorsed: Coppy of Ogle's letter to Ld Bristow, 24 Nove. 1643.

(2.) PROPOSITIONS SENT BY THOMAS OGLE TO THE EARL OF BRISTOL.

[Tanner MSS. vol. lxii. fol. 334.]

Since its undeniable that nothinge can bee added to the happines of thys Church and State, if the benefitts proposed and promised in his Ma^{ts} many and frequent protestacions and declaracions, confirmed and attested by Oathe and Sacrament, can bee reallie inveyed,[b] and that through diffidence of his Ma^{ts} performance and reallitie this unnaturall civill warre, with all the miseries of the same, still rageth amongest us, which difference principally is caused through a beliefe that all these late acts of grace in satissfaction of the former misgovernement, for prevention of the like in tyme to come, and for a through reformacion, were compulsivelie and by constreant, and not voluntarilie and for the compassionate weale of the subject passed by his Ma^{tye}; hence it is that the people beleive that they cannot safely enjoy religion and lawes by the proffered reformacion, nor bee free from the former cou^{rt}[c] incroachments upon theire soules, bodyes, and estates, by any other meanes then an utter extirpacon and allteracon of Episcopalle governement, which haveinge a strength in and uppon the civill power, and by diver-

---

[a] Information given by the copyist.   [b] *Sic.* ? injoyed.
[c] This may stand for "court" or "covert."

sion weakeninge his Ma^{ts} auctoritie his Ma^{tye} is necessitated to defend the same, from whence ariseth the bloodie quarrell of the militia. To settle therfore a confidence in the people of his Ma^{ts} reallitie in mayntenance of religion, the just priviledges of parliament, the lawfull libertie and propertie of the subject, and his future government by the knowne lawes of the land, without the alteracon of Episcopalle governement, and the trust of the militia reposed in the Crowne.

1. Theese meanes are heartilie proposed and desired that his Maiesty wilbee gratiously pleased to consent unto, and that all the ould Bishopps, what have brought in and practised the late innovations in the Church, whoe have tyranised and oppressed his Ma^{ts} subjects in theire severall judicatures, bee forthwith displaced, and that his Ma^{tye} choose the ablest and most consciensious divines, whoe through theire unblameable livs and doctrine have interest in the peoples affections, in theire steade.

2. That his Ma^{tye} doe graunt out a commission as was doune 1mo Elizabeth, to certeyne visitors for regulateing of ceremonies, and appointinge certeyne orders in the Church untill a free, nationall, and right composed Synod can bee called for setlinge the distractions of the Church, whoe may ymediatelie pull doune all allters, superstitious pictures, and prohibitt the practise of the former innovacons, as boweinge to or towards the allter att the name of Jesus, standinge att *gloria patri*, and the diviscon of service, etc.

3. That a proclamacion bee forthwith published, as *in primo Hen.* 8^{vi}, that all those whoe have byn oppressed in the former misgovernement shall[a] uppon theire repaire to Court shalbee[a] with all speade repaied and the oppressors punished accordinge to justice, that thereby the world may see his Ma^{tye} will doe justice against the Bishopps and the culpable ceremonious abettors, that the warre is not mainteyned for defendinge delinquents from due punishment.

4. That all delinquents accused both by his Ma^{tye} and the two

[a] *Sic.*

Houses bee tryed either by a knowne lawe, or in a full and free Parliament, or that his Majestie bee pleased to graunt such a generall and free pardon as by the advise of the two Howses of Parliament may secure all men's feares.

5. That his Mat^{ye} bee pleased to pass such an acte of parliament as the two Howses shall advise for the repaireing the breach of priviledges in his courte[a] to the House of Commons and secure the Howses from the like hereafter.

6. That his Majestie bee gratiouslie pleased to graunt a safe conducte and give audience to some whoe shalbee appointed to attend his Mat^{ye} by many thowsands of inhabitants in and about London, to propose to his Mat^{ye} the humble desires of the rest comeing for easeinge of theire consciences from such heavye burdens as have byn layd uppon them by Byshopps, and for givinge them assurances for enjoyinge theire freedome from such oppressions and penalties, submittinge themselves unto and obeyinge and mainteyninge his Mat^{ye}, the lawes of the land, of the kingdome in all civil affaires.

Indorsed: Propositions from Ogle to Ld Bristoll, sent with letter to Ld Bristoll, 24 Novem: 1643.

---

(3) LIEUTENANT-COLONEL MOSELY TO THE EARL OF BRISTOL.
[Tanner MSS. vol. lxii. fol. 418.]

Though my man be so trusty as I dare commit my life unto his hands, yet the ever watchfull eyes of my enemys are soe over all my actions that I conceive it very dangerous to send him often unto your Lordshipp, which consideration had more startled me, had not he informed me that it was your honour's expresse command

[a] *Sic.* ? coming.

that he should attend your Lordshipp on this Thursday.[a] Yet I question not (if any jealousy should arise by any misfortune) but I should be able so to bleare their eyes as that noe degree of discovery should followe; and I wish my ability to expresse the zealous affection I have to the peace of this kingdom and the prosperity of his sacred Ma^{ty} were such as could answere all objections your Lordshipps not knowing me can possibly suggest to your thoughts; for then I should rest assured of your favour in a speedy returne of the signification of his M^{ties} and your Lordshipps will concerning the busines in hand. But I knowe the matter requires most serious deliberation, though the agents in it heere even faint with expectation of the issue. I need not trouble your Lordshipp with a declaration of my particular condition; my servant informs me he hath informed your Lordshipp thereoff, only thus much I humbly beseech your honour to know from me, that I accompt myself only happy in this world in being made an instrument capable of doing his M^{ty} and the kingdome service. My Lord, my man told me your Lordshipp signified unto him that he which should have been the prime actor in this busines is nowe a prisoner with us, which I am not a little sorry for.[b] Mr. D.[c] (who is a very friend of mine, and he which ingaged me in this service) with myself (as privy therunto) had a way to procure the liberty of my L. Mack Mahoone,[d] and had accomplished our designe had not the tumultuous spirits of some citizens crossed

---

[a] Mosely was at Aylesbury at the time he wrote this letter, indorsed Dec. 6, which was a Wednesday. "This Thursday" would therefore mean the following day, Dec. 7. He went to London about the 9th, "taking with him Bristol's reply (No. 4) to his letter, and also other documents (Nos. 5, 6, 7, 8, 9) received from Oxford on the 8th or 9th, connected with the proposals made by Ogle in his letter of Nov. 24. *See* No. 14 and note.

[b] As appears from Bristol's reply (No. 4), the person on whom he had his eye was Thomas Ogle. But Mosely is either not aware of this, or affects not to be so.

[c] Devenish, the keeper of Winchester House, as appears from Bristol's reply (No. 4).

[d] The allusion is obscure. Lord Maguire and Hugh MacMahon, both of whom had taken part in the conspiracy to surprise Dublin in Oct. 1641, were at this time

our desire by complaining to the house of his remove (I question not but your Lordshipp hath heard thereof), whereuppon he was committed close prisoner to the Tower; yet our designe goes on and I hope will shortly come to good effect. If we may doe any service in the like kinde for the person your Lordshipp means (whom I cannot guesse) upon the least intimation from your Lordshipp we shall be as active as possible. I know not whether your Lordshipp be acquainted with Major Ogle that sent yow the letter by my hand; if not, Sir Nic. Crispe can informe your Lordshippe of him; he is a man of a very working braine, and may possibly doe good service, [*Last words obliterated.*] JOHN MOSELY.

Indorsed: L.-Col. Mosely to Lord Bristow, 6 Dec. 1643.

---

(4) THE EARL OF BRISTOL TO LIEUTENANT-COLONEL MOSELY.
[Tanner MSS. vol. lxii. fol. 419.]

For yourself.

Though the party you send to[a] be a stranger to you, as as[b] likewise to him,[c] I made the last addresse by this messenger, yet both your desires seeme to be so reall for the procureing of peace and

prisoners in London. In May 1643 they had been removed from the Tower to Newgate. On Oct. 13 there is the following notice in the *Commons' Journals:*

"Mr. Corbett reports the examination of the business concerning Colonel Read, Macquire, and MacMahun; the endeavour used to procure their escape.

"Resolved, &c. that the Lords Macquire and MacMahun shall be committed to the Tower, and kept close prisoners there." MacMahon, one of the chiefs of the sept of the MaçMahons in the county of Monaghan, may have been spoken of in London as Lord MacMahon. He was condemned of treason, and executed at Tyburn in 1644."—C. J. vol. iii. p. 297. *A Contemporary History of Affairs in Ireland,* edited by J. T. Gilbert, vol. i. part. ii. p. 563.

[a] Bristol himself.   [b] *Sic.*

[c] The meaning of this passage is not clear and has probably been mis-copied. The "him" may perhaps have been originally followed by "to whom," and so refer to Ogle. It can hardly refer to Bristol himself, because the words "both your desires" point to a third person.

quietness in the Church and kingdome that yow shall finde all the assistance and incouragement he can give unto yow. And to the purpose heere goeth a very punctual and exact dispatch of all things that can be desired,[a] the delivery whereof (with safty and speed) is earnestly recommended unto yow, neither can yow employ your paines in a better errand. For the close prisoner you mention in your letter, and for whose release you make the kind offer, it was spoken to your servant that he might conceive that the letters he brought were only for the inlargment of a prisoner, but the prisoner is the Major[b] yow write of. Mr. D. (if it be meant by one Mr. Devonish, of Dorsetshire) if he be hearty and trusty therein the busines will be the better liked of, for that he is knowne (by the party that writeth this) to be an able and dextrous man. If the busines on that side be carried prudently and calmly it shall not here want secrecy nor assistance. Finde meanes (as soone as posibly yow can) of advertiseing of the safe comming of this dispatch to the partyes yow know of; let both yourself and all others (that shall have a hand in this good work) be confident to finde cleere and reall proceeding.

Examined to bee a true coppy of the letter to L. C. M. 11th Dec. 1643, by us,

[c] P. WHARTON.
GILBERT GERARD.
JOHN CLOTWORTHY.

Dec: 7, 1643.

---

[a] Ogle's letter of 24 Nov. and the Propositions reached Oxford Dec. 2. *See* No. 8.
[b] Ogle.
[c] This is the first of the documents to which Wharton, Gerard, and Clotworthy affixed their signatures. Mosely, no doubt, showed them a copy that he or some other made of his letter, written to Bristol from Aylesbury (No. 3), but they could not attest its genuineness. The fact that their names do not appear on the copies of Ogle's letter to Bristol of Nov. 24, and the inclosed Propositions (Nos. 1 and 2), suggest the inference that they did not see the original documents but only copies of them.

(5.) ROYAL WARRANT TO THOMAS DEVENISH.

[Tanner MSS. vol. lxii. fol. 429.]

CHARLES R.

Whereas you have under your custodye att Winchester Howse the person of William[a] Ogle, gent. detayned prisoner there. Our will and pleasure is [and we] doe heereby strictly charge and commaund you upon sigt heereof to release and sett att full libertye the person of the sayd William Ogle, gent. Of this yow must nott fayle, as you will aunsweare the contrary att your perill, and for soe doeing this shall bee your sufficient warrant. Given under our hand and signett att our court att Oxford this 6th of Decemb. in the ninetenth yeare [of] our raigne.

By his Ma^{tys} commaund,

GEORGE DIGBYE.

To   Devenish, keeper att the
present of Winchester Howse in Southwarke.

Examined to bee a true coppy this iith [b] of Decem. 1643, by us,

P. WHARTON.
GILBERT GERARD.
JOHN CLOTWORTHY.

---

(6) SIR GEORGE STRODE TO SAMUEL CRISPE.

[Tanner MSS. vol. lxii. fol. 434.]

COZEN,

Monies doth grow scarce with us, háving lyen heere long with wyfe and chyldren (although not soe many as God sent me); my meanes is kept and taken from mee, and my rents detayned. Tho. Greene, of this cytty, will pay me 100^{li} on a noate of soe much paid in London, unto Mr. William Ogle, who I know not. I have

---

[a] The name "William" was inserted in mistake for "Thomas." *See* No. 12.
[b] *i. e.* 11th.

geiven him a byll at syght which I prey see punctually paid, and, God willing, your said 100^{li} shall be repaid yow, with dammages; but yow may not fayle to pay my byll, my credite resting theron, which is all wee have left to subsist by. I shall neede say noe more. Your brother[a] is well in the west, from whom I have a letter this morning. Restinge

Y^r kinsman to serve you,
GEOG. STRODE.

Oxon, the 7° x^{br}, 1643.

Brother Samuell, I pray pay this 100 pownd for Sr Gorg Strod.

ANN CRISPE.[b]

For my honored kinsman Mr. Samuell Crispe, at the twoe Black boys in Breed streete, these present, for London.

Examined 11th 10^{bris}, 1643.

P. WHARTON.	JOHN CLOTWORTHY.
GILBERT GERARD.	OLIVER ST. JOHN.

(7.) BILL OF EXCHANGE INCLOSED IN A LETTER TO OGLE FROM SIR GEORGE STRODE.

[On the same sheet as the preceding.]

FOR MR. SAMUELL CRISPE IN LONDON.

At syght heerof I pray pay this my only bill off exchange for the some off one hundred powns, unto Mr. William Ogle, gent., and put it to account, returninge unto mee his discharge for soe much; the 7° off x^{ber}, 1643.

Your servant,
GEO: STRODE.

Examined 11th 10^{bris}, 1643.

P. WHARTON.	JOHN CLOTWORTHY.
GILBERT GERARD.	OLIVER ST. JOHN.

[a] Sir Nicholas Crispe.   [b] ? the wife of Sir Nicholas Crispe.

(8.) Letter of Sir George Strode to Thomas Ogle.

[On the same sheet as the preceding.]

For Mr. W. Ogle.

Your letter of the 24 of November came safely to hand the 2^d of this month, but the party that writeth it is unknown to him to whom it was directed;[a] and the knight[b] mencioned in your letter, with whom former correspondence was had, is absent in the west; yet ther appearing therein soe greate a desyre of peace, and the quiett of the Church and kingdom, all is effected that in your said letter is desyred, and is sent, according to your directions therein gieven, by which it will appeare how willingly all motions tending to peace and accomodation have admittance heere ; and that party that makes you this answere[a] as hee hath endevoured to satisfy you in these fyrst beginnings, soe shall hee bee most redy to contribute any thing further in his power that may conduce to the ending off these miseries and dystracsions, by which this church and kingdom are made soe unhappy, which he conceiveth (suitable to what you write) can only be effected by ways of moderation and temper; the parties may com and goe,[c] most assuredly, and what is don, I conceive, will geive you noe dyscouragement.

Dec. 7, 1643.

You must be careful that the bill of exchange and letter of advice [d] together and that it bee dyscreetly carried.

The letter dyrected for Mr. W. Ogle hath bin examined, and what is written on the other side is a true copy theroff together with a byll of exchange inclosed therin.   P. Wharton.
                                                                        Gilbert Gerard.
11 Decemᵣ 1643.   John Clotworthy.

Indorsed : Coppy of letters to Ogle and Crispe, with letter of Exchange for 100^{li}. 7 Dec. 1643.

[a] Bristol.
[b] Sir Nicholas Crispe. *See* No. 1.
[c] Between Oxford and London.
[d] A word lost, the page being torn.

(9.) SAFE CONDUCT SENT BY THE KING FOR THREE PERSONS, WITH A BLANK LEFT FOR THEIR NAMES.

[Tanner MSS. vol. lxii. fol. 437.]

CHARLES R.

Charles, by the grase of God, King of England, etc., to our generals, lieutenant-generalls, gouvenours of townes, collonells, captaines, and all other officers and soldiers belonging to any of our armies or garrisons, and to all other whom it may conserne, Greeting, Wheras the three persons heerin named, viz.:

are to repayre unto our Court at Oxford about our spetiall affayres, we do by thes present streightly charge and comand you to let them passe freely from place to place unto our Courte att Oxford from our cittye of London without lett or interuption. And of theis our comandes we shall expect a due observance from you and every of you, as you will answre the contrarey at your perille.

This safe conduct untill the tenth of Januari next ensuinge the date hearof.

By his Ma^{ts} commaund,

GEORGE DIGBYE.

Examined this 11th of Decem: 1643, to bee a true coppy by us

P. WHARTON.
GILBERT GERARD.
JOHN CLOTWORTHY.

Safe conduct.

(10.) MR. SAMUEL CRISPE TO SIR GEORGE STRODE.

[Tanner MSS. vol. lxii. fol. 438.]

HONOURED SIR, London, the 12 December, 1643.

Your letter dated the 7th[a] I have received, and according to your letter and bill of exchange on me I have paide it on sight the summe of one hundred pounds, and have take[n] up your bill of exchange and a reciept for it, of which summe[b] is payde to Mr. Will. Ogle, as will apeare with acquittance I will send by my cousin Cox; he tell me will goe this weeke. Sir, heere is a most miserable time of trading and no mony to be had from any man allmost that oweth me mony. I pray God send better time, or else this kingdome will suffer much. Sir, the halfe of our gould[c] that came is voted in the house, and saith will pay us againe in March next. God knowe howe it be performed. We could not help ourself, being all the gould were in their possession, and as yet we have none power to recover the other half, but shall. The Parliament sent it all to the Tower to be guined[d]; we gave the Parliament all that the company were indebted, and want to pay debt. All would not serve turne. I pray God to worke in the heart of the parlia-

---

[a] No. 6.   [b] *Sic.*

[c] Sir Nicholas Crispe, Knight (the brother of Samuel Crispe), formerly a farmer of the customs, had been found by the committee of the navy to owe to the State more than 16,000*l*. On Feb. 18, 1643, the Parliament had ordered that "the stock and adventure in the Ginny Company," belonging to Sir Nicholas, should be sequestered in the hands of John Wood, treasurer to the company, towards payment of this debt. On the arrival of a vessel, "The Starre," laden with gold ore, Wood and the other partners agreed to lend the half for the supply of the wants of the navy, until it should be shown what part belonged to Sir Nicholas. Accordingly, the two Houses ordered that whatever sums belonged to the said Wood and partners, over and above the said Sir Nicholas Crispe's part of the stock and adventure, should be repaid to them upon the following 25th of March, out of the customs collected in the port of London, with allowance of 8 per cent. interest. 2 Dec. 1643.—C. J. vol. ii. p. 326; L. J. vol. vi. p. 321.

[d] Coined.

ment to preserve this kingdome. Sir, I pray remember my service to my Lady and all with yow. So praying God in his due time to send us a joyfull meeting, so shall ever rest

Your to be commanded,
SAMUELL CRISPE.

To my much honoured kinsman, Sir George Strowde, knight, this present.

Attested to be a true coppy by
JOHN MOSELY.
THO. DEVENISH.

(11.) ACQUITTANCE OF THOMAS OGLE TO SAMUEL CRISPE ON RECEIPT OF £100.

[Tanner MSS. vol. lxii. folio 436.]

The xii[th] daye of December, 1643.

Receaved the day and yeare above written from the hands of Mr. Samuel Crispe the som of on hundred pound of currant English mony. I say received by me, WILL. OGLE.

Attested by
JOHN MOSELY.
THO. DEVENISH.

Indorsed: Coppy of Ogle's acq. to Crispe.

(12.) THOMAS DEVENISH TO THE EARL OF BRISTOL.

[Tanner MSS. vol. lxii. fol. 450.]

RIGHT HONOURABLE,

Tusday[a] last I received a vissite from two freuds of my old acquaintanc, whose erand mad them the better welcom, and for answering both ther expectacons I shall not fayle to contribut

[a] Dec. 13, the day this letter is dated, was Wednesday; Tuesday last would be Dec. 12.

my best endevors; one hath his erand, and the other I hope shall not stay long,[a] which at first I resolved to have performed in silenc on my parte, not presuming to trouble your honour especially at this time, but my duti and affection to the buysnes (which it concerns), the progresse whereof I apprehend to conduce so much to the publique good, that mad me wilfully repell all reasons that might dissuade me, and adventure to give your Lordshipp this best accoumpt, not only of my readeynis to do servic, but allso of the hopes which I conceave of the suckcesse (ther being so good a foundacon laid) if the maiors[b] zeale doth not in the prevention overballance his prudence, which I hope your wisdom will prevente, and in that hope I humbly tak my leave.

    Your honours to be
        Commanded in what I may,
            D.

London, 13° Decem. 1643.
 Concordat cum originali.
  ex^r per Tho. Devenish.
Indorsed: Coppy of letter of Devenish to Ld. Bristoll, 13 Decem. 1643.

(13.) THOMAS OGLE TO THE EARL OF BRISTOL.

[Tanner MSS. vol. lxii. fol. 458.]

MY LORD,

On Munday night last [c] late, I received your honours dispatch, whereby I perceive your Lordship did not remember me. Tis

---

[a] Presumably Mosely and Ogle. Mosely came to London about Dec. 9. Compare (No. 14) Mosely to Bristol.   [b] Ogle's.

[c] Dec. 15, the day on which this letter is dated, was Friday; Monday last, therefore, Dec. 11. All the letters, &c. written in Oxford Dec. 7 (Nos. 4, 5, 6, 7, 8, 9) were examined by Wharton, Gerard, and Clotworthy on Dec. 11. We have no letter of that date from Bristol to Ogle, and the word "despatch" does not necessarily imply a letter. Bristol may merely have sent the other letters by a messenger of his own. Ogle probably refers to the opening words of Strode's letter to himself (No. 8).

trew I did not presume of any perticuler interest or acquantance with your honour. But I was confident that, besides Sir Nicholas his informations, your Lordship would easily call me to mynd when you did but heare of Mr. Smart's [a] cause, to which your honour and my Lord Digby [b] were pious and just freinds, in the respective houses. But principally the matter conteyned in the letter did emboulden me to presume upon my generall acquantance (begun at Rippon at the pasificatione; and continued since in par[liament] upon occasione of my father's cause) with your honour, to make that addres unto your Lordship, by the happy effectinge whereof I hope with approbatione to be booth knowen and admitted by your Lordship hareafter to be your honours faithfull and trusted freind and servant.

My Lord, on Tusday [c] night last (as this enclosed letter and acquittance will shew) I receved the money, for which I retourne your honour most humble and hartie thanks, with assurance that I will never faile upon occasione to requite soe greate a favour. And the fulness of your Lordship's retourne shall spedily and really (God willinge) be answered by a faithfull performance of the intimatione given, which I assure your honour is heightned to that degre of resolutione (by his M^{aties} and your Lordship's effectuall resentment) as ther is more resolved and wilbe actually done then I did hope for before our arrivall at Courtt. And to give your honour the better ground to assure his M^{atie} hereoff, I send hereinclosed a letter

---

[a] Peter Smart, a prebendary of Durham Cathedral, who, for preaching a sermon against the use of ceremonies, had been degraded from the clerical office by the northern High Commission Court in 1629. In 1640 Smart brought his case before the notice of the Long Parliament, and Dr. Cosin, who had taken a leading part in his prosecution, was impeached. As Ogle was Smart's son-in-law it is probable that he came from Durham, where a branch of the Ogle family, of Causey Park, Northumberland, had long been seated.—Hodgson's *History of Northumberland*, vol. ii. part ii. p. 135.

[b] Bristol's eldest son.   [c] Dec. 12.

from Mr. Devenish,[a] whose harte is as right and indeavours wilbe as cordial for establishinge his M^{aties} full, just, and antient power and authoritie, as can be desired. And fore that end he did first ingage the partie who conveyes thes letters, who is most firme, as the effectuall fruites, shortly answeringe your Lordship's expectation and your promise, will evidently declare. Though for the present I am found to delay my cominge (for strengthening our preparations prudently and calmely as your honour advises) thereby to make the event more certayne and infallible; yet within a few weekes your honour may expect us, and I hope shall[b] *   *

My Lord, I beseeh your honour pardon me for beinge thus generall; the names, the particulers, I am forced to conceale for secrecies sake in case of miscarradge, that whatever becomes of me the busines may happily goe on. And for I have noe more to troble your Lordship with att this tyme, save to desire a few lines to assure me of the receit hereof; and alsoe a kynd and effectuall letter to Mr. Devenish for his and. his freinds incouradgementt, that his Mag^t will take them into his protectione and satisfy ther disbursements about this busines; with the presentment of my unfeined service to the Right Honourable the Lord Digby, craveing your honour's pardon and patience, I rest

                Your Lordship's faithfull and
                    Devoted servant till death,
                              TH. OGLE.

Winchester house,
  X^{ber} 15, 1643.

My Lord, my name was mistake Will. for Thom. Pray pardone my bad wreitinge.

---

[a] Ogle, therefore, inclosed in this letter, dated Dec. 15 (1), Devenish's letter to Bristol (No. 12), dated Dec. 13, and (2) Crispe's letter to Strode (No. 10), dated Dec. 12, which contained his own acquittance for the 100*l*. Mosely was probably the bearer of all at least as far as Aylesbury.

[b] Here follow five words, which I was unable to read with certainty; but they look like "shell a Christenmas pye in it."

Attested a true copy, 15 Dec. 1643,
JOHN MOSELY.
THO. DEVENISH.

Indorsed: Coppy of Ogle's letter to Ld. Bristow, 15 Decem: 1643.

---

(14) LIEUTENANT-COLONEL MOSELY TO THE EARL OF BRISTOL.

[Tanner MSS. vol. lxii. fol. 462.]

MY LORD,

I have beene in London these eight or nine daies[a] to get money for the regiment,[b] but have had farre better successe in my more intended businesses. I hope your Lordship doth not thinke it long, when you concider how much it stands us upon as yet (on this side) to be most circumspect, especially my selfe, who having a command am more deeply ingaged both in life and honour should it come to be discovered. My Lord, I delivered the dispatch safely into the person's hands to whom it was directed: the money is paid, the

[a] Mosely probably arrived at London from Aylesbury, Dec. 10 or 11. The papers that he brought with him (Nos. 4, 5, 6, 7, 8, 9) were all read by Wharton, Gerard, and Clotworthy on Dec. 11. On Dec. 12 he visited Devenish. *See* No. 12.

[b] Mosely must have come to London with the double object of getting pay for the garrison at Aylesbury, and of showing the letters which he had received from Oxford. That the Commons were uneasy about the town is apparent from notices in their Journals. The soldiers were unpaid, and threatening to disband. On Dec. 9 there is the following order: "Mr. Browne, Reynolds, Dacres, Fountaine, Sir Jo. Clotworthy, Captain Wingate, Mr. Holland, are presently to go forth to receive informations from the gentleman that is come from Aylesbury, and to consider of some speedy way for the security of that place." Very probably this gentleman was Mosely himself. But, however that may be, it is evident that after his arrival in London the question of finding money for the garrison was recognised to be an urgent one, and that he was not so unsuccessful in his endeavour as he sought to represent.—C. J. Dec. 23, 25, Jan. 8; L. J. Jan. 10.

maior is at his owne will, and intendeth, I thinke, to waite upon your honour the next weeke, unlesse your Lordship upon any service of greater concernement shall command him to stay longer. I percieve their doubtfullnesse, what answer it would please his sacred Matie and your Lordship to give to their motion caused them a little to suspend their activenesse, whereby they are not so fully prepared as I hoped I should have found them; but (may it please your honour) *sat cito si sat bene*. Mr. D. is that Mr. Devenish of Dorsetshire, whose fidelity, discretion, secrecy, and care, I hope your Lordship shall never find cause to question, being a man who (I am persuaded) would spend willingly his dearest blood in opposition of the C[ovenant], which we are all cleare in (and so are thousands in London) will lie heaviere upon us then Episcopacy ever either did or can, which (if his Matie shall please to give a gracious answer to our desires) I question not will be prevented.

My Lord, the only thing I am jealous of is discovery by occasion of my sending to Oxford, both in regard of my many enemies, as also the fate (I thinke) of the towne, which ever hitherto hath had strange successe in discoveries: this doth a litle trouble me, and I should be very happy if your honour would please to give me some direction in it. Many waies have runne in my fancy to secure me; this stratagem doth like me best, if I may have your Lordship's approbation (for without it I will doe nothing). I may pretend to have large proffers made me to deliver up Alesbury to his Matie, which I may discover to my Lord of Essex, and if I can get a warrant from him to treat, *omnis res erit in vado*, I humbly conceive it can be no prejudice to any service to be done (either in that or any other kind) within the spheare of my power; it will worke in them a great confidence of my fidelity, and make them secure of me; and if my servants comming to Oxen be observed, and it come to my Lord Generall's care, your Lordship knows how I may frame my answer; thus armed I shall be bold to serve his Matie and your Lordship in anything you shall command.

Your honours devoted servant.

Attested to be a true coppy by
JOHN MOSELY.
Indorsed: 18 Dec. 1643, copy of L. C. Mosely to Lord Bristow.

(15.) THE EARL OF BRISTOL TO LIEUTENANT-COLONEL MOSELY.
[Tanner MSS. vol. lxii. fol. 466.]

Your desyres are such for the publicke quiett that yow may be confident of all assistance from hence. Yow goe upon a good grounde and such a one as must unite all honest Englishmen, although in other thinges of different miudes, which is not to be overrunn by an invasion of the Scotts, who if they should prevayle will tyranize both over our estates and consciences.

As for the pretexte you speake of, a way can hardely be sett downe on the suddayne, but use your owne discretion to make such papers and invitations as yow thinke fitt to serve for a pretence uppon any occasion that should happen. But for your going to the Earle you write of, stay a little befor yow resolve on it, untill yow see thinges brought to a little more ripenesse.

Tuesday, at three o'clock, 19th

Send no oftner then ther is necessity. The party is directed whether to goe privately.[a]

(16.) THOMAS DEVENISH TO THE EARL OF BRISTOL.
[Tanner MSS. vol. lxii. fol. 494.]

MY LORD,

I hope by this time Ogle is arrived att Oxford.

The contrivance of his passage was soe happyly layde and ordered, thatt noe reflection of prejudice reacheth mee, which in relation to further services I ame nott sorry for.

---

[a] This letter has no indorsement on it to the effect that it is a copy.

Before hee went wee tasted some, and perticularly Mr. Ny and Mr. Goodwin, whoe as they are very eminent and have great interest in the most active people, soe wee found them—and theire principles leade them to itt—to bee very desirous of theire liberty. They may proove very instrumentall when they shall have afterwards from the King whatt they may trust too; till when as they will not have sufficient grounds to bee thouroughly satisfyed in theyre owne breasts, soe will they nott engage themselfes with confidence to act upon the cyttysons for soe great an alteration, for if they have nothing to moove them by way of allurement and that all shall be left to theyre jealousy and feare of the Scotch and presbitery, itt may prevayle with them perhapps to retire; but nott to apply themselfes to the King without some reasonable invitations, which these very feares and jealousyes may make way for the embracement of.

By Ogle your Lordship receaved a character whereof hee hath noe key, because I desire hee should know noe more then your Lordship shall thinke fitt, and for the farther and better prevention of any discovery of this great busynesse of consequence in case of intercepting any lettors of or on, itt may please your Lordship by your next to commaund mee to whome and whither I shall superscribe my lettors, and your Lordship may bee pleased to direct yours to mee to Mr. Christopher Vine, in Peeter's Streete, in Westminster.

There is a way layde to gitt the names of the officers in the trayne bands of the militia in London, and thatt beeing had, itt shall bee seriously considered whoe will bee the fitter to worke by, and your Lordship shall have an account thereof very speedyly.

Tis conceaved the fitt choyse of persons of severall vocations to bee the first steppe to bee made in this worke, and therefore having already chosen some few of the clergy and of the army (of which I dare boldly reccommend L.-Coll. Mosely as a person of faythfulnesse and ingenuyty) twas thought convenient to make this enquyry into the cytty officers.

The time of the safe conduct will bee exspired the 10th of th[is] instant, and therefore your Lordship will procure and send some of a larger date for three or foure, and yow may bee pleased to cause them to bee single ones, for 'twill be occasion of lesse suspition to have persons goe singly, and there may bee occasion of severall dispatches. However, itt can bee of noe disadvantage to have itt in our choyce.

The bearer heerof is a person whome your Lordship may trust. Hee is (without beeing made acquainted with perticular persons engaged) in some measure made privy into the designe in generall, as one whoe heereafter good use may bee made of, his interest in that sort of people beeing greater then his outward condition promiseth.

Reade to my Ld. Genrall, Sir Gilbert Gerard, Mr. Sollicitor, and examined to bee a true coppy by us this 5th of January, 1643.

P. WHARTON.
THO. DEVENISH.

Indorsed: Coppy of Devenish letter to Ld. Bristow, 5 Jan. 1643.

(17.) THOMAS OGLE TO THOMAS DEVENISH [a]
[Tanner MSS. vol. lxii. fol. 498.]

SIR,

On Weddensday [b] att night last late, I arrived safely here about 9 a cloke, where I found all the portes shutt, but upon informatione thatt I was come by spectiall directions from his Maity they were opened and I brought to the partie yow know off, where, after a lardge discourse, his Lordship sent a gent to se me provided for that

---

[a] The words in italics are in cipher, with a contemporary decipher written above them. The MS. is probably a holograph, as it is hardly likely that the copyist would have taken the trouble to copy the cipher. The address on the outside of the MS. and the remains of a seal also suggest that the paper is that which Devenish received.

[b] Jan. 6, the day the letter is dated, was Saturday; Wednesday, Jan. 3.

night, and the next day provisione made of *chambers* in *Mawdlen Colegge* to the end they should be *secretly treated* with all. There is nothing further can be *don in the busines yntill they be*[a] *come*. Pray therefore in case they *be not,* then *send them hither* with all possible speed, especially Mr. *Nye whom*[b] *yow* may assure to be *admitted his Majesties chaplain and highly preferred* upon the conclusione. Pray therefore faile nott to send Mr. *Nye to me,* and lett him make haste hither, as *yow* and *he wish wel to the business.* I have no more to write until we mete, save only that all things are in as good a posture and equipage here as your harte can wish; and in perticuler grea[t] care and respect had of yourselfe, of which yow will assuredly injoye the benefitt in an ample manner; and so with my harty commendations to yow and your bedfellow I rest your assured

Lovinge faithfull freind,
THOMAS OGLE.

Jan: six[t], 1643.

Addressed: To my honored freind Mr. T. D. att W. in London.

Indorsed: Ogle to Devenish, 6 Janur: 1643.

---

(18) THOMAS OGLE TO PHILIP NYE.
[Tanner MSS. vol. lxii. fol. 500.[c]]

SIR,

I hope before my letter come to London to se yow here with me, yet doubtinge ther might be some occasione of longer stay than I expected, 1 did thinke it very necessarie to give an account what truly I find the state here since my short comminge

---

[a] "They be" is the correct decipher, though in the MS. an unintelligible word is written.

[b] So by the cipher; the word written is "thom."

[c] The handwriting is the same as in No. 17.

On Weddensday^a att night last, after the ports were shutt, I came to Oxford, which were commanded by his M^{atie} to be opened upon intimatione that I was there, and after my cominge and stay at court about an hower a lodginge provided for me alsoe, where I made a lardge discourse and received as large a satisfactione as can be desired : which was that those thinges desired should be confirmed, not only by his M^{atie} but by the generall consell^b appoynted here to mete very shortly, which I assure yow was either caled or at least hastned for this very busines upon my intimatione.

Sir, you are principally loked upon in this busines, and your presence or absence here will mutch hinder or further the effecting therof. Therfore, since your uttmost endeavers and abilities have bene always bent this way, let nothinge hinder your presence here to attayne the desired end, which is as sincerely intended on this side as it is desired of you. Pray therfore, Sir, make some excuse for your absence for 4 or 5 dayes, as you respect either the cause or your owne preferment, and faile not to come to your very lo. freind to serue you.

THOMAS OGLE.

Directed: *for my reverend friend Mr. Nye one of the assembly* give this in *Westminster*, to his owne hands.^c

Indorsed : Ogle to Mr. Nye, 7 Janu: 1643.

---

(19) HEADS OF INSTRUCTIONS GIVEN BY THE EARL OF BRISTOL.

[Tanner MSS. vol. lxii. fol. 502.]

The demandes in particular.
The particulars that may induce therunto.
That persons be imployed into all places, etc.
That the partyes be hastned away.

---

^a Jan. 3.   ^b *i.e.* the Oxford Parliament.

^c The cipher is the same as that used in the previous letter, but is not deciphered in the MS.

L. Say, etc.
Independents wilbe.
Assembly goes on the same grounds.
A disguised hand.
To leave the papers.

[Another hand.] Direct letters sometimes to Mr. John Squire at Mr. Chesterman's house over against the Crosse Inn in Oxon, and sometimes to M^ris Emma Brome at the president's lodgings at Magdalen Colledge.

Indorsed: Ld. Bristoll's Heads of Instructions to the Messenger. 9 Janu: 1643.

(20) THOMAS OGLE TO THOMAS DEVENISH.

[Copy. Tanner MSS. vol. lxii. fol. 503.]

HONEST FRIND,

Here is inclosed a letter[a] from the Lord that write unto yow. I did mutch admire yow write not to me, and send his letter[b] open that I might understand the contents of it. Pray hereafter let me receive your dispatches, and nothing be concealed from me in this transactione, for it can serve for no end, but to doe great harme, to create jelosies and suspitiones, and to bringe me into a disesteem here: and the mayntenance of my reputatione here wilbe a principall meanes to effect as the means, soe the end, I and yow proposed in this busines. I assure yow I have already met with mighty clashes here, and shall every day have more, if I be discountenanced. Pray therefore send me a coppy of the letter yow sent the partie yow write unto, and me hereafter receive all the dispatches, that therby I may be inabled happily to conclude this busines. I have write to Mr. God.[c] for money. Pray let me have your

[a] No. 21.
[b] Devenish's letter to Bristol of Jan. 5 (No. 16).
[c] Mr. Goodwyn. *See* No. 22.

best assistance herein, for I assure yow, upon ther cominge, my repayment of the 100ˡⁱ I received will doe them, me, and the busines an extraordinaire advantage and creditt; for as I know yow doubt not my care and fidelitie herein, soe yow need not questione a full, clere, reall, and ingenious dealinge here. This bearer will informe perticulerly of his and my interteynment and conditione here. Ther[fore] I shall write noe more, only dy[sire] yow to hasten them here, to speake to Mr. G. for the money I write for, and let Mr. M. goe to my wife from Mr. G. with the money I mentioned in his letter.

Remember me, and recommend the busines to God in your prayers. *Vale!*

Yr. lo. and assured freind.

9ᵐᵒ Jan. 1643.

Remember Wind[sor ᵃ] and your sone. Ther is somethinge in your letter that seems a contradictione to what I have saide about that busines. Pray avoyde this roke ᵇ here after by your addresses and open letters to me.

Indorsed: Coppy of Ogles to Mr. Devenish, 9 Janu. 1643.

(21.) THE EARL OF BRISTOL TO THOMAS DEVENISH.ᶜ

[Tanner MSS. vol. lxii. fols. 505-508.]

Yours of the 5ᵗʰ of Jan. is come safe to hand, and all things are dispatched according to your desire, and I doubt nott butt the readynesse yow find heere will bee a just ground to begett confi-

ᵃ See No. 23.   ᵇ *i.e.* "rock."

ᶜ There are two copies of the Earl's letter. The one partly in cipher, with a contemporary decipher, possibly the paper transmitted to Devenish from Oxford; the other a transcript of the whole, without any cipher. The opening words show that Bristol was writing to Devenish—" Yours of the 5 Jan." (No. 16).

dence, which is the first thing yow must labor to settle, of which this bearar hath instructions to speake with yow. Ogle is heere, and I beleeve will be hearty; yett if itt were nott for the reliance I have upon your discretion and affection in this cause I should nott have those hopes which I have of good successe. I hope God will make yow an instrument of doeing much good and meriting much.

The grounds that in the first place are to bee layd are these:

Thatt men bee induced to unite themselfes agaynst the invasion of the Scots, whose intent can bee noe other then to overrunne this nation.

Thatt men bee convinced in theire judgements that if the presbittery bee once brought in, all sorts of men thatt shall not conforme to them must exspect more severity and persecution in poynt of conscience then from the Spanish inquisition itselfe.

Agaynst this tiranny both over men's fortunes and consciences there must bee an absolute union and conjunction settled in the first place, and this nott onely in London but over all the kingdome of England, thatt the odiousnesse of the Scotts invasion may possesse all true Englishmen's mindes.

In the second place for the securing of the Independents of theire owne ease and liberty, I noe wayes doubt but when the particulars shalbe propounded there will be such satisfaction as will give content to yow or any discreete person or persons that shall be imployed therein. Wherein I most earnestly intreate yow that noe more tyme may be lost, but that some trusty and able parson or parsons be speedily imployd, for it wilbe of greate importance that the buisinesse be in some sort settled before the assembly heere begins the 22th of this month.[a] And as this care is taken for satisfying of Independents, soe they must lay the grounds of the assistance and advantages that may acrew to the King by which he may be induced to this favour and indulgence towards them. And truly it will be expected that those which have above all men bin most active in another way should now be as active in all things that

[a] Charles's Oxford Parliament.

may conduce to the King's service, and resisting this wicked invasion of the Scotts, and they must endeavor to make themselves as considerable to the King as possibly may bee.

January 9th, 1643.

Sir John Digby, brother to Sir Kenelme, is in some place prisoner in London. I shal intreate yow to enquire after him and to afford him as much friendship as with discretion yow may, and if hee should bee in any want I pray yow supply him, and I will see yow satisfyed, and lett him know that yow have such order from mee.

---

(22) THOMAS OGLE TO THOMAS GOODWIN.
[Tanner MSS. vol. lxii. fol. 504.]

REVEREND SIR,

This bearer can informe yow what interteinment I and he have had here. And what yow, your brother N.[a] and the rest are like to find; therefore I shall add nothinge, save to desire yow and him, as yow love the cause and your owne contrie and preferment, make haste to me. This bearer can tell yow what I have done in your busines; my care and interest shall not be wantinge to finish itt, which certainly wilbe if yow be not wantinge to yourselfes, for as yow shall receive full satisfactione soe it is here expected that yow give assured testemoneye of your strength and abilities to doe the works proposed; for that end bringe the remonstrance with yow which your brother N.[a] toold me of, and a list of the mil[itia] and com[manders] C[ity] of L[ondon], with an estimate of your strength in booth Ar[mie]s. And alsoe I pray bringe 100^{li} or 200^{li} alonge with yow, for I am in veric great want of money, etc. Ther is none to be had here to supply either me or themselves. Except, therefore, as I labour in your worke, soe you in some measure assist me to live, and follow it, I cannot continew in this

[a] Nye.

place, but must retire myselfe elsewhere into employment. I know your credit is soe good amongst your con[gregation] that yow may have 200^h for askinge. In the meane tyme pray furnish my wife with 40^h or 50^{li}, that she spedily come to me with her children. And leave something with her disstressed father[a] towards his releife untill I can take further care for him. This gent. hath promised me the utmost asistance for the procuringe this money. Mr. D. will tell yow wher to find and how to send to my wife. Remember me in your prayers, and make what haste you possibly can to

Your assured lo: faithfull
frind to serve you.

9no Jan. 1643.

Indorsed: Coppy of Ogles to Mr. Goodwin, 9 Janu. 1643.

(23.) THOMAS OGLE TO THOMAS DEVENISH.

[Tanner MSS. vol. lxii. fol. 533.[b] *Undated.*]

HONEST FRIND,

The newes we received from London of Mr. Roylies and the other committment[c] haith made a stay of my first dispatch. Thes inclosed copies will instruct you sufficientlie of the trew state of that busines and its originall here, which was upon an overture from London by an unknowne man. I conceive its some that I have discoursed unto of the moderate sorte of men, who had not patience to tarry my addres, beinge soe longe delayed. Now your worke is to se if this partie and our correspondents can be joyned firmly together, since the busines is soe sowne brooke outt. Assure yourselfe that ther is

---

[a] *i.e.* Peter Smart.

[b] This letter, and No. 25, are neither dated, signed, nor indorsed. The handwriting in both is the same, and both, as internal evidence shows, were written by Ogle, the one to Devenish, the other to Mosely. The handwriting is not the same as in Ogle's letters to Devenish and Nye (Nos. 16 and 17). If, therefore, these two last are holographs, Nos. 23 and 25 must be copies.

[c] As Ryley and Violet were committed to the Tower on Jan. 6, it seems most probable that this letter was written before Bristol's letter to Mosely of Jan. 15, and I have, therefore, reversed the order which the two hold in the Tanner MSS.

the most reallytie here can be imagined, soe gratiouse a kinge, soe willinge expressiones he made to me, as would have moved an harte of stone. Pray use your utmost dexteritie to joyne the strenght of booth thes parties together, and be confident of all the helpe and assistance from his Matie thatt can be possiblelie. Upon any way we shalbe advertised, inquire exactly of the busines, the state of itt, and write bake to me in my owne caracter.

I have sent yow a gratious and fre warrant[a] from his Mag^{tie}, who is soe well pleased with your affectiones and the settlementt of the desinge for Windsor before my cominge away, thatt yow may be assured of the benefit. Pray therefore actually and really intend it, and withe all speed settle it accordinge to this warrantt, that att worst will preserve us all, and abate the furie of this presbyterian factione.

The Lord direct us all aright. *Vale* [?]

Your assured faithfull freind.

Pray scind me bake all those papers I left with yow while yow kepe [?] att Westminster. Haste our frind's letter.

---

[a] In the list of documents in the *Commons' Journals* (iii. 378) is mentioned, "The King's warrant to Mr. Devenish to raise 200 men, under his son's command. to be put into the garrison of Windsor." In the *Lords' Journals* (iv. 395) "The King's letter to Mr. Devenish, keeper of Winchester House, dated from Oxford, 12 Jan. 1643." The *Kingdom's Weekly Intelligencer*, No. 41, tells the tale as follows: "Mr. Devenish, finding his addresses so acceptable, writ again in figures to the Earle of Bristoll and propounded unto him a design he had to betray Windsor Castle at the same time into his Majesties hands, by taking advantage of a fear that would possess them upon the surrender of Aylesbury. His Majesty and the Earl of Bristol well approved of the design, and both of them in severall letters, signed with their own hands, highly extolled his wisdome, promised great rewards, as by the letters appeares." (*King's Pamphlets*, E. $\frac{40}{19}$). The only letter written by the King to Devenish, of which report is made in the *Journals* of either House, is the one mentioned above. We possess only two letters of Bristol's to Devenish, and in one of these (No. 21) there is no mention of a design upon Windsor.

(24) THE EARL OF BRISTOL TO LIEUT.-COLONEL MOSELY.

[Tanner MSS. vol. lxii. fol. 510.]

You are intreated to deferr your journeye and wholy to tende the bussinesse. The tyme holdeth the first day and all thinges wil be readye, according as is settled. You must not fayle to sende your man hether on Friday, to retourne to yow on Saturday,[a] and then advertise the major of all that is further needefull. You may assure your frendes that all goeth here to their mindes, and they and yow I doubt will have much comforte insteede of certeyne distraction otherwayes if Scots prevayle.

This is written by my Ld. of Bristow, my man standing by.[b]

Indorsed: Ld. Bristoll to L.-Coll. Mosely, 15 Janu: 1643.

(25.) THOMAS OGLE TO LIEUT.-COLONEL MOSELY.[c]

[Tanner MSS. vol. lxii. fol. 535. *Undated.*]

HONEST FREIND,

Last night I tarred at Court till past 11 a cloke. His ^{Matie} read, debated, consulted, upon the paper we booth signed; the result whereoff you have in this inclosed paper which I received from that Honourable Lord you write unto,[d] which yow must punctually observe, and in case my Lord Wharton should press yow to goe up

[a] 15 Jan. the date of this lettter according to the indorsement, was Monday; the following Friday and Saturday would therefore be Jan. 19 and 20. On Sunday, the 21st, the royalist forces approached Aylesbury, and the allusion must relate to the design upon the town.

[b] These words are written in another hand to the letter.

[c] *See* Note to No. 23.

[d] His Majesty's instructions to Lieutenant-Colonel Mosely, to blow up the magazine, in case of sudden discovery, mentioned in the *Commons' Journals*, which may be identical with the document mentioned in the *Lords' Journals:* "The King's letter to Lieutenant-Colonel Mosely concerning the surrendering up to him of the town of Aylesbury."

about those coates yow must faine yourselfe sicke, and wholy intend the busines in hand. Send this bearer to me on Friday[a] without faile by whom Ile retourne the instrumentt, and for the dispatches you have for our frinds send them to London by your brother Sheifeild and pray send up ten pound to my wife that she may come to me; and write by your brother Sheifeild to my L. Essex secretary for a pass to be given your brother for Mrs. Marshall, her two children, and Mr. Welbye. I have here taken order for a wach one Mr. Simsone, which hath a pass to come to the French Ambassador[b] on Weddensday or Thursday. Pray therfore send away Mr. Sheifeild the morrow early and give our frinds all assurance of reallitie, but intimate nothinge of the busines in hand. I know your dexteritie and zeale attend the busines in hand   [Last words defaced.]

---

[a] Probably Friday, Jan. 19. The Royalist forces advanced towards Aylesbury on Sunday, Jan. 21. This letter is probably identical with "Captain Ogle's letter to Lieutenant-Colonel Mosely about the time of delivery up of the town," mentioned in the *Commons' Journals,* vol. iii. p. 378.

[b] The Prince of Harcourt, a special ambassador, came to England to mediate between the King and the Parliament. The two Houses, in answer to his overtures made through the Earl of Northampton, replied "that if the Prince D'Harcourt have anything to propose from the French King to the Lords and Commons assembled in the Parliament of England, the Houses have done nothing to bar or hinder the Prince D'Harcourt from the usual and fitting ways of address to them." Dec. 6. (C. J. vol. iii. pp. 319, 330.) As Charles at this time refused to recognise the two Houses as the Parliament of England, Harcourt's efforts to bring about a negociation were necessarily unavailing.

INDEX

Aylesbury, promise to surrender, 6

Bristol, Earl of, prepares to correspond with Ogle, 12; Accepts overtures of Moseley, 25; promises liberty of conscience to Independents, 32

Charles I. authorises the release of Ogle, 14; sends a safe conduct to Ogle and others, 17

Crispe, Sir Nicholas, called before the Commons, escapes from London, 1 (Note b).

Crispe, Samuel, pays money to Ogle, 18

Goodwin, Thomas, overtures made to him by Devenish, 26

MacMahon, projected escape of, 11

Moseley visits London, 23

Nye, Philip, in Scotland, 5; overtures made to him by Devenish, 26; offered a chaplaincy to the King, 28

Poole, attempt on, 6 (Note c)

Strode, Sir George, sends money to Ogle, 14

Ryley, commitment of, 34

A LETTER

FROM

THE EARL OF MANCHESTER

TO THE HOUSE OF LORDS,

GIVING AN OPINION ON THE

CONDUCT OF OLIVER CROMWELL.

EDITED BY

SAMUEL RAWSON GARDINER, LL.D.,

DIRECTOR OF THE CAMDEN SOCIETY.

PRINTED FOR THE CAMDEN SOCIETY.

M.DCCC.LXXXIII

PREFACE.

The following letter is ascribed in the Catalogue of the Tanner MSS. to Sir William Waller. Its real authorship is unmistakable, and if it had fallen into Mr. Bruce's hands it would have formed part of the collection which, after his death, was edited for the Society by Professor Masson. Its importance as showing what were the grounds on which Manchester quarrelled with Cromwell is at once evident.

LETTER

FROM

THE EARL OF MANCHESTER

TO THE HOUSE OF LORDS.

[Tanner MSS. vol. lxi. fol. 205.]

Dec. ? 1644.

MY LORDS,

In obedience to your commands I shall give your Lo^{pps} an account of that which with much trouble I have of late laboured under; the discontents that have bin in that army wch I have the honor to comaund. My Lords, when I found these differences in my army to grow to some height, and considered the inconveniences thatt might thence ensue, I brought to London twoe persons of my army that were most concerned in these differences, and did represent to the Comittee of both kingdoms the danger and prejudice that might thereby arise to the publique service if some speedie course should not be taken for removeall thereof. But the Comittee of both kingdoms, holding it unfitt at that time to take them into their consideracion, when there was a necessitie of putting the armies to present action against the common enemic, directed mee to endeavour that they should be composed, or at least laid aside till further leasure, in the time of our winter quarters. This advice I willingly embraced, and did apply myselfe wth my full endeavours to quiett those distraccions for the present; but this hath not satisfied the aimes of some who I heare (upon what grounds I cannot imagine) doe fixe upon mee the character of being a discountenancer of honest and godly men.

I cannot but wonder at soe high a slaunder, and if this relate to those of my owne army, wherein I hope there are many honest men, though differing in judgement to what I profess, yett I shall appeale to them whether I have at any time been failing in my respects unto them; and I can say that upon some of them I have looked wth that value and esteeme, as that the choice and approbacion of most of the comaunders in the army have bin in their power. Lieftennant Generall Cromwell shalbe my compurgator in this particular. Hee knowes that I alwaies placed him in cheefest esteeme and creditt with mee. But it is true that of late I have not given soe free and full a power unto him as formerly I did, because I heard that he used his power soe as in honor I could not avowe him in it, and indeed I grew jealous that his designes were not as he made his professions to mee; for his expressions were sometimes against the Nobillitie; that he hoped to live to see never a Nobleman in England, and he loved such better then others because they did not love lords. He hath further expressed himselfe wth contempt of the Assembly of Divines, to whome I pay a reverence, as to the most learned and Godly convention that hath bin this many ages, yett these he termed persecutors; and that they persecuted honester men then themselves. His animositie against the Scottish nation, whome I affect as joyned wth us in solemne league and covenant, and honor as joyntly instrumentall wth us in the common cause; yett against these his animositie was such as he told me that in the way they now carried themselves, pressing for their discipline, he could as soone draw his sword against them as against any in the king's army; and he grew soe pressing for his designes as he told mee that he would not deny but that he desired to have none in my army but such as were of the Independent judgement, giving mee this reason:—

That in case there should be propositions for peace or any conclusion of a peace such as might not stand with those ends that honest men should aime at, this army might prevent such a mischeife.

I must confess these speeches, some of them spoken publiquely, others privately, yett soe as I saw they had a publique influence on the army, made mee jealous of his intencions; and therefore I did not communicate my councells to him wth that freedome that formerly I had done; and I hope this shall not make such an impression upon the hearts of others that are godly, even of such as are of his judgement soe as to derogate from my esteeme in soe high a measure as to thinke mee fitt to be stiled an enemie to Godly men. My conscience bears mee witnes that my affeccions are still sett upon such as love Christ in sincerity with the highest value; nay, I can in the cleerenes of my heart profess that to those who have sought thus to traduce mee my prayers shalbe that God of mercy would pardon of their uncharitable and unchristian carriage, and my endeavours shalbe as farr as it may stand with the vindication of my owne integritie to returne good for evill.

Indorsed: Concerning Leiutenauant Generall Cromwell, referred x^{ber} 4°, 1644.

LETTERS

ADDRESSED TO THE

EARL OF LAUDERDALE.

EDITED BY OSMUND AIRY.

PRINTED FOR THE CAMDEN SOCIETY.

M.DCCC.LXXXIII.

PREFACE.

The Editor hopes in a future volume of the Society's publications to offer a selection from the correspondence comprised in the Lauderdale Papers. That selection will be framed with the view of illustrating with some fulness the main stream of the political history of Scotland during the reign of Charles II., or, rather, during the supremacy of Lauderdale in Scotch affairs. The letters now printed have been taken out of that correspondence as being, to a great extent, isolated in their interest, while in themselves curious. The first eleven are written by John Kennedy, Earl of Cassilis, father of Lady Margaret Kennedy, with whom Lauderdale entertained so close an intimacy, and who afterwards became the wife of Gilbert Burnet.

"Don John," as he is familiarly called by Tweeddale and others, was one of the most marked figures in Scotland at the beginning of the reign. He was noted, and is continually referred to in the Lauderdale correspondence, as a proud, obstinate old man, dressed in strange fashion, and eccentric in language and opinions. His eccentricity was perhaps most to be noted in the sturdy integrity with which, alone among the politicians who surrounded him, he refused for fear or favour to betray his rigid Presbyterian principles, by taking the oath of allegiance, which in his eyes implied the royal supremacy in ecclesiastical affairs. He died in April 1668. Anyone who reads the letters of Lady Margaret Kennedy, published by the Bannatyne Club, will be struck by the similarity between father and daughter in style and tone alike.

The remaining thirty-three letters are from two of the most distinguished of those numerous soldiers of fortune who left Scotland to command the regiments of Scotch guards always maintained by the French sovereign. Those from Lord Rutherford, afterwards Earl Teviot, give a vivid picture of the harassments attending the command of an outstanding garrison, as well as many curious scraps of information. It is interesting too to notice in them that the wild and varied life in foreign countries seemed never to weaken the strength of the national feeling. Rutherford is always a Scotchman in the first place, and we are vividly reminded of the picture which Scott drew of his class in the character of Lord Crawford in " Quentin Durward." He was killed in or about the year 1665, in a skirmish with the Moors at Tangiers, of which he was made governor after the sale of Dunkirk.

The letters from Lord George Douglas illustrate the complications which necessarily arose between the French government and these mercenary troops, when disagreements occurred between the two crowns; and they as well as Lord Rutherford's form an interesting addition to the information given us by Mr. Burton, in " The Scot abroad," and M. Michel in " Les Ecossais en France." The papers are taken from the Additional MSS. in the British Museum.

The Editor reserves for a future occasion the pleasure of acknowledging the assistance so courteously rendered to him at the MSS. Department of the British Museum, while engaged upon the Lauderdale correspondence.

LETTERS ADDRESSED
TO THE
EARL OF LAUDERDALE.

EARL OF CASSILIS TO THE EARL OF LAUDERDALE.

MY LORD,   Edinb. 28 de^r, 1660.

I waited for yours with anxietis and reseaved it with muche satisfaction, returning your Lo^p now manie heartie thankes for your respect to my cousin, tho for hazard of the monosillabes reputation I wishe it had onely come two dayes sooner. Your Lo. may give assurance that whatsoever my thoghts wer long since for kingly autoritie I am not come so farre to anie extremitie as to forget my dutie to our native prince, or prove ingrate for his M^s kindness to Scotland. Bot my earnest desire is that hee may so regulate his power that the lustre of his government may keep his subjects with delight under him and prove ane attractive to strangers, who (as all men) love to embrace there apprehendit happines. If anie should enquire why the king's plantations are so farre scattered, since by vicinitis they may bee the more help full to cache other, and with lesse trouble to the croŭne, I wold know what to answer. It is thoght the Spanishe monarchie is the lesse formidable by the great disfraction of her limbes. Whatsoever bee undertaken by these dominions, that the blessing may be expected, let it bee on cleer grounds. Jamaica gives mee some occasion of this. I doubt not bot your stay there may bee of great use, yet it vexes me to thinke with whom I shall communicate and advise the following one the project that is not yet communicable,[a] and which untimeously vented may bee marred. The instructions your Lo. mentiones please mee well and conduce to the end. If you shall procure ane addition by letter in serious termes to the commissioner for laying to heart and promoving what shall bee propond by your incatenato[b] for inlarging his Majesties dominions and multipliing his subjects, it may doe well being timely delivered by mee. If you bee instrumentall to increase our king's greatnes in a Christian and heroik way I hope a greater then man will give the reward like himselfe, that you may doe and get that from his free grace is the cordiall wishe of

Your mere incatenato.

EARL OF CASSILIS TO THE EARL OF LAUDERDALE.

4. MY LORD,   Edenb. 1 Ja. 1661.

Since my writing the other, beside my differing from the rest in parl[iament] for choosing our preesident, I differd upon the oathe preposid,[c] and whatsoever there determination bee, except I see a a more cleer ground for it then I judge possible to shou, ere I take it, I resolve to leave his Majesties counsels and dominions, whiche

---

[a] The project mentioned in this and succeeding letters is probably the confirmation of the Presbyterian government, which Lauderdale urged upon Charles as being the best way to secure Scotland in his interest in case of complications with his English subjects. Burnet mentions a long letter written to Cassilis' daughter, Margaret Kennedy, by Lauderdale on this subject. *See*, on the whole matter, *Burnet*, vol. i. sect. 108.

[b] Italian "incatenare," to bind.

[c] The oath of allegiance which acknowledged the King's supremacy in ecclesiastical matters. *See* Mackenzie's *Memoirs*, p. 23.

He was declared incapable of trust on April 10, after a second refusal, when summoned as an extraordinary lord of session. *See* 23116, ff. 17, 19.

is as ill as anie thing that ever Oliver threatned mee with, tho he knew I abhorid him and his way. If I sit and can bee of anie use for promoving that project whiche you onely knou, it will bee expedient letters bee written seriously to such as bear suey besides the commissioner which was shewed to your Lo. at my being there by

Your *incatenato*.

I pray your Lo. let mee not long so muche for the answer of this as of my former.

If his Majestie thinke I merite anie trust I hope hee will intrust the letters and timeing of the deliverie to mee, and let mee kenn somewhat of the tenour.

EARL OF CASSILIS TO THE EARL OF LAUDERDALE.

MY LORD,   Edenb. 8 Ja. 1661.   23115,

Since your stay is necessitat, if I by our parlaments command bee made incapable to acte in that bussines whiche I communicate to you onely, I hope his Majesties justice will not put mee to worke when my hands are cut off. The causes of there proced . I have set doune in a paper aparte under a more legible hand. If I had leav to prosecute that project, the helpe of the monosillabe of whom I wrote lately to you might have beene of great use; he is nou to his home in the countrey, upon his disabling to sit here as a member, and that (as I suspect) by the cumming and his fliing of one against whom you formerly at Striveling[a] protected him. Tho you onely knou the whole, yet I glanced at severall things conducing to it with him long since, which makes me knou, hee wald

[a] Stirling.

sympathize and assist powerfully by his pen when a doore opens if hee bee not put in a capacitie to acte otherwise. I have made bold to write a line to his Majestic, and if there bee need I hope you will helpe to read it to him, and imparte more at large upon conveniencie what I have written to you. I shall trouble your Lo. no more now bot to shew that your returne will bee longed for by

Your *incatenato*.

EARL OF CASSILIS TO CHARLES II.

MAY IT PLEASE YOUR MAJESTIE,

Whil upon your command I was here attending your Majesties service in parlament ane oathe was urged whiche I desired to bee explained that I might take it with freedome, and tho they without contradiction   agreed, that what I propond was there true meaning, yet they refused to adde it in write. If upon this I bee secluded from a capacitie to prosecute, as I intendit that project which I imparted to your Majestie, and by your command more at large to another (whom you and manie of your subjects confide in), I hope your Majestie will not blame mee to sit idle when I am disabled to worke, and till I deserve worse must presume you will esteeme mee that whiche I resolve to live and die,

Your Majesties faithfull and humble subject,

CASSILLIS.

Edenb. 8 Ja. 1661.

EARL OF CASSILIS TO THE EARL OF LAUDERDALE.

MY LORD, 23115,
It might appear to some you had missed the copie of my reasons inclosed in one of my last to you, for you nether ansuer nor mention them, and I thoght you kneu mee too well to send mee offers instead of ansuers, bot I hope wee shall not bee hastie to mistake. As to the places which his Majestie pleases to nominat mee for,[a] you knou I am free from moving for them, and if the barres that ly in the way bee taken out I shall endeavour to serve him faithfully in them, if my former cariage deserve not so muche as the removeall of these. I should be sorrie that his Majestie should wrong himself, the people, and you, whom I take mee to as the remembrancer at least, to nominat suche a one. Wee have not manie newes here. It is said they are going on with the processes, and that contest about the acte craved to bee past betuixt creditor and debitor is like to make heat, manie being interest on bothe sides. What is more to bee exprest looke in another paper hirewith under a sure hand from

Your incatenato.

Edenb. 7 Mar. 1661[?].

EARL OF CASSILIS TO THE EARL OF LAUDERDALE.

MY LORD, 23116,
I hope you will beleeve I am sensible of his Majesties favours, and my gratitude for them obliges to keep my selfe free of that staine of ambition by suallowing doune nou the pilles I have so long stucke at, as may make me unserviceable to him, in that designe whiche I conceave may be of consequence for him.

[a] Cassilis was nominated a member of the Scotch Privy Council, 1661, Feb. 13.

Whether for that upon the proofes his Majestie hes alreadie had of my fidelitie he will please to dispense with neu tyes it belongs to himselfe to consider. What more I had to say is set doune otherwise, being unwilling you should receave unnecessar trouble by

Your incatenato.

Edenb. 6 Apr. 1661.

[a] Whether your friends saying his Majestie was at Whitehall and his commissioner here merites the castle threatned and confinement to the toune execute you may enquire at conveniencie.

More of this if not nou with the next.

Earl of Cassilis to the Earl of Lauderdale.

17.
Apryle 6, 1661.

The Notte to which the letter of your incatenato relates.

What past anent the oath in the beginning of the parliament is showen; and now the Earle of Cassilis being required to come to the parliament as one nominat to be an extraordinar on the sessione he appeared (tho he had a promeise before from the Commissioner his grace of a post warrand to waite on his Majestie), and being required to give his oath and subscrybe a declaratione which wes large and never formerlie seene be him, he acknowledged he had seene the oath long since, bot the declaration being new and large he desyred tyme to consider. Withall declared he wes willing to serve his Majestie in whatsoever statione he wes capable of, bot for shunning misconstructione of his ansuer desired there allowance to waite upon his Majestie. The Chanceller[b] in passione and heate ansuered: "The King's power and authoritie is heire." The Earle ansüered, "That is not denyed, bot yet the King is at Whythall."

[a] *See* following letter.   [b] Glencairn.

Then the Chanceller said, "You dissoune the King's Commissioner," which the said Earle contradicted, bot wes still interrŭpted in passione and removed, and reinformed by eare witness that it wes moved by some to send the Earle to the castell, and the result wes that he should appeare and give his ansŭer on Tŭisday the 9th, and remaine confyned in Edinburgh in the meane tyme.

What the designe wes to hinder him from going up is best knowen to the actors.

EARL OF CASSILIS TO THE EARL OF LAUDERDALE.

MY LORD,   23116,
    If I have not merited the libertie to wait upon his Majestic for representing my reasons in reference to my cariage upon the oathe and declaration of parlament, when I conceave it for some advancment of his oune service, I shall regrate it and studie to deserve better in whatsoever condition I bee under his Majestie. I have writ so muche to your Lo. on this subject as I shall spair further till to-morrou ordaind for a finall ansuer to bee given by ^a
Your incatenato.

Edenb. 9 Apr. 1661.

EARL OF CASSILIS TO THE EARL OF LAUDERDALE.

MY LORD,   East Roxburghe, 28 7^{ber} [1667].   23128,
    I have muche satisfaction by yours of the 20th, and heartily wishe a progresse sutable to the actings mentiond in it. I intind not to

^a *See* footnote, p. 2.

make evill use of it, in reference to him most concerned.[a] The going on that way is thoght a surer mean for quieting spirites then raising of oppressing men under whatsoever name. I shall be brief henc, purposing by a surer bearer tho slouer, that you shall have the trouble of some lines more from

Your incatenato.

Earl of Cassilis to the Earl of Lauderdale.

78. My Lord, East Roxburghe, 30 7^{ber} [1667].

It appeares by yours of the 20th that Donald[b] hes fallen on a handsome way to discharge himselfe,[c] and the going on at that rate you write,[d] a probable mean to the ends whiche honest men desire bee aimed at. It will not bee secure nor noble to doe his worke by halfes. His keeping stedfast friendship with those of our profession beyond sea[e] is a goode meane for making him indeed Donald on that element, probably likewise in plantations, and for breaking the bridge[f] whiche his great neighbour might have troubled us by. It is no shame to imitate a woman (who ruled famously) in the support of the protestant cause bot glorious to outgoe her. I wishe hee had a true convert in his bosome,[g] I am sure it is a dutie to use the meanes, and I can imagine nothing obliging to a tolleration of

---

[a] Probably referring to Earl Rothes, the King's Commissioner, who at this time had his commission taken away. In a letter to Lauderdale, dated Sept. 7, 1667, Tweeddale says: "For God's sake, let us but have a trial of securing the peace and quiet of the country without a commissioner, having a chancellor and the old form of government."

[b] Charles II.   [c] From the war with the Dutch.
[d] Probably the negociations which ended in the Triple Alliance. Holland.   [f] French conquest of Holland [?].
[g] The Duke of York [?].

superstition and idolatrie. The actings of those in his station are exemplari. I need not repeat to you the poets sentence to that purpose. If it bee a goode worke to gain one soule what must it bee to bring in millions running headlong in the broad way, either plainly worshipping divils, or at best ther oune fancies without neglecting our oune ignorants at home. Hou well might a parte of that wasted in the 3 kingdomes on belligods bee bestowed for præserving worlds of heathen. If parents providing temporall things for there children bee a great addition to the naturall obligation, hou muche should providing spirituall and faithfull steuarts to distribute ingage the hearts of suche as doe or shall beeleeve (on right grounds) ane immortalitie. I have sent abroad a youth on whom paines have beene tane for advancing him in knouledge, perhaps not without successe, some advise it for lousing his tongue and making what hee hes more communicative. My designe is that hee may bee made more serviceable to our almightie king and his vicegerent and generally to all to whom hee oues dutie. I hope you will not bee spairing of advice to him and so comme another incatenato, and likewise to Mr. Pat. Lyon, who hes attendit him these five years past you may use freedome with him, for hee will bee found muche above the pitche of those who take them to suche employment. I wishe they may be hasted away when the youth hes done his dutie to his Majestie and the rest of the royall familie as you will direct. I hope you will please to signifie your minde in reference to a students cariage to the Prince of Orange and others there at his comming or afterwards, I thinke hee will not have occasion to fall in that ceremoniall solæcisme which Hemfleet in haste made a friend commit. This occasion makes mee præsume to bee the more large, whiche I trust you will not mistake in

Your incatenato.

If you shall procure from his Majestie suche allowance for going abroad or recommendation as hes been given to others of his condition, it will bee a further obligation.

Earl of Cassilis to the Earl of Lauderdale.

85. My Lord, East Roxburghe, 1 Oct. [1667].

Since the writing of my other of yesterdayes date I have thoght of some things which the bearer, Henry Kennedy, can informe and concern his Majestie to knou. He is so well knoune to you and others employed as you wer, as it seemes needles to write how faithfully he did acqüit himself in everie station hee was set in, and how well hee deserves trust. Hee is to speake of some particulars whereof you have heard (as I thinke) muche alreadie. I hope you will make your best use of what hee speaks. If anie of his relations have beene wrongd, or himselfe frustrat of what is due to him, your help will yet further oblige,

Your incatenato.

Lord Rutherford to the Earl of Lauderdale.

2. My Lord, [30 March, 1661.]

Displease your Lo. I must, since little better as stealing I ame casting your l: moneys at the cocks. Your two sutes of cloaths are bocht with the consent of three different enouch fancies other wayes of taylours and courtiers, all the other things contained in the memoire are also bespoken so yt your Lo. sall hav them w^t in the tyme prefixed. Your 200^{lb} ster. will pairt fro your Lo. thoe to Mr. Kinlochs great grudging, soit dit entre nous, I did buy all myself, he looking on w^t ready moneys, which saved allwayes 5 of the hindred.

At my arryval heir Mr. Le Tellier,[a] secretaire of State, caressed

[a] Noted for his persecution of the Huguenots. His last signature was given to the Revocation of the Edict of Nantes. *See* Felice, *Histoire des Protestants de France*, pp. 399, 411.

me much, prodigalising the King's favors on me, and did propose to keep our regt at 20 companies, making them to 2000 sogers, but be the reduction of Lo. George Douglas regt into ours, but when we came to conclude our traitte he told me I behoved to renonce the title and qualitie of Scots Gardes. This did so move me y^t I replyed (in good earnest) y^t not only would I loose all my pretensions and fortune, yea, but rather suffer the rake befor I condiscended to so base ane agreement. The regiment belonged to the nation not to me, and y^t no man heirafter could w^t assurance treat w^t the King of France since he would violat his bargaines made so authentiquely and signed be his secretaires of State. He seing me so hotanosed, left me to myself, and I went immediatly to my Lo. St. Albans and related what had passed. The Duk of Anious fiancailles are to be this day, to-morrow the marriage: till this be past nothing will be acted. I ame affrayed y^t betwixt stooles—I begg of your Lo. to let me hav your counsell and orders heirin whither his Majestie our maistre hav use for me or not befor I undertake any thing to chocq our nation or below myself. I rather renonce all and goe fere abroad.

The Queen hath told publicqly heir to several of the French grandes y^t the King hath made me governeur of Dunkerk. I know not fro whom her Maiestie hath it.

   Beggs most humbly pardon for, my Lord,
    Your Lo. most humble, most obedient, most
     obliged serviteur,

          RETORFORT.

LORD RUTHERFORD TO THE EARL OF LAUDERDALE.

MY LORD,   [beg. April, 1661.] 23116,

Yesterday my man pairted with your Lo: coffres. I wisch they come to a good port, for this day news cometh y^t on all hands robberies are committed be the cavaliers y^t wer disbanded without moneys or recompense, which hath so desesperated them y^t they attacque all they meit with. I hav used all diligence to let your Lo. hav them in tyme as also all necessarie precaution, soe my man is gone w^t them on the chassemaree^a to Calais. I will not sleip sound till I hear of them frō thence.

I hav given him instructions how to doe at his landing, and a letter to Mr. Burnet at Heth,^{b} ane other to Mr. Touris, the searcher at Dover, at the signe of the Prince of Orange, to keip them up and not let them be visited till orders come frō your Lo. as belonging to your Lo. All things are very dear heir be reason of the great number of buyers for the coronation.

My Lord Ormond and others will find theirs very dear passing be the hands of merchands and taylors. I daresay I hav saved something to your Lo.^{c} thoe I find all very dear, for I did buy all myself w^t ready money, which hath so incensed the taylors y^t heirafter if your Lo. hav any commissions for me you will be pleased not to astrict me to any in particular, but let me choyse my man.

I send heirin a little memoire of what is in the coffres. I hav not got Mr. Kinloch's compts for the faschion and garniture of your Lo. cloaths, which sall cause the compts be differd at this tyme. Kisses most humbly your Lo. hands, and be your Lo. permission, my Lady Countesss, and my Lady Mary's,

My Lord,

Your Lo. most humble most obedient serviteur,

RETORFORT.

(Enclosed with 23116, f. 5.)

7. In the coffre for my Lord ane sute w^t black cloak lyned w^t velvet chamared, w^t breeches chamared, garnisched with bleu rubans, and the doublet brocurd dor chamared, lyned with whyt satin.

^{a} Fishing smack. ^{b} Hythe [?].
^{c} During the early part of his career Lauderdale was comparatively needy.

A sute of rich oliv-coloured stuff chamared w^t a rich gold dental cartison, the cloak lyned w^t a cloath of gold and silk sutable, the breaches chamared, also garnisched w^t a cherie-colored ruban.

Two pair of gloves of dogg leather deiply parfumed, garnisched according to the sutes, a bever very good and lairge w^t a gold hate band, a boderier of gold and black fond, w^t a sword or couteau of silver guilded sett with turquois, and a base blade, but damasced and musqued.

Their are 4 bands w^t two pair band strings rich, wheirof on is very rich; of the other three your Lo. may choyse and leav the other two for Mr. Mercer. The bands I say will mount to 400^{li}, the two best, yea the on cost 285^{li} 10s. w^t the handcuffs. This is the dearest merchandise.

For my Lady Countess.

A black goune of Venetien stuff, w^t two paire of gloves and garnitures conforme, and two musqued eventailes.

For my Lady Mary.

A goun of coloured brocard, w^t a petticoat of whyt satin faschioned in chamarrure of the new mode, w^t two paire gloves and garniture, and two eventails conforme.

In a sappin boxe or coffre.

A little boxe with 12 little phiales of Essence of Roses and six of Jessemin. Ane other w^t a silver little box guilded, set w^t turquois (good or bode), full of eau d'ange, and half a douzen bottels of essence of orange; a bigg bottell of water of flower of orange, a bigg boxe of fyne pomode w^t jessemin poudre, a paire of very great tables or trick-track, w^t 4 rame of paper and musqued waxe and black waxe, w^t ane escritoire as was desyred.

For Sir Robert Morray.

A black sute of Venetienne brode plain doubled w^t velvet, garnisched w^t black salined rubans and dogg, musqued gluffs conforme.

Their are a sute of cloaths for Mr. Mercer, w^t sword and belt and feathers and perruque, and garniture conforme, w^t two bands, as your Lo. will leav to him.

LORD RUTHERFORD TO THE EARL OF LAUDERDALE.

74. MY LORD,

I arryved heir yesternicht and hav schowen my Commission under the Royal Seal, his Maiesties lettre to me, and M. Secretarie Morice's. The Governeur hath delt most civilly with me and is ready to resigne the chairge, only desyrs for his own dischairge y^t as his Maiestie hes been pleased to wryt to me to receav and take the place in my hands, so his Maiestie will be pleased lykwayes to wryt to him y^t he may delyver it to me, and on sayd of this lettre or ordre being for his dischairge he will immediatly after resigne.

Meantyme he is to schow me and giv accompt of all the munition, artillerie, and other materials belonging to the place. I sall begg of your Lo. to sollicit his Maiestie y^t w^t all diligence the ordre may be sent to Sir Edward Harley, for he tells me himself y^t at his pairting fro Court some ten dayes agoe his Maiestie did tell him of my coming, and y^t he sould hav at Dunkerke his Ma. directions for resigning.

Your Lo. will be pleased to remember to send me a cyphre w^t the key.

I ame advysed be Sir Edward to desyre y^t in my Commission (wheiras it is sayd to the Governeur of Dunderk w^t command of all the forces, forts, and strenths their-to belonging) it may be specified of Mardik fort Royal and all others which I begg of your Lo. may be told to the Secretaire Morice to be inserted in my Commission under the Great Seal.

My Lord,
Your Lo. most humble most obedient serviteur,
RETORFORT.

Dunkerke, 30 May, 1661.

LORD RUTHERFORD TO THE EARL OF LAUDERDALE.

MY LORD,

At my arryval heir Sir Edward Harley did send ane express to his Maiestie, and be his means I did wryt to your Lo. He hath gotten a returne frō his M^{atie} to surrender me dunkerk, wheirof I ame in possession, but I hav had no news of your Lo.

However, my most noble Lord, I sall begg of your Lo: to be kynd and gratious to this noble cavalier. Sir Edward, of whom I hav receaved great and reall civilities, and who will sympathise w^t your Lo: both in point of policie and religion, for he is a most honest wyse gentleman.

And in case my commission under the great seal of England be not as yet expected suffer me, my Lord, to begg y^t it may hav the same termes and latitude y^t Sir Edward's had, specifying both ports, forts, and strenths, and mardyk and others in particular. If your Lo. secretaire, Mr. James, will be pleased to doe me this grace I hope your Lo. will ordain him to dce it. I expect w^t impatience your Lo. instructions and ordres. Kisses most humbly your Lo. hands.

My Lord,
Your Lo. most humble most obedient serviteur,
RETORFORT.

Dunkerk, 8 Juin, 61.

Lord Rutherford to ————*

Dunkerk, 18 7bre, 1661.

I did wryt a long confused piece to my Lord Lauderdaile last weik amongst others my grievances on was about the sending over Sir Philip Monkton heir to be controlleur to my preiudice and affront, if he sculd hav the latitud he pretends.

And becaus I hear now my Lord is indisposed, and y^{r}for not to be importuned, and y^t the sayd Sir Philipp is pairted frō this yesternicht for London not weell satisfyed w^t me, no mor as I ame with him I must hav recours to you to imploy my Lords credit and your oun to keip me frō Sir Ph. his bade impressions of me to my Lord Tresorier Southampton or any els, and y^{r}for first remitting you to y^t pairt of my Lord's lettre to instruct you concerning Sir Phil. and his chairge, I sall next giv you ane accompt of the rest.

Sir Philipp Monkton it seimeth is a favorit of my Lord Tresoriers hath obtained a patent to be controlleur of the customes heir, to which I have nothing to gainsay, but be vertew of his patent pretends to hav a general inspection in all business and to reduce and bring in the droits of the governour into the King's tresorie, a thing never practised be any befor in the tyme of any governour, Spaniard, French, or Inglisch, and since it hath pleased his Maiestie to giv me a patent not only to inioy what any of my predecessours had, but what they ought to hav if any thing be omitted, I cannot without jealousie of ane affront to me or my nation suffer any novelties come in upon me to crye down my authoritie heir, which is every day a brauling too the malignant humors of the old ill principled officers, who as they abhorr as they call it arbitrarie power, so if they get their will the King sall never be absolut maistre heir nor will I undertak to command and assure the place on y^t accompt.

It is trew the King is maistre, and I ame ready when he com-

* Unaddressed, but doubtless to Sir Robert Moray, Justice Clerk, Lauderdale's most intimate friend, and appointed his Deputy-Secretary, 1663, June 5.

mands to resigne not only any interest but the chairge of gouverneur yea to expose my lyf for his service, but for others to get patents be surpryse to my preiudice in things wheirof my predecessors hav all bein possessors and never troubled theirin this is of hard digestion. Au pis aller, if my Lord Tresorier will hav all in on the King's accompt, which I ame confident his Maiestie doeth not intend, I can be as answerable my self as any els to giv accompt, and on pain of my body, confiscation of goods, and all els, give full satisfaction and safe the expenses and chairges of a supranumerarie officers.

The particular disput is about a droit heir called the brewers' gulden. Col. Lockart and Sir Rob. Harley have inioyed it, and yet I must be questioned. It is enouch I ame a Scot, yea thoe I never received a pennie of the sayd droit and yt I ame not so avaritious to prey having few or non successors to my tresors.

If you can doe any thing heirin during my Lord's indisposition, act as you think fitt.

The King promised me at pairting y^t no commission nor patent sould be given in dunkerk w^{t}out my advyse or advertisment. Heir is a new creation be surpryse, all others Governours inioyed what they incroach upon in my tyme. I ame as ready as willing and w^{t}out vanitie able to rendre compt as any of them my predecessours. Why treat me thus I hav done.

Your own man.

LORD RUTHERFORD TO THE EARL OF LAUDERDALE.

MY LORD,   Dunkerk, 23 7bre, 1661.   23116,

I was overioyed at the recept of your Lo. the other day. Your Lo. sall not want a sogers prayers for your health becaus I ame so much interessed therein.

Your coach will be ready next moneth. Let me know if I sall cause put on your armes or if your Lo. will not hav her, for I will make use myself als, and y^r for let me ones mor hav your Lo. armes with the colours for I hav lost the former.

I must recommend the bearer heirof to your Lo. Lieut. Col. Knichtly; he is a very prettie gallant gentleman, most necessare for this Garnison, he is casseird be a Court Martial heir. Thoe be vertew of my authoritie I could remitt him, yet I rather hav it from his Maiestie, be an lettre and ordre to me to receav and rehabilitat him again his Maiestie having pardoned him he will giv your Lo. an accompt of alle, and truely he is not so criminel as they make him; had he don it in France he had never bein called to a Court Martial, but bein reconciled without much pain. Ones mor I recommend him to your Lo. to sollicite for him with his R. H. to whom I hav made my supplications too in his behalf.

Since your Lo. commands me to tell you what was layed out for your Lo. in france I sall say freely I have not tyme to cast upp the compts exactly, but I conceav it will amount to two hundred and betwixt twentie fyv and threetie punds sterling.

I begg y^t your Lo mak no hast, but when your Lo. is resolved to giv it to Mr. Willschaw Scots, Merchands.

My Lord,
Your Lo. most humble most obedient serviteur,
RUTHERFURD.

LORD RUTHERFORD TO THE EARL OF LAUDERDALE.

MY LORD, Dunkerk, 6 9bre, 1661.
27 8:

At the very houre I receaved your Lo. with your Lo. seal of armes and colours, your coach arryved heir, for I had sent ane Captn to Bruxelles, who brocht it be land be four horses from thence;

it would hav bein spoyled be water as they informed me, and would hav coast as much be reason of frequent changing of boats they say the coach is cheap but I find it dear. All the nails of harnois and coach are double guilded, their are six harnois w^t the postillons sadles. If it doe not fit your Lo. I sall take it back again for it will cost nothing the transportation having sent this hoys express. It comes to 1700^{li} permission silver, and twentie four crounes for the bringing, with 8 crounes for other little compts, making in all (as they compt to me) ane hundred seventie on pund, fyf schilens ster. nay if it pleas not your Lo. and y^t any other will hav it, I hav set the pryce for y^t end, for els I sould not compt so exactly with your Lo.

I sall hav the honor to wryt to your Lo. be the next ordinare and giv ane accompt of all things heir. I have constantly 700 men at work yet advanceth but slowly. Rome was not built in on day.

My Lord,
Your Lo. most humble most obedient servant,
RUTHERFURD.

I send your Lo. a piece of new wyn of daye,[?] it is entiere rare heir, and nou cometh this way; when I find any good your Lo. sall hav pairt.

MY LORD,   Dunkerk, 13 9bre, 1661.   23116,

I ame advertised by his grace my Lord of Albemarle y^t Sir Rob. Harley's regiment is destined for Tangiers and sould pairt from hence schortly; if they get not their decompts and arriers they will make a hurlie burlie, or a richt doun mutinie, and the poor scot may suffer.

If England wer farther frō us heir I would be mor a tease and securitie. Never officers loved their countrey so weill as ours heir doeth, for I beleiv giv them their pay and let them stay in England they would hardly weary many of them, yea our very ingenier thoo a Dutch mate hath left me in the heat of our business, but I forgiv him. Many of our officers are sick heir and mor as the tenth of our sogers payeth tribut with sickness. I dare not tell how I am keipt in hot water heir, only beleiv me my good Lord je ne suis pas icy pour casser des noix. Pray God make me and continue me a loyal fidel subiect and creature to his Majestie.

I intend to sell my coach mears and three Spanish horse I hav heir, on my word of honor botht with the French kings moneys, of whom since my pairting I hav gotten 10,000^{lb} currant. If your Lo. hav a mynd for the 7 coach gray dapled mears, I sall send them over; if not and y^t any of your court hav a mynd for them and my horses I sall send them on your Lo: advertisement, it is too much macquinioned [?] begs most humbly pardon for

My Lord,
Your Lo. most humble most obedient servant,
RUTHERFURD.

LORD RUTHERFORD TO THE EARL OF LAUDERDALE.

155. MY LORD, Dunkerk, $\frac{5}{15}$ 9bre, 1661.

The Doctor General of this garnison is dead, thoe I hav the power to place ane other, yet because Doctor Burnet (on whom I hav cast my eyes for his abilities rather as his relations to me) being a Scot, and fearing to giv ether subject or appearence of jealousie to the garnison y^t two Bretheren Burnets, both Scots and of my relations, sould have chairge and direction of soul and bodie over

the Inglisch heir. Theirfor doe I supplicat your Lo. that his Matie may be intressed in it, that the commission for the sayd chairge may come frō the secretaire his Majestie, and your Lo. hav the thanks and acknowledgement only my consent attached becaus this was the treatie betwixt Sir Edward Nicolas and me about the creation of any officer. This is the humble requeist of,
My Lord,
Your Lo. most humble most obedient servant,
RUTHERFURD.

LORD RUTHERFORD TO THE EARL OF LAUDERDALE.

MY LORD,   Dunkerk, $\frac{12}{18}$ 9bre, 1661.   23116,

Not having receaved any ordres of your Lo. of a long time, I hoped my man sould bring me some whose arryval without a lettre frō your Lo. did a little trouble me, supposing it was be his cairlesness.

I intended to hav sent in a little paper to your Lo. a memoire of some things to be presented to his Ma. but being certainly informed be M. de Puij, the Duk's valet de chambre, y^t his H. R. will be heir this nicht, I will not trouble your Lo. he being on the place to take connoisance. I have written a letter to Sir Will. Waller in his son's behalf. I sall plainly tell your Lo. he is not fitt for this service or trade, he may prove other. It is not but he is very honest, deutifull, and willing, but their is something wanting. I hav written so categorically to his father y^t whatever he desyrs sould be done I sall obey, thoe to my preiudice and others. I sall desyre your Lo. with all secrecie to let me know if the cloaths y^t cometh over heir to the King's regt. be payed be his Maiestie, or if the regt. must pay for them.

Becaus my L. Wentworth sends me ordres or word to send him over the moneys y^t is due in arrieres to that regt be reason of the payement must be made for them cloaths at London. This is most inst in y^t case, and if the King pay for them I think as iust he may dispose of those moneys, for he is not rich enouch to giv in all and all, and to hav so many Iron in the fyre to me it is all on, for I have the moneys. It would help heir the fortifications when moneys lacketh. I begg your Lo. service, kisses most humbly your Lo. hands.

My Lord,
Your Lo. most humble most obedient servant,
RUTHERFURD.

LORD RUTHERFORD TO THE EARL OF LAUDERDALE.

168. MY LORD,

I receaved two of your Lo. at ones, next day after his H. Royal was pairted frō hence, whose arryval as it did surpryse us no less did his sudden depairture deiect us. He was pleased to leave ordres for the modelling and ranking the companies of those regts. destined for Tangiers. Our Scots regt. of Neubruch is reduced to two companies, and they cast in to ane Irisch reg. Sir James Hamilton's sonn commandeth on of the companies. It is not my pairt (because too much interessed) to say y^t his Maiestie having so many Englisch reg. on foot, and four Irisch regts. with his H. R. micht have on poor Scots regt. I ame sorry his Maiestie sould hav promised anything to Doctor Burnet, but it floweth frō his unparalelld bountie to accord to all what men desyr. This is a little ruffle to me so much the more sensible, becaus my own lieut.-col. without my knowledge did wryt over to M. Halsey, cupbearer, to sollicit the chairge of Doctor for y* man Vial, as also heir at Dunkerk w*out my knowledge did sollicit his H. R. I will not say it is ingratitude in him, but Dieu m'en garde des ces gens cij peice and piece they will wear me out of all authoritie. Pardon, my Lord, this digression.

Never any sets forward this way but it is to put me out of Dunkerk. Sir Will. Compton was the man in his tyme, and now my Lord Gerald, who sould have comed with the Duke, my Lord Tresorer, and Lord Roberts will hav me out. What a poxe w* permission aileth the world to persecut so a poor Scots body. God save the King, and make me a constant loyal subiect, even to spend my heart blood for him, thoe he sould chass me away.

My Lord,
Your Lo. most humble, most reall, and obedient servant,
RUTHERFORD.

Dunkerk, 6 X^{bre}, 1661.

LORD RUTHERFORD TO THE EARL OF LAUDERDALE.

MY LORD,
I receaved your Lo. of the 10th instant, which sould make me proud be the relating of his Maiesties most kynd and charitable expressions towards me. I pray God keip me allwayes constant and loyal. I will bragg no mor. I hav merited least of any of his subiects and creatures. On thing I must communicat to your Lo. y* wer it not his Ma. service in a most particular way to be heir in conscience and point of honour, I sould be presently wearied of the imploy. I hav 4000 spyes about me, and nou I dare impart myself too, since he that was confident hath acted against me and the principles of freindschipp. I must confess that I make profit of this

strait, it makes me mor circumspect and goe the cheirfuller for the King's service, teste elevee malgre l'envie.

Because this year is at ane end, and I have many compts of the garnison on my hands to dischairge myself, and let my Lord Tresorer and others see y^t sogers may be frugal, honest, and able to menage. I sall beg of your Lo. that his M$^{a tie}$ will permitt me to come over for 8 days only to rendre compt to his Ma. or my Lord Tresorer (but be his Ma. special ordre alenerly[a]), of my recepts and despenses heir for this garnison. If it be graunted it must be speidily, for we must beginn to hasten our new works with the new year. I expect with impatience the honor of your Lo. return to this prayer.

My Lord,
Your Lo. most humble most obedient servant,
RUTHERFURD.

Dunkerk, $\frac{22}{12}$ X^{bre} [1661].

LORD RUTHERFORD TO THE EARL OF LAUDERDALE.

59. MY LORD,   Dunkerk, 26 Jun. 1662.

I hav vowed (beggerly to) to importun your Lo. till I get my ansuer. The subiect theirof be your Lo. weilfaire in body, Court, and State, and my being in your Lo. good graces I told be my precedent in a prophetique humor y^t a body of our own C.[b] men would prov usefull heir and not chairgeable.

I had ane lettre of his Grace of Albemarle last day with ane inclosed petition which had bein presented to the Counsell, signed be several officers reduced of Dunkerk. I know not how you relisch those petitions signed in England be so many sogers hands, having

[a] Only   [b] Country.

bein all at their several homes and theirfor behoved to hav a rendevous to doe it, but wheir I hav bein bred it would hav passed for richt down mutinie. God giv us all as much of honestie and loyaltie as I see we hav of interest. Then sall his Matie be happie in his subiects.

       My Lord,
        Your Lo. most humble most obedient servant,
            RUTHERFURD.

LORD RUTHERFORD TO THE EARL OF LAUDERDALE.

MY LORD,   [No date.] 23117,

I hav reason to suspect your Lo. silence, the rather that I ame informed some good godly soules had dreamd and vented in Ingland or your Court that this place was to be betrayed to the frenches be my muschipe, yea some of our oun countrey peers contributed with their good opinions to the same. God rewaird them all. I sall not be obliged to burne Dianar's temples. They will save me those paines. Our trouppes for Tangers are embarqued, all well satisfyed with me and I most satisfyed with them.

I hav advertised his Maiestie be Secretarie Nicolas that the report is heir that M. de Caracene[a] is in arrest be M. de Marsine. May be yow know mor and sooner as I doe heirof. My Lord, thoe your Lo. doe not honour me with your commands, be not affrayed of me, I beseich your Lo. In good earnest I hope to proof steal to the back. God make every subiect alyk.

       My Lord,
        Your Lo. most humble most obedient servant,
            RUTHERFURD.

---

[a] Spanish ambassador at the Hague.

Lord Rutherford to the Earl of Lauderdale.

84.   My Lord,   Dunkerk, 21 7bre, s. v. 1662.

I receaved your Lo. of the 18th with the inclosed, to both which I retnrne ane succinct ansuer, being surprysed and galled at the contents theirof.[a] I hav ever professed to be your Lo. most in all obliged servant, and now if I wer not touched with your concerns, and hazard all that is dear to me for them, I sould prov but a scholem[b] and a farfarr. I signify but little in this world, but what I ame good for I begg your Lo. will make use of, for still I say I ame most perfectly,

   My Lord,
    Your Lo.
      A vendre et dependre.

I ame affrayed that my designe on teviotdaill will prov ridiculous. God keip me from it if you continue so at home—I mean Scotland. It will be better to supp a french potage neir orleans.

Lord Rutherford to the Earl of Lauderdale.

f. 88.   My Lord,   Dunkerk, 3 8bre, 1662.

I receaved your Lo. of the 27 7bre, as I hav receaved the lettres wheirof your Lo. wryts, so hav I returned ane ansuer to that freind with ane other inclosed which I hope are safely comed to hands.

For my proiect in Teviotdaill I sall not be very instant in the sollicitations till it be fairer weather.

[a] Probably Lauderdale had written to him regarding the Billeting Conspiracy.
[b] Schelm.

But for my pass to France I hav got it at such a tyme that I ame quyt disoriented and to giv your Lo. accompt yrof I sall begg your Lo. patience and attention for a little. Their hath runn a bruit heir neir this moneth of the reddition or exchange of Dunkerk, every day confirmed frō all places (safe Whythall) with all imaginable appearences of truth. I did wryt to Sir Edward Nicolas theirupon to know his Ma. will and pleasure, answered it was y^t their was no such matter.[a] Yet last day 1 see a lettre frō the Maior of Graveline, saying in positiv terms y^t Mr. d'Estraches was Governeur of Dunkerk and M. de Belfont in his place of Graveline. This I confess alarmed me, wheirupon I did wryt to Sir Edward again and inclosed ane narrativ of all business heir to be schonen to his Ma. containing the inconvenients may arryes be concealing it frō me (en tel cas). I expect every moment news theirof.

Last nicht the same reconfirmed be a letter frō Count de Charrois in doun richt terms, yea Batillier the sec. il embassade, passing last day at Calais frō Paris, told he had the contract signed be his Ma. of France. This is knowen to all the officers and sogers, who are in a most deip consternation. This begets a contempt of me in all their spirits, either y^t I conceal the veritie, or y^t I ame not worthie it sould be communicated; whatever be the matter, provyded it be for his Ma. weil, I ame aboundantly satisfyed. It wer too tedious to tell your Lo. the number of inconvenients following thir news, but in particular all my measurs are broken for the next year's proiect, and had I knowen only 20 dayes agoe (if it be trew) I had saved his Maiestie neir 2500^{li} ster.

Now, my dear Lord, most pressingly I supplicat your Lo. with all hast let me to know in particular of his Ma. if it be so or not, and how I sall behav myself, for at present I signifye little heir in the opinion of all. Most cheirfully sall I retyre, and wheirever his

---

[a] The first mention in Pepys of this transaction is Oct. 19, 1662. The charge for maintaining this garrison had greatly increased under Rutherford's management, amounting to 120,000*l.* a-year.

Ma. service call me, runn and hazard for it the best of my blood till their be no mor. God bless his Ma. with all felicities, and in particular with wyse and fidel counsellors.

  Pardon, my Lord,
    Your Lo. most humble, most obedient servant,
            RUTHERFURD.

---

21. LORD RUTHERFORD TO THE EARL OF LAUDERDALE.

MY LORD,   Doil, 27 April, 1663.

This nicht we schipp all in with a resolution to pairt to-morrow. I hav the reserv his ^{Maties} schipp w^t me and three other loadned w^t sogers and munition. Their are tuo behind in the river, and so ame forced to leav them with 100 sogers to wait on Sir Jhon Lauson or ane other convoye. I hav nether my commis nor instructions nor the Establischment, nor my old compts of Dunkerk closed with a quietus est, yet to serv his ^{Matie} I goe most willingly. I wisch we could flye, he is so good a maistre their is pleasur to serv him weill. God giv me the grace and force to doe it till my last breath.

  [Torn away.]
to be recommended to the Embassadeur particularly.

Next to advertise his Matie y^t I may hav a secret ordre for keiping up a Scots companie and cap. in Col. Geraldin's reg^t, becaus befor ever his own reg$t$ was in the King's service my Lord Neuburg's was, and it is iust, if not the reg$t$ at least on companie be keipt up. I hav done. God preserv yow long, y^t I may hav the confort of your freindschipp. I sall provyd your Lo: w^t a M[?] for Mr. Jean and a Lyon for Prince Rupert. To your Lo. and all those y^t honor yow. I ame most really,
         My Lord.

  [Torn away.]

LORD TEVIOT TO THE EARL OF LAUDERDALE.

MY BEST OF LORDS,

Since my pairting frō England the 28 Apryl we hav seen the ennemy tuo tymes in great bodyes and w^t him spoke. We built fyv redouts of stone and lyme, whither he would or not, and afterwards made peace, concluding it on the head of his armie, he and I sitting in two chaires. It is only for six moneths and to our King's pleasure herein w^t intention to giv him accompt of all. I pairted frō Tanger the 27 Agust, leaving it in good ordre w^t 9 moneths provisions, abondance of merchandise. I passed throw the kingdome of Algarves, kissed the King of Portugal's hands at Lisbone, arryved at Portsmouth the 16 7bre, wheir I had the honor to kiss the Duk and Dutchess hands, frō thence came to the Baith, kissed their Maties hands and Sir R. Morray and passed be Chichester, wheir was the Earle of Middleton^a and Neubourg,^{b} kissed the Chancellour's hands at Corneberry, and now iust now arryv at London.

Now since your Lo. hath given me the libertie to be saucie and too familiar, I sall make a humble petition to your Lo. y^t yow will favorise me in the purchase of Rutherfurd, be persuading the owner to pairt w^t it in just and reasonable termes. I will take no advantage on him, but submitt myself to tuo freinds whatever they judge the valeur of a land without ane house, holding ward not seigneur of the church, according to its rents I ame content to pay. I hav written to my Lords Bellenden and Whytkirk to make their addresses to your Lo. about this subject. I intend to pairt w^{t}in a moneth at fardest to come kiss your Lo. hands in Scotland. The

^{a} Royal Commissioner for Scotland from 1660 to the summer of 1663, when the rivalry between him and Lauderdale ended in the victory of the latter. He succeeded Lord Teviot at Tangiers.

^{b} Lauderdale's competitor for the Scotch secretaryship: appointed captain of the King's Guards. He was in strict alliance with Middleton, and came with him to Court after the failure of the Billeting Conspiracy.

King pairted yesterday frō Baiths. Dynes on Wednesday at Corneberry, wheir the Duk meits him and cometh y^t nicht to Oxford, wheir he is to stay 7 dayes.

My best Lord,
Your Lo. petit valet,
TEVIOT.

London, 22 7bre, 1663.

LORD TEVIOT TO THE EARL OF LAUDERDALE.

57. MY BEST OF LORDS,

I waited at York on his Grace and your Lo. coming, but when I learned that yow pairted frō Newcastel yesterday I came this lenth thinking to find your Lo. heir or at Alerton, but Mr. Mackie[a] incertain what way yow are to come and affrayed to miss I giv your Lo. the trouble of this, begging most humbly pardon if I wait no longer on his G. or your Lo. My tyme prescryved for my returne is so schort y^t I will hardly adiust my business w^t it. Your Lo. hath many ennemys, at least envyers at Court, and I lyk you all the better for it. God's blessing on yow. I leav yow to Sir Rob. for those things.

The Duke of Buckinghame professeth much freindschip to yow and told me the same y^t yow had illwischers. I hope you will thryv the better. I kissed the King's hands on Thursday at 11 of the clock coming out frō the Queen's bed chamber. Very sade Her M^{atie} abandoned be all and speechles; when I pairted schee was not dead but without miracle depairted y^t nicht or next morning.

If his G. or your Lo. hav forgot anything in Scotland or on the waye let me have your ordres. Thoe I did kiss my Lady Countesses hands at Highgate and got regales w^t Sir Ro: yet hearing your

[a] A confidential servant of Lauderdale, often employed in carrying despatches to and from Scotland.

Lo. to be on the way hither I did not receav her commands at pairting.

My best of Lords,
Your Lo. petit valet,
TEVIOT.

Borrowbridge, 27 8bre, 1663.

LORD TEVIOT TO THE EARL OF LAUDERDALE.

MY BEST OF LORDS, Tanger, 24 Jan. 166¾. 23121,

We arryved safe at this place the 14th instant with the loss of 9 horses. I hav payed for them all but ame not sure as yet how to be reimbursed. Our deputie governour fearing my stay in England had continued the peace for two moneths, but becaus I intend to make our new fortifications which is contraire to our peace already made, I ame of opinion we sall break, for work I must and hav advertised Guyland. The Kent fregat, Cap. Teileman, will bring your Lo. a pype of Cery wyn and some orange waters,

My best of Lords,
Your Lo. most humble and most obedient valet,
TEVIOT.[a]

Our deputie Governeur hath acted with great prudence in my absence, we are most entyre, and I begg your Lo. will be kynd to his at his arryval.

Earle Lauderdaill.

EARL OF ROTHES TO THE EARL OF LAUDERDALE.

MY DEAR LORD, Julay the 6 [1665.] 23123,

I am much trublid that by the courts remuffal it uill be impossibell for you to leat me hear so oftin ffrom, bot I most intreat ffor it als oftin as posiblie you can. The taym ffor the conuensioun dus nou

[a] He remained in charge of Tangiers until his death in a skirmish with the Moors, 1665.

draue nier, and I shall by the nixt post or tuo giff you acaunt of uhat I shall in all humilatie expeckt ffrom his Majestie as letiers or instruxions in relasion to the conuensione. You may remember a great uhayl ago his Majestie did in a prayffit letier ureatun by your Lo. comand me to retard the leues of the ffranshe ofisiers undier my Lord jorge duglies, of thos thrie hunder men uhich hie brought a uarant ffor. I uas tu long of geating the comand ffor me to meack a stop bot that it uold have esalie bin perseued, and tho I haue indeuoried it to put all the stop I could prayfitlie yit I ffaynd thay uill be in redines aganst the tuintiethe of this munthe, ffor thay ar uerie dilieant ouer the kingdum, and the ships uill be hear presislie aganst that day sent by the ffrenshe king ffor transporting of them, so that I most expeck a positiff comand uhat I shall du, ffor iff a stop be put to them it nill in my opinion be luckt upon as a breathe and the considerasion of that meacks me not enou uhat to du, bot iff ther be not a spidie breath layck to be I shuld thinck so small a number of men is not much uirthe of being notified, bot leat me haue an ansuier to this als sun as you can, and so ffor this post adeaie my dear Lard

[ROTHES.]

LORD GEORGE DOUGLAS TO THE EARL OF LAUDERDALE.

11.   Since that our kings ambassadeur hes takin his leuve of this court, and that it is thothit that ther shall be wars betuixt his Majesté and the king of France,[a] I wold intrait thet faveur of your Lo. as to assour his Majesté of my most faithfull loyalnesse and all the regiments that I dow command, as also that I might know what is his Majestes will that I should dow, for altho as your Lo. dis know that I have nothing in my ouin contray and no other livlyhod but

[a] In 1666 France was in alliance with Holland.

be my regiment hier, yet whatever commands his Majesté will honnor me and my regiment with shall be most punctuall and faithually obeyed; as your Lo. hes alweis doun me the honneur as to be my frind I hop you will continued now and lat me know what is the kings intention we should dow. I should wish that your Lo. wold lat me hier from you as soun as possibl can, for I belive I may may be commanded to go towards jttallie or cattalloing. I begge your Lo. will excusse me for this fridom I tak as to give you this trouble, since I am most really,

        My Lord,
      Your Lo. most humbl and obedient servint,
            DOUGLAS.

Paris, 9 Janvir, 1666[6$\frac{2}{3}$].

LORD HOLLES (English Ambassador at Paris) TO THE EARL OF LAUDERDALE.

MY LORD,   Paris, $\frac{14}{4}$ February [16]6$\frac{5}{6}$. 23124.

This is but to acknowledge the receite of your Lo^{ps} letter and to present you with my most humble service, for my Lord Douglas doth himself give your Lo^p an account of the little which wee both of us yet know will be done in his busines as to the transporting of his regiment, of which some difficulty as yet seemes to be made here; by the next post more may be knowen, of which he or I or both will give your Lo^p an account. In the meane time lett me begg the continuance of your Lo^{ps} favor to esteeme me as I really am,

       My Lord,
      Your Lo^{ps} most humble servant,
           HOLLES.

Thierry Charpentier (Secretary to Marquis of Louvois) to Lord George Douglas.

70. Monsieur, A St. Germain en laye, le 2 Mars, 1666.

J'ay pris les ordres de monseigneur le Marquis de Louvois sur ce qui vous regarde. Votre regiment doibt estre assemblé a St. Quentin et estre embarqué a St. Vallery. Je travailleray des demain a ce qui est a faire pour faire rendre toutes vos comp[agnie]s a St. Quentin, mais vous scavez, Monsieur, qu'elles ne peuvent partir des quartiers ou elles sont qu'elles n'yayent esté remplacées. Ainsy je ne croy pas qu'elles puissent estre avant trois sepmaines icy? toutes ensemble. Je ne perdray aucun moment de temps a ce que je doibt faire en cette occasion. Et je cheriray toujours beaucoup celles qui me donneront moyen de vous tesmoingner combien je suis,
　　　　Monsieur,
　　　　　　Votre tres humble serviteur,
　　　　　　　　　　　　　　　　Charpentier.

Lord George Douglas to Earl of Lauderdale.

72. My Lord, Paris, 3 Marche, 1666.

According as I did wryt to your Lo. by my last, the King of France has given me my pass conforme to our capitulation, and as your Lo. will si by the enclosed which I have just now recevid from Monsieur de Louvois, his secretaire, we ar to be embarqued at St. Vallery, so your Lo. most be plaissed to send the passes for the wessells that will transporte us from thence. I cannot spessefie the number so your Lo. most procure passes for such wessells as shall serve for the transpotation of the regiment. By my last I dissaired your Lo. to let me know in what place the king dissaired we should land at ; now that yow dow know the place that we ar to be imbarqued at your Lo. will be plaised to lat me know his Majesties plaiser in it, which shall be punctually observid, wind and wather serving. St. Quentin, which is the place of our randevous, is six days' march from St. Wallery, and it will be thri weiks before we can be ther, so it will be the last of this month before we can be imbarqued. My Lord Holles dis pairt from this, he dis tell me with in ten or tualve days; so, my Lord, what letters yow dow send to me efter his pairting, addresse them under a cover, A Monsieur, Monsieur Richard, maistre de la poste d'Anglettere. I am with respect, my Lord,

Your Lo. most humbl and obedient servint,

DOUGLAS.

LORD GEORGE DOUGLAS TO THE EARL OF LAUDERDALE.

MY LORD, Paris, 6 March, 1666. 23124,

Sinc my last to your Lo. things ar changed, for now the King of France dis trait us in the most crouel way that ever was, for he hes told me that he has no mony to pay us what is oning us, and that we shall have our rout according as I did wryt to you by my last, and ships at St. Wallery, but no mony to pay us what is ouing us, that we might pay our debts in the places we ar in, nor to carry us to the seaside. He dis this thinking to make our sojers stay behind and distroy the regiment. I hop this shall not have the effect they belive, for I am assowred non of our sojers will stay, and they should beg ther bred thorow the contray. I beliv ther was never such a crouel and barborus action doun efter so many years services, spending our bleuds and fortuns in his service, to be nessesitate to beg hom, and perhaps putt in prison for my debts, and refuss the payment of our arriers as also my pension. I believe such a traittement as this will be a warning to all my contremen or any of our kings subject. I have sothit my pass presently with our rout that we may go to the sea sid the best way we can, and ships for our transportation according to ther last promis which the secretaire of state said I should have, but that before I but to give him the pasports for the saif retourne of the ships, so my Lord I pray you to lat me have them by the first post, as at so to lat me know what I should dow in this. I refer other particullaires to my Lord Holles letters to your Lo. and my Lord Arlington, only I intrait a spidy and diligent ansur, for befor I can recev it I will presse them, so that I hop to gaitt all my ordres and pass from them, and will pairt immediatly upon any account out of this most ungraitfull countray, wher thy begin to louk now opon me in a most strange way. So expecting with impatiance to hier from your Lo. and to be in Ingland, I dow remaine,

My Lord,
Your Lo. most humbl and obedient servint,
DOUGLAS.

LORD GEORGE DOUGLAS TO THE EARL OF LAUDERDALE.

87. MY LORD, *Paris, 10 Marche, 1666.*
Yesterday I did disaire of the King of France that since he was not plaissed to pay us what he was ouing us, that he would be plaissed to give me immediatly my congé and routté and ordres for my transportation according to his promis to me. He told me, Je vous ay deja ditte que je suis court d'argent pour le present, mais je donné ordre a Monsieur de Louvois de vous donner tous vos

ordres nessesaires, et vous depecher; and he did immediatly call for Monsieur de Louvois and commanded him to dispache me, who told me he should dow it with all diligence, and for that effect the ordres dis pairt to morrow to . . . . . thri companies marche that is towards Lorraine. He told me also that we should have estapes upon our routte, which is so much flech, bred, and drink for every sojer, and to the officirs a proportion, and that we should find our shipes redy at St. Wallery for to cairy us over, and as for our tow months pay which was ouing us and my pension, that the king wold pay us when he had mony if I would live an officire behind, so that I had no raison to complaine of the King, and that he did kip our capitullation to us. The raison why thy dow not pay us our arriers was that thy thothit that that wold brek the regiment and oblige the officirs to stay, of the which thy ar extraimly desseved, for we shall cairy over seven hundrid as good sojers as is in the world; this is now ther last dessein how thy will traitte us, which your Lo. may belive for certine, as all so that we shall be imbarqued against the first of Appryll. Now that I have had my congé of the King of France I will not si him no mor till I be redy to pairt for to tak my liv of him. I dow expect with impatiance the passports for the wessels, for the secretaire told me that befor I went from court I but to delivre them to him. I told him that it was litle honnor for the King of France for to reffuse to pay us our arriers and si us put in prison, or at list striped naked for our debts in our quarters. His ansur was that the King had a dow[a] with his monyes, for to richen out shipes to fight against us. I shall not faill to advertis your Lo. when we marche from St. Quentin, our lieu d'assamblé, and at our arrivall at St. Wallery, and I hop your Lo. will pardon me for the trouble I give you by my letters, and that I am,

      My Lord,
          Your Lo. most humbl and obedient servint,
                             DOUGLAS.

[a] [?] enough to do.   [b] Rig.

Lord George Douglas to the Earl of Lauderdale.

94. My Lord,   Paris, ce 13 Mars, 1666.

Immediatly after the wryting of my last the secretaire of state send for me and told me that the King had maid une efort, and had borrowed moneys for to pay us, and that we shall be payed to the day of our embarquement, and at the King's retourne from the reveu at Compienne, wher he is gon this day and will be againe this day agithit [eight] days I should have my orders, so this will retarde us aight or ten days longer nor I expected, but my Lord I shall mak all the heast that can be, and I hop to cairy over a good regiment and at leist seven hundred men, for ther was never men so overjoied and willing as all the officirs and sojers ar. I asked the secretaire if the king wold not pay me my pensions he was owing me; he told me that he had no ordres from the King to dow it, for it was a particullaire bissinis that regardit myself, and that for the capitullation the king wold kip it, and bad me spik to the king; what he will dow I know not, but I am affrayed of the warsit. I dow expect with impatience for thos pasports for the wessills as also to know in what place I should land at. I pray yow my Lo. to lat me know if your Lo. will command me anything hier for your service, for now we have the foire de St. Germaine hier, and I can be abl to cairy over things with me conveniently. I shall wish to God I may be abl to testifie how much I am your Lo. servint, and sensibl of thos obligations I have to your Lo. and in particullaire in this last, which shall be the greatest passion of him that is with respect,

                 My Lord,
                    Your Lo. most humble and most obedient servint,
                                       Douglas.

Lord George Douglas to the Earl of Lauderdale.

My Lord,   Paris, 24 March, 1666.

At the retourne of the court to St. Germains, I went ther, so yesterday the secretaire of stat told me that he should send presently the ordres for to casse the regiment assembl at St. Quenten, and that he had ordres from the king to command me to rettire me self immediately to my regiment, that the king was not satisfied with me, and that for my pensions the king wold not pay me. I told him that I was ouing a great daill of debt hier and I had not a farding mony; he told me the king wold pay the regiment but as for me not, and that I must be going presently, so my Lord you may juge in what a sad condition I am in. My Lord Ambassadeur hes bein plaised to casse lenne me opon his credit thri hundrid pounds sterling for to pay my debts and to retir myself, so I will pairt within thri or four days for St. Quentin, wher I wold stay till my regiment be assembled. The secretaire of stat told me he should send me what ordres should be nessesaire to me you may jug my Lord how things stand with me hier by this hard usag I recev. I know not if I dar trusit ther promis in what they say they will dow concerning the regiment; therfor my Lord if they should put me aff with delays (as I dow not think thy will) lat me know what I shall dow. I have recevid yesterday the passes for the waissels, but no ordre for my landing nor wher I should dow it. My Lord Ambassadeur does wryt by this post to my Lord Arlington of it, as also to addresse his letteres and ordres for me in our queen mothers pakit, for his Lo. does pairt within tow or thri days, if thy should braik ther words to me hier concerning my regiment. I have told Collonel Gerardin what may be douin in that conjunctur, who will acquaint your Lo. with it. I am,
                My Lord,
                     Your Lo. most humble servint,
                             Douglas.

Lord George Douglas to the Earl of Lauderdale.

f. 140. My Lord, Diepe, the 16 Octobre, 1667.

I dow send over this officire for to intraite your Lo. to spik to the King, that his Majestie will be plaised according to his word to me (upon the which I payed my regiment four days pay of my ouin mony) to order me the payment of it, which was four days I stayed longer nor I receved pay for, and his Majestie did assour me I should be payed for it befor the Duke of York, and my Lord Generall told me so to. I dow assour your Lo. that insted of gaining upon this bissinis I will be a grait lousser, for ther was sum personnes that was plaised to mak a reporte go amongst my regiment that I was going for Tangere, so that ther runeaway almost thrie hundred men the day befor I shiped, so that with thos and the sik men I was forced to live be hinde; all that I have broght over is seven hundred and six men in sted of twelve, so that I most repay the superplus, which really my Lord will putt me extraimly to it, what with the weknisse of my regiment, so my Lord I will have nide of the continuatione of your Lo. faveur to spik to the King for me, and if his Majestie wold be plaised to confer that honor upon me that I dissaired your Lo. to spik alredy to his Majesty of, it wold be extraimly for the advanement of my fortune, so if your Lo. thinks fitt to spik againe to the king of it, you will oblige me extraimly in it, and to assure his Majesty that whatever service he hes a dow with me or my regiment I shall obey his commands most faithfully and punctually. I hop your Lo. will pardon me for this trouble I give you, and belive I am,

My Lord,
Your most humbl and obedient servant,
Douglas.

LORD GEORGE DOUGLAS TO THE EARL OF LAUDERDALE.

My Lord,   Paris, 9 May, 1668.   23129,

Now that the peace is maid hier thy ar going a mak a wery great reforme a mongst the troups, and I am affrayed that it faill havily upon my regiment, ther for I wold intraitte your Lo. that you wold be plaised to spik to the King that he wold be plaised to wryt a latter hier in my faveurs, and also to Sir Jhon Trever to spik to the King of France and Monsieur de Louvois. If your Lo. will be plaised to dow me this faveur it must be doun by the first post; for the reforme of troups ar to be presently doun, so ther is no tyme to be lost. I shall begg the honnor of your ansur, and to belive I am,
        My Lord,
               Your Lo. most humbl and most obedient servant,
                                   DOUGLAS.

LORD GEORGE DOUGLAS TO THE EARL OF LAUDERDALE.

My Lord,   Paris, 19 Decembre, 1668.   23131,

I have receved from Major Monro the letter your Lo. was plaised to honnor me with. I dow assour your Lo. all of us in the regiment ar extraimly sensible of your Lo. faveur in this last particulaire as we ar also of the formers we have to your Lo.; and I begge of your Lo. to assour his Majesty that ther is non of his subjects shall be mor redy to obey his commands nor I and all my regiment, which we shall allwais dow most faithfully and punctually. My

Lord Major Monro told me that it hes bein reported to your Lo. and to several others that I was maryed hier. I dow assour your Lo. it is most false, for upon my word of honnor I had nevr any such thothits, and I pray your Lo. to dow that justice to belive that I am incapable to dow a basse actione; and, my Lord, if you hier any such thing spok you will oblige me extraimly to assur the contraire, and to belive I am,
    My Lord,
     Your Lo. most humbl and most obedient servant,
       Douglas.

Lord George Douglas to the Earl of Lauderdale.

89. My Lord,   A Paris, 16 Feb. 1669.

By the last post I gave your Lo. notis of our merche for Vienne en Dauphine, and being destined for Candy, as this will be the absolat rouing and destructione of my regiment, our only resource is to your Lo. to intraite you to spik to the King to spik to the French Ambassadeur, and that his Majesty wold be plaised to wryt hier in our faveurs; for, if my regiment com to be weik, as it will most certinly, we will never be in conditione to mak it up a gaine; and your Lo. knowis that it is all my fortune and my officirs. As you have alwais bein our frind, now is the only and last strock for to help us. I have bein with Monsieur de Rouvigny and shoed him how we war not fitt for that service, and how strange it is to send us for our absolut roning, which he conffessed and hes spok of it to Monsieur de Turenne. But ther is sum other raisons, for all the holl world admirs why my regiment should be sent. So, my Lord, our last refuge is to the King and you, that his Majesty wold be plaised to tak our intrests and spik for us serieusly. But what his Majesty dis most be sudenly; and, my Lord, as I wryt to you by my last, I dow not knòw but the Kinges Ambassadeur and the Jnglishe merchants my suffer by it that is in Turky. So, expecting your Lo. speedy ansur, I remaine,

My Lord,
Your Lo. most humbl and most obedient servant,
DOUGLAS.

INDEX.

Albemarle, Duke of, 19
Anjou, Duke of, 11
Arlington, Lord, 36, 39

Bellenden, Lord, 29
Buckingham, Duke of, 30

Charpentier, letter to Lord George Douglas, 34
Caracène, M. de, 25
Cassilis, Earl of, i.; letters to Lauderdale 1-10, inclusive; to Charles II. 4
Compton, Sir William, 23

Douglas, Lord George, letters to Lauderdale, 10-30, inclusive; his regiment mentioned, 11
Dunkirk: *see* letters from Douglas and Rutherford, *passim*

Fort Royal, 15

Gerald, Lord, 23
Glencairn, Earl of, 6

Harley, Sir Edward, 14, 15
Harley, Sir Robert, 17, 19
Holles, Lord, letter to Lauderdale, 33; mentioned, 35, 36, 39

Knichtly, Lieut.-Col. 18

Lauderdale, Countess of, 13
Lawson, Sir J. 28
Le Tellier, 10

Lockhart, Col. 17
Louvois, Marquis de, 34, 36, 37, 41

Maitland, Lady Mary, 13
Mardyke, 15
Marsine, M. de, 25
Middleton, Earl of, 29
Monckton, Sir Philip, 16
Moray, Sir Robert, 14, 29, 30
Morrice, Secretary, 14-15
Munro, Major, 41, 42

Newburgh, Earl of, 29
Nicholas, Sir E. 21, 25, 27

Ormond, Duke of, 12

Roberts, Lord, 23
Rothes, Earl of, letter to Lauderdale, 31
Rouvigny, M. de, 42
Rupert, Prince, 28
Rutherford, Lord (afterwards Earl Teviot), letters to Lauderdale, 10-30; letter to Sir Robert Moray, 16

Southampton, Lord Treasurer, 16, 17, 23
St. Albans, Lord, 11

Tangiers, 19, 22, 25
Trevor, Sir J. 41
Turenne, M. de, 42

Waller, Sir W. 21
Wentworth, Lord, 22
Whytkirk, Lord, 29

York, James, Duke of, 21, 22

ORIGINAL LETTERS

OF

THE DUKE OF MONMOUTH,

IN THE BODLEIAN LIBRARY.

EDITED BY

SIR GEORGE DUCKETT BART.

PRINTED FOR THE CAMDEN SOCIETY.
M.DCCC.LXXIX.

ORIGINAL LETTERS

OF

THE DUKE OF MONMOUTH.

It is unnecessary to recapitulate more of the history of James, Duke of Monmouth, son of Charles II, than is already known; how he raised the Standard of Rebellion in 1685, and how, after the Battle of Sedgemoor, he was eventually taken prisoner, and committed to the Tower.

Our object in the present paper deals exclusively with the autograph letters which are extant of him. Those which he wrote to the King and the Queen Dowager from Ringwood, the place of his capture, on the 8th and 9th of July, have been often published,[a] as far as their substance goes; but the originals of all, save that to the Queen Dowager, are now in the Bodleian Library, and of these, two appear never to have been published; in fact, from what Roberts (Monmouth's historian) quotes from the "Clarendon Papers" of a non-delivered letter to the King, and that which another version of the account (given hereafter) has on the same subject, we have no hesitation in asserting, that not one only, but both these letters, were suppressed.

There are four original letters of Monmouth in the Bodleian;[b]

---

[a] Roberts's "Life of Monmouth," II, 112, 119; Fox's "History of James II.;" Ellis's "Historical Letters," III.; "Lansdowne MSS.," 1236, art. 230; Harl. MSS. 7006, 7198.

[b] Rawl. MS. A. 139 b.

one to the King from Ringwood, dated 8th July; another to the King from the Tower, dated 12th July; one to the Queen from the same place, and on the same day; and lastly the Declaration, made just before his execution, in the presence of the Bishops of Ely and Bath and Wells and Drs. Tennison and Hooper.

The following are the unpublished letters in question with the exception of the first, which is that dated from Ringwood:—

"S^r

"Your Ma^{ty} may think it is the misfortune I now ly under makes me make this application to you, but I doe assur your Ma^{ty}, it is the remorce I now have in me of the rong I have done you in severall things, and now in taking up Arms against you, for my taking up arms, it never was in my thoughts since the King dy'd; the Prince and Princess of Orange will be wittness for me of the assurance I gave them, that I would never stir against you, but my misfortun was such, as to meet wth some horrid people that made me believe things of your Ma^{ty}, and gave me soe many false arguments, that I was fully led away to belive, that it was a shame and a sin before God not to doe it; but S^r, I will not trouble your Ma^{ty} at present wth many things I could say for myself, that I am sur would move your compation, the cheif end of this letter being only to beg of you that I may have that hapiness to speak to your Ma^{ty}, for I have that to say to you, S^r, that I hope may give you a long and happy Rain. I am sur, S^r, when you hear me you will be convinced of [the] zeal I have for your preservation, and how hartily I repent of what I have done. I can say noe mor to your Ma^{ty} now, being [seeing?] this letter may be seen by those that keep [me]; therefore, S^r, I shall make an ind in beging of your Ma^{ty} to belive so well of me, that I would rather dy a thousand deaths then to excuse any thing I have don, if I did not realy think myself the most in the rong that ever any man was, and had not from the bottom of my hart an obhorance for those that put me upon it, and for the action it self, I hope, S^r, God Almighty will strick your hart wth mercy and compation for me, as he has done mine wth the obhorance of what I have done; therefor I hope, S^r, I may live to show you how zealous I shall ever be for your service, and could I say but one word in this letter you would be convinced of it, but it is of that consequence that I dare not doe it; therefor, S^r, I doe beg of you once mor to let me speak to you, for then you will be convinced how much I shall ever be your Ma^{tys} humble and dutifull,

(Signed) " MONMOUTH.

(Addressed)
" For the King."

[Seal in red wax, broken.]

" S^r,

I had forgot to tell your Ma^{ty} that it would be very nesessary to send some troupes down into Chesehire, for there ar severall gentlemen there, that I beleive wear ingaged in this re . . .[a] I hope your Ma^{ty} will not be angry wth me, if I take this opertunity to put you in mind, that there ar severall doe wish me out of the way for there own sakes, without considering your Ma^{tys} service, but I am sur, S^r, you ar soe just and soe good, that noe such people will have any credit wth you. Pray, S^r, doe not be angry wth me, if I tell you once more that I long to live to shew you, S^r, how well and how trully I can serve, and if God Almighty sends me that blessing, tis all upon earth I will ever aske, being that I hope I shall end my days in showing of you, that you have not a truer and a faithfuller subject than your most dutifull,

(Signed) " MONMOUTH.

(Endorsed)
" D: of Mon: Letter
" July 12, 1685."

[Seal of red wax, abstracted.]

[a] Erased in the original; the word being evidently " rebellion."

"Madame,

"I would not take the boldness of writting to your Mat^y, tell I had shew'd the King how I doe abhor the thing that I have done, and how much I desire to live only to serve him. I hope, Madam, by what I have sed to the King to day, will satisfy him how sinceir I am, and how much I detest all those people, that has brought me to this. Having done this, Madame, I thought I was in a fitt condition to beg your intersesion, wch I am sur you never refuse to the distresed, and I am sur, Madame, I am an object of your pity, having bine cousened and cheated into this horid busines. Did I w^ch [wish], Madame, to live, for living sake, I would never give you this trouble, but it is to have life to serve the King, wch I am cable to doe, and will doe, beyond what I can express ; therfor, Madam, upon such an account as that, I may take the boldness to presse you, and beg of you to intersaid for me, for I am sur, Madam, the King will harken to you ; your prairs can never be refused, espetially when tis beging for a life, only to serve the King. I hope, Madame, by the King's generosity and goodness, and your intersession, I may hope for my life, wch if I have, shall ever be employ'd in shewing to your Mat^y all the sence immadginable of gratitud for your great goodness, and in serving of the King, like a true and faithfull subject, and ever be your M^tys most dutifull and obedient servant

(Signed) "MONMOUTH.

"To the Queen."

The main consideration in the present inquiry, which will be apparent by the annexed correspondence, is the presumed suppression of these concluding letters. The account given by Roberts from the "Clarendon Papers," of the non-delivery of one of Monmouth's letters,[a] and that given, hereafter, by Dr. Rawlinson's friend,

---

[a] Roberts, II. 135.

though differing in detail, still agree as to the main fact, that a letter to the King was kept back. There is a discrepancy in the version of these two narratives, which is decidedly in favour of the Rawlinson account, for Dr. Samuel Jebb, of Stratford, in Essex, who relates it, was present at the hearing of the story by the principal actor in it, Colonel Scott of the Guards, and vouches for its accuracy. The same may be said of another particular, related by Roberts, in which the interview between Ralph Sheldon and the King, in respect of a message from Monmouth, by which the Earl of Sunderland (James's Lord President of the Council) was implicated,[a] is differently related ; the probably real account of the same being, as with the former, in favour of Dr. Jebb. According to this gentleman, Bridgeman, an Under-Secretary of State and Clerk of the Council at that time, and of course under the direct influence of Sunderland, or, in fact, his devoted servant and creature, was the person said to have suppressed the letter delivered to him. This is rendered more than probable, from the knowledge we have of Sunderland's character, of whom the Princess Anne said that he was "the subtilest working villain that is on the face of the earth";[b] equally so from the fact, that he had been all along plotting and intriguing with Monmouth as to the future, but, above all, that in the very letter (this presumed suppressed letter) the Duke points to him as one of those "who wished him out of the way for their own sake." These circumstances go far to invalidate the accounts handed down to us as historical, and very much tend to complicate the general opinion of James the Second's character. Relying upon the veracity of Colonel Scott's interview with the King, and what he said on the occasion, it would certainly seem that James, receiving no reliable intimation of the Duke's sincere remorse and contrition, or, to use

---

[a] Roberts, II. 114; Clarke's Life of James II.

[b] Dalrymple's Memoirs, Appendix, Part i. 301. The Princess Anne on several occasions expresses her bad opinion of Sunderland. In a letter to her sister the Princess of Orange she says: "You may remember I have once before ventured to tell you that I thought Ld Sunderland a very ill man, and am now more confirmed every day in that opinion."

his own words to Colonel Scott, " his sincere discovery," became less susceptible of any merciful impulse, and supported, as he undoubtedly was, in this frame of mind by his chief adviser the Earl of Sunderland, there is a want of generosity and a harshness about his acts in respect of Monmouth which the evidence now brought forward would seem to qualify if not to contradict; indeed, it is evident from his own " Memoirs," if they are to be trusted, that the King regretted being forced to carry out the execution of Monmouth. On the other hand, all testimony points to James as a man void of all feeling, inexorable and unrelenting. That one of the letters was not delivered we have ample proof, and it is reasonable to infer the same of the other.

Before, however, we proceed to give the correspondence in evidence of this assertion, we may observe as to the way in which the Monmouth letters came into Rawlinson's possession. They formed part of a collection of State Papers of about the same period, and their authenticity is proved from having at one time been in the possession of the aforesaid William Bridgeman, in his official capacity as Clerk of the Privy Council and Under-Secretary of State to James II. They were purchased by Rawlinson at the sale of the library and pictures of William Bridgeman's daughter (Catherine) in 1743, and this fact is alluded to by him in a letter on the subject among the Ballard MSS. [ii. No. 78].[a]

At this lapse of time one can only hazard a conjecture as to the cause of Bridgeman's visit to Monmouth at the Tower. At that time he would appear to have been Clerk of the Privy Council to James II., but in 1694 (or earlier) he was Secretary to the Admiralty. Some years before these events, *i.e.*, in 1677, Monmouth had been one of the Commissioners of the Navy (or, as now termed, Lords of the Admiralty), so that the visit is as likely to have been in a private as in an official capacity. Catherine Bridgeman, to whom the Duke's autograph letters descended, married her cousin Orlando, son of Sir John Bridgeman, and was therefore one of the same family since promoted to the Earldom of Bradford.

[a] For this last information we are indebted to the recently published Catalogue of the Rawlinson MSS. by the Rev. W. D. Macray.

It is on the acquisition of these original letters that Dr. Rawlinson is congratulated in the first part of the ensuing correspondence.

[Letters from Dr. Samuel Jebb to Dr. Rawlinson.]

"Hon^d S^r

"I heartily congratulate you upon your late acquisition. The D. of Monmouth's letters is one of ye greatest curiositys extant. They were never deliver'd to ye King. If they had been given him, they might possibly have prevented his ruin. I have a strange story to tell you about 'em, for wch I can produce authentick vouchers. The inclos'd parcel I am afraid is of no great value, but, such as it is, it is at your service. I shall hope for ye pleasure of seeing you soon at Stratford, and in ye mean time am, wth all due regard, S^r, y^r most ob^t S^t

"Feb 19, 1743 "S. JEBB.
"Stratford.
(Addressed)
"To Dr Rawlinson
 "at London-house in
  "Aldersgate-Street
    "London."

"Stratford
"Hon^d S^t "March 1, 1743.

"I had ye favour of both y^r letters.

"Y^e Story you give me in y^r former, stands in need of some little correction. The person sent to ye D. of Monmouth by ye K., was Ralph Sheldon, ye brother of Dominck, but was not sent to him when in ye Tower, but immediately upon his been seiz'd in ye West, before he was brought up to town. When this gentleman return'd, he found ye King in ye Circle, & upon his saying, ye Duke had engag'd him to deliver his message only to ye K., his Majesty ordered all to withdraw, except my Ld Sunderland. Upon M^r

Sheldon's pressing y^t ye Lord Presid^t might likewise retire, & urging y^t ye D of Monmouth had oblig'd him to swear, y^t he would tell ye secret he had entrusted him wth to none but ye K. in private, ye K. warmly told him that 'twas an unlawfull oath, & charg'd him upon his allegiance to declare what it was. He then said y^t ye D. had bid him tell his Majesty, y^t if he had succeeded, my L^d S^d was to have been his first Minister; to wch ye K. answer'd wth a smile—'Poor Monmouth! he was always easy to be impos'd on'— But this was not ye story I refer'd to. When I was at Boulogne in ye year 1723, amongst other gentlemen I found there, was one Col. Scot, formerly an officer in ye Guards, who upon ye Revolution follow'd ye fortunes of K. James, & attended upon him at St Germains. Whilst ye D. of Monmouth was in ye Tower, it was this gentleman's office to be one day there upon guard, w^{ch}, if I mistake not, was ye day before his execution. The D., who knew him, desir'd to speak wth him, & upon his coming into ye room, ye D., wth great earnestness press'd y^t he would immediately deliver to ye K. a letter he had wrote, & ^{Wch} then lay before him upon ye table, assuring him y^t he had reason to believe, he might still find mercy, if that letter was rightly delivered. Col. Scot excus'd himself from deserting his post before ye proper time of his being reliev'd, & laid before ye Duke ye hazard he should incurr by doing it, but at ye same time assur'd him, y^t when his duty was over, if that would suffice, he would not fail to give the letter into ye K.'s own hands. In ye mean time a third person enter'd ye room, wch if I misremember not, was Mr Bridgeman, (tho' I cannot certainly charge my memory with it)[a], upon sight of whom ye D. said, 'Col. Scot, here comes one upon whom I can rely no less than upon y^{r}self, I will send my letter by him;' & accordingly he sealed it up, & gave it him. This letter I suppose to be the letter you have

[a] According to Roberts, a certain "Captain Blood" (whom he calls the "infamous") was the person intrusted with the letter; but, if this person is intended to be identical with the notorious Colonel Blood, it cannot be correct, for he was not then living, having died in 1680.

purchas'd, & suppress'd by ye person to whom it was intrusted. For as this gent^n (Col Scot), about four years after the Revolution was walking in ye garden at St Germains, ye King call'd him to him, & told him he had ye night before been inform'd, y^t ye conversation mention'd above had pass'd betwixt him & ye D. of Monmouth, whilst he was a prisoner in ye Tower, & desir'd to know if he had been rightly inform'd; and upon Scot's answering in the affirmative, ye K. averr'd, y^t he had never receiv'd any such letter from ye D., nor ever heard of it till that time, & y^t it was in his inclination to have sav'd the D.'s life, if he could have had any proper assurances y^t ye D. was dispos'd to have made a sincere discovery. This story Col. Scot[a] told in ye presence of Mr Cotton, Mr Panton & several other English gentlemen of reputation & credit, at that time residing in Boulogne. The particulars of ye letter, Col. Scot declared, he was a stranger to, but ye letter itself, he said, was a long one. The last parcel of letters I sent you, I apprehended, would not be judg'd of equall value wth ye former, but as in ye letter I receiv'd from you some time ago, you was pleased to say you sometimes reserv'd letters of acc^ts, I was willing to lay these before you, to be dispos'd of as you thought fit; tho' ye letters from ye B^ps daughter, Mrs Goulston, & her husband, to Dr Turner, I should think might be worth saving, & if they are not agreeable to you, I should be glad to have 'em return'd. I have look'd over some of ye sermons I have by me, & find abundance of ye B^ps, but have not been able to pitch upon one, y^t I have had reason to think the Doctor's, unless this wch I have sent you be his, wch yet I doubt. I mention'd some time ago a large collection of controversial tracts & letters, wch are still remaining, & of wch I sent you a specimen. These I have not yet been able to digest in proper order, & I imagine are some of 'em printed, but when you favour me wth a visit, you shall look over ye whole, and have such of 'em as you have not already. In Mr Dodwell's life by Brokesby I suppose too we shall

[a] Colonel Scott was evidently one of the Buccleugh family.

find some of 'em. I am much oblig'd to you for ye catalogue, & should be glad of a book or two therein, if they are not of too high a price; the one is in ye third nights sale, N° 122, & call'd Cooper's Anatomy, but I suppose is Cooper's Anatomical Treatise of ye Muscles; in ye 5th night's sale is also a little piece of Caius, bound up wth a treatise of Lommius, N° 66, wch would be of use to me, as also ye Oxford Aretæus in ye 6th night's sale, No. 108, if ye price of it did not run too high. But as these are books, wch I w^d not chuse to buy, unless they were penny worths; so neither would I trespass upon y^r good nature to lay out any considerable sum for 'em upon my account. I am, S^r, wth all possible regard,

" Y^r most obed^t &c.

" S. JEBB."[a]

[a] The identifying history of the Monmouth Letters being, in a great measure, due to Dr. Jebb, a short notice of him may not be out of place. He was decidedly a remarkable man for the age in which he lived, and was probably born somewhere about 1696, for in 1716 we find him a member of Peter-House, Cambridge, being ordained Deacon among the Non-jurors by (Bishop) Jeremy Collier, and Priest in January of the year following, at which time also he published a translation of "Martyn's Answers to Evelyn." In 1722 he was Editor of the "Bibliotheca Literaria," and appears at different periods to have been the author of several learned and important works, His name is associated with an Epitaph, written by him in memory of four English gentlemen, who, with their servants, were murdered in 1723, between Haut-Buisson and Marquise, on the road from Boulogne to Calais, but the pyramid on which it was inscribed, marking the site of the murder, has long since vanished, a chapel or oratory having been afterwards erected on the spot. According to Chalmers's Biographical Dictionary, Dr. Jebb was, in 1749, in possession of all Bridges' MSS. relative to the "History of Northamptonshire." He practised, nearly until his death (in 1772), with great success and reputation as a physician, at Stratford, in Essex, and the works which he commissions Dr Rawlinson to purchase for him, on medical and chirurgical subjects (in the above letter), have an interest at this day, in respect of a profession, at that time more or less in its infancy. His son, Sir Richard Jebb, followed his father's calling, and was created a Baronet by George III., having been made Physician-Extraordinary to the King in 1777, and employed about the Royal Family from that time till his death.

INDEX.

Anne, Princess, afterwards Queen, 7
Aretæus, the Oxford, 12

Bath and Wells, Bishop of, 4
Bibliotheca Literaria, 12
Biographical Dictionary, Chalmers's, 12
Blood, Captain (supposititious), 10
Blood, Colonel, his death, 10
Boulogne, 11, 12
Bradford, the Earl of, 8
Bridgeman, Catharine, 8
Bridgeman, (Sir) John, 8
Bridgeman, Orlando, 8
Bridgeman, William, 7, 8, 10
Brokesby, Francis, 11

Caius, 12
Cambridge, Peter House at, 12
Catharine of Braganza, Queen Dowager, 3
Chalmers, Alexander, his Biographical Dictionary, 12
Cheshire, rebels in, 5
Clarendon Papers mentioned, 3, 6
Collier, (Bishop) Jeremy, 12
Cooper, Sir Astley Paston, 12
Cotton, Mr. 11

Dalrymple, Sir John, 7
Dodwell, Henry (the elder), 11

Ellis, Sir Henry, his original letters, &c. 3
Ely, the Bishop of, 4

Fox, Charles James, his History of James II. 3

George III. 12
Goulston, Mr. and Mrs. 11

Hooper, Dr. 4

James II. *passim*
Jebb, (Sir) Richard, 12
Jebb, (Dr.) Samuel, 7, 9, 12

Lommius, 12

Manuscripts : Ballard, 8 ; Bridges, 12 Harleian and Lansdowne, 3; Rawlinson, *passim*
Marie Beatrix, Queen, 4, 6, 8
Martyn's answers to Evelyn, 12
Monmouth, James Fitzjames, *alias* Scott, Duke of, his rebellion, 3; letters from Ringwood to James II. 4, 5; from the Tower, 5; to the Queen Marie Beatrix, 6; his intrigue with Sunderland, 7; visited by Bridgeman, 8; earlier by Ralph Sheldon, 9; his interview with Colonel Scott, 10; the same related to the King, 11

Northamptonshire, History of, 12

Orange, William and Mary of, 4

Panton, Mr. 11

Rawlinson, Dr. 6, 8, 9, 12
Ringwood, 3, 4
Roberts, George, his Life of Monmouth, 3, 6, 7, 10

St. Germains, 11
Scott, Colonel, 7, 10, 11
Scott, James: *see* Monmouth
Sedgemoor Fight, 3
Sheldon, Dominick, 9
Sheldon, Ralph, 7, 9, 10
Stratford, in Essex, 7, 9, 12
Sunderland (Robert Spencer), Earl of, 7, 8, 9

Tennison, Dr. 4
Turner, Dr. 11

CORRESPONDENCE

OF

THE FAMILY OF HADDOCK

1657—1719

EDITED BY
EDWARD MAUNDE THOMPSON

PRINTED FOR THE CAMDEN SOCIETY
M.DCCC.LXXXI.

PREFACE.

Settled from remote times in the little town of Leigh, in Essex, at the mouth of the Thames, the family of Haddock, we may be sure, took early to the sea, as was befitting their name. There are traces of Haddocks of Leigh to be found as far back as Edward the Third's days; but we need not search for earlier generations than those which sprang from Richard Haddock, a captain in the Parliamentary Navy. That the family had followed the sea from father to son in bygone times, and had so established a tradition to be observed by their descendants, might be argued from the regularity with which the Haddocks of the seventeenth and eighteenth centuries served in the Navy for upwards of a hundred years. This regularity is only to be equalled by that with which they named their children Richard, to the perpetual confusion of their biographers.

Captain Richard Haddock, to whom reference has been made above, served under the Commonwealth. In 1642 we find him in command of the ship Victory, and in 1652 he received a reward of £40 for good service. He died in 1660 at the age of 79. His eldest son William, also a Parliamentary captain, commanded the ship America in 1650, and the Hannibal in 1653. He survived his father only seven years, dying in 1667, aged 60. Captain Richard Haddock had another son, Richard, who was probably a good deal younger than his brother. He served with distinction in the Dutch war in 1673 ;* and was in all probability the father of William Haddock whom the family papers show to have been a lieutenant in the Cornwall in 1696-1697, and who commanded a ship in the action off Cape Passaro in 1718 (p. 54) and died in 1726.

William Haddock, the Parliamentary captain, had at least four sons: Richard, Andrew, Joseph, and William. Richard will be noticed presently. Andrew is mentioned in the first letter of this Correspondence. William was at sea with his brother Richard in 1657 and 1658. Joseph was a lieutenant in the Lion in 1672, and in the Royal Charles in 1673, and served in the Dutch war in those years ; and afterwards held a command in the East Indies, whence he wrote an interesting letter here printed (p. 37). Richard Haddock was born about the year 1629, and must have entered the service at an early age ; for in 1657, when the present Correspondence begins, he was already a captain in command of the Dragon frigate, which formed part of the squadron cruising off Dunkirk. In 1666 he was captain of the Portland ; but from 1667 to 1671

---

* See p. 19 in the Correspondence. Charnock in his *Biographia Navalis*, i. 334, has made him out to be the son of Andrew Haddock, his own nephew.

PREFACE.

he appears to have temporarily left the Navy and engaged in trading to the Mediterranean. On the breaking out of the Dutch war, however, he was made captain of the Royal James, the ship on which the ill-starred Earl of Sandwich hoisted his flag in the battle of Southwold Bay. He was one of the few officers of that vessel who survived the day, though he did not escape unwounded. He next commanded the Lion; but early in 1673 he was appointed to the Royal Charles, Prince Rupert's ship, and within a few weeks followed the Prince into the Royal Sovereign, when the bad qualities of the former ship in action became evident. In July of the same year he was made Commissioner of the Navy; and on the 3rd of July, 1675, he was knighted. In 1682 he was appointed to the command of the Duke and to the chief command of ships of war in the Thames and narrow seas ; and in the next year became First Commissioner of the Victualling Office. After the Revolution he was named Comptroller of the Navy, which office he continued to hold till his death, and received a pension of £500 a year. He was one of the joint commanders-in-chief of the fleet in the expedition to Ireland in 1690. He died on the 26th of January, 1715, in his eighty-sixth year, and was buried in his native town of Leigh.

Sir Richard represented the borough of Shoreham in the parliament of 1685-1687. He was twice married, his first wife being named Lydia, probably a member of the family of Stevens, which was settled at Leigh. The maiden name of his second wife Elizabeth is unknown. He probably married her not earlier than 1670, when she was about twenty years of age, the inscription on her tomb recording her death in 1709, at the age of 59.

Sir Richard appears to have had at the least six children, three sons and three daughters. The sons were Richard, William, and Nicholas. Of the daughters the name of only one, Elizabeth, has survived, who married John Clarke, of Blake Hall in Bobbingworth, co. Essex. Another daughter married a Lydell. The third daughter died unmarried. William, apparently the second son, died young. Richard and Nicholas both entered the Navy.

Richard, the eldest son, was, in 1692, fifth lieutenant of the Duchess, and was present at the battle of La Hogue. He afterwards served in the London, and in 1695 was in command of the Rye. At the beginning of 1702 he received his commission as captain of the Reserve, and in the following year succeeded to the Swallow. In the latter ship he served with Sir George Rooke in the Mediterranean. But in 1707 he had the misfortune to be surprised by the French when convoying the Archangel merchant fleet and to lose fifteen ships; and, although appointed to the Resolution early in the following year, he seems to have soon retired from active service. In 1734, however, he re-appears as Comptroller of the Navy, and held the post for fifteen years, dying at an advanced age in 1751. From the entries in Leigh parish registers it seems that he was married thrice and had issue, none of whom, however, survived him many years.

Of Nicholas, the youngest son of Sir Richard Haddock, we first catch sight in the following pages (p. 43) as distinguishing himself at Vigo in 1702, and serving in Spain in 1706. In the following year, on the 7th April, he received the command of the new ship Ludlow Castle, being not yet twenty years old. At the battle of Cape Passaro he fought his ship, the Grafton, with great gallantry; and indeed at all times proved himself a very skilful and dashing officer. He rose eventually to the rank of Admiral of the Blue, and commanded the squadron sent into the Mediterranean to overawe the Spaniards in 1738-1741. He returned to England invalided and did not long survive, dying in 1746, aged 60.

About the year 1723 he purchased Wrotham Place, in Kent, where he occasionally lived. He left three sons: Nicholas, Richard, and Charles. The first died in 1781; Richard served in the Navy; Charles was still living at Wrotham in 1792.

Here the male line of the Haddocks fails: and it is not necessary to follow the family history further. A pedigree, which may be found useful, is appended.*

It will be seen that the letters and papers here printed belonged, for the most part, to Sir Richard Haddock. His long life enabled

---

* The best account of the Haddock family is to be found in a paper written by Mr. H. W. King and printed in *The Archæological Mine*, a work relating to Kentish history by A. J. Dunkin, vol. ii., pp. 41-51. Charnock's *Biographia Navalis* of course gives particulars of the services of the family; and a number of original naval commissions of its different members are still extant in Egerton MS. 2520. See also *The History of Rochford Hundred* by Philip Benton, 1872, pp. 35 *sqq*.

him to embrace four adult generations in his correspondence. The collection of documents from which they have been selected was purchased by the Trustees of the British Museum in 1879, and now forms the Egerton MSS. 2520-2532.

It is to be regretted that the Correspondence is so comparatively scanty, for no doubt at one time the collection was a good deal larger. From Nichols's *Literary Anecdotes* (vol. v. p. 376) we know that the Haddock papers were placed in the hands of Captain William Locker, the Lieutenant-Governor of Greenwich Hospital, who contemplated a publication of naval biography which was carried out by Charnock in his *Biographia Navalis* from the same materials. There is also evidence among the papers themselves, in the form of a letter written by Charles Haddock in 1792, to show that they were placed in Locker's hands. The fate of borrowed books and papers is a mournful one.

But, few as they are, a selection from the Haddock Papers has been thought worthy to appear in print. As specimens of the letter-writing of a seafaring family of the seventeenth and eighteenth centuries, the letters have a value of their own, even apart from the personal interest which they inspire as the record of long and honourable service.

E. M. T.

24 *March*, 1881.

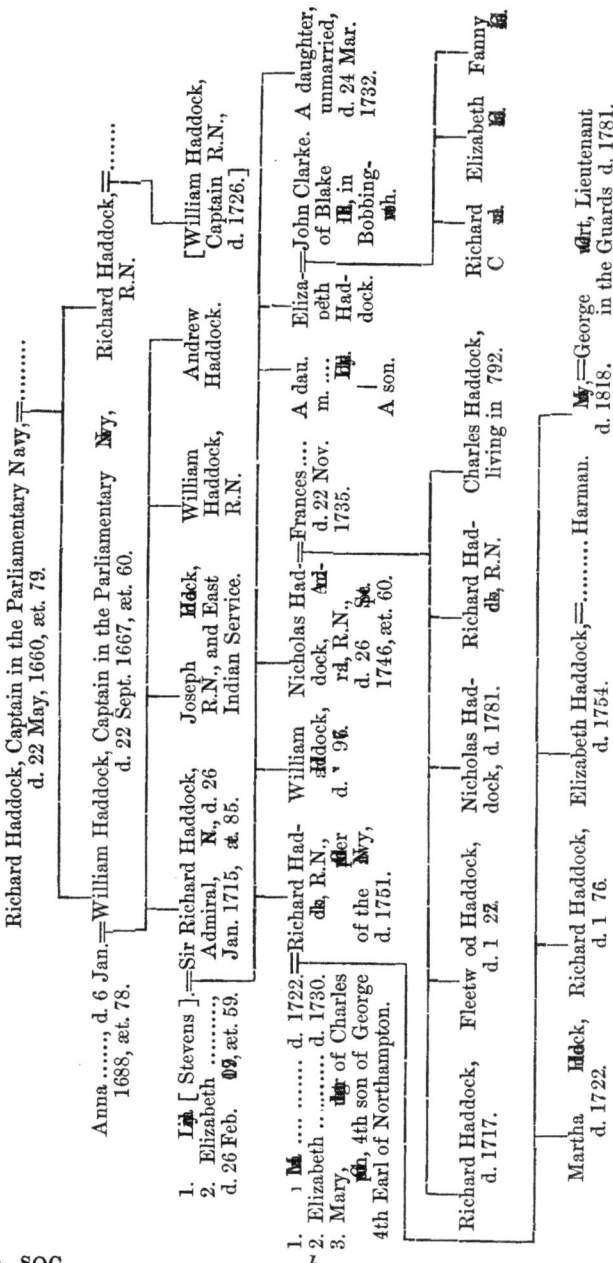

CAMD. SOC.

CORRESPONDENCE

OF

THE FAMILY OF HADDOCK.

CAPTAIN RICHARD HADDOCK [a] TO HIS FATHER.

HON^d FATHER,   Dragon frig^t in the Downes, this 30th May, a° 1657.

Sir, these I hope will congratulate yor safe arrivall at Leghorne, wch God graunt may be with yor health and well fare, for the continuation whereof I shall ever pray.

I cannot yet forgett my unhapynes y^t soe short a tyme and small distance hindred me the inioym^t of seeing yo^u before you gote out ye Channell, seeing I made it my aime and bussines to performe it, but pleased God to frustrate me of my intended hapynes. I hope y^t our next interview may be with the greater ioy and comfort. Indeed, when I returned to Dover, which was the Sunday following yor departure, I was not a little greived when Major Gen^{ll} Kelsey [b] tould me ye unwellcome news of yor being past by; and himselfe was very sory when I gave him an acc^t y^t I mett yo^u not, and tould me, if I had in ye least desired not to have gone for Zeinhead, he would have ordered an other ship in o^r roome. I was very thankfull for his respect he exprest towards yo^u, but I knew not before y^t I might be soe bould wth him as to desire such a favor. Yo^u saild hence ye Fryday evening; and Satuarday, by 10 in ye forenoone, we were soe neare ye head of Beachy y^t noe shipp could or did passe

---

[a] Afterwards Admiral Sir R. Haddock.
[b] Major-General Thomas Kelsey, commanding in Kent and Surrey.

by us, but we spake wth in hopes of meeting yo^u. Surely the wind blew the harder to deny me y^t hapynes. God in mercy goe alongst with yo^u and preserve yo^u from the rage of unreasonable men. I shall not be wanting, as I am bound in duty, to make it my earnest request to God for yor preservation. My wife, in good health, presents her humble duty to yo^u, and hath ever since bine very sorrowfull she stayed not behind to present her duty and respects to yo^u at yor departure.

Sir, litle of novelty ofers at present, only of great preparations for ye fitting out seavrall great shipps, as ye Resolution, Naiesby, and Andrew, from Portsm°; ye Tryomph, Victory, Vantguard, and Entrance, from Chatham. I cannot give you an acc^t, ye occasion or upon w^t designe ye shipps are prepared; only suppose it may be to be in a readynes to defend our selves if any treachorus act should be ofered by the Hollander, who will have 70 saile men of warr out very sodainely, as is certainely reported. I hope noe act of hostillity against us is intended. We have iust cause to feare ye worst; and I think, as farr as I am able to aprehend, yo^u will have little occasion to trust or put any confidence in them abroad. God send us peace at home and abroad; but, if these faile us, peace wth God will beare up our spirits in the greatest dificulties y^t doe atend our earthly pilgrimage.

Sir, my wife desires yo^u please, at yor arrivall at Ven^a, to buy for her a foiled stone of the measure I conseave was given by her sisters to Brother Andrew at Leigh; as alsoe a pott ketle and 2 stue panns, one lesser than the other; as alsoe a jarr from Leghorne, with w^t other things nessesary for a howse, to ye value of £3 in fower pound in all, which shall be thankfully repaved. I intend to wright yo^u to Ven^a, when [I] conseave you may ataine thither, and what ofers shall not be wanting of advizeing yo^u.

My Lord Protector hath denyed ye governm^t of the Comonwealth under ye title of King,[a] and since, its established to him in the title he now beares.[b]

---

[a] On the 8th May.   [b] On the 25th May.

I have not heard from home since yor departure. My intire love with my wives remembred to our 3 brothers wth all o^r freinds on bord yo^u. Brother Wm., in health, pres^{ts} his humble duty to yo^u, wth his love to his Bro^r. My saluts to Mr. Holder; and, with my most humble duty presented to yor self, I remayne,

   Sir, yor ever lo. and obedient sonne till death,
          RICHARD HADDOCK.

My wife being present desires, wth ye presenting her humble duty to yo^u, to subscribe herselfe yor lo. daughter till death,
          LYDIA HADDOCKE.[a]

Since ye wrighting ye above lynes I have rec^d order to goe over and ryde before Dunkerk, and to take ye comand of y^t squadron now riding there. This day is arrived hapy news, Gen^{ll} Blake's burneing and sinking 16 saile of the K. of Spaine's gallions and shipps at Sta Cruse, most welcome and true.[b]   R. H.

To his hon^d. father, Capt. Wm. Haddock, Comander of the
 shipp Hanniball, these present, Livorno.

THE SAME TO THE SAME.

       Dragon frig^t in Dunkirk Road, this 15th June, a° 1657.
HON^d FATHER,

S^r, my most humble duty w^{tb} Bro. Wms. presented unto you wth o^r intire loves to o^r loveing brothers and freinds wth you. These only serve to advize yo^u of our wellfare, hoping and earnestly praying to the Lord that ye like good health atends you y^t, blessed

---

[a] Richard Haddock's first wife. Perhaps her maiden name was Stevens. (See letter of 1 May 1658, in which Haddock sends his duty to "Father and Mother Steevens.")

[b] Blake's last victory at Santa Cruz, in the Canaries, 20th April. He died on his voyage home, in sight of land, on the 17th August.

be God, we injoy. These I hope will find yo^u safe arrived at Leghorne. My last from the Downes gave yo^u an acc^t y^t we were ordered over hither to take the command of this squadron that now lyes wth us before this place.[a] Since o^r arrivall heere, wch is 14 dayes since, not anything of action hath ofered worth yor advice; the good we doe heere is only to keepe there men of warr in y^t are in, and prevent those comeing in wth there prisses y^t are abroad. But they want not harbours in Holland to secure them and w^t they ketch from us. I conseave yo^u want not letters of caution from yor owners to be carefull of trusting the Hollanders. I feare they will prove treacherous to there ingagem^{ts} wth us in the peace agreed betwixt us. They are almost ready to saile wth 50 or upward men of warr, besides 16 saile now in o^r Channell. My Lord Protector is not wanting to prevent there treacherous actions, if any intended against us. I conseave in 14 dayes we may have upwards of 40 saile, considerable men of warr, in the Downes, to answer any atempt may be ofered by them; and doe beleive both we and the squadron before Ostend may be called of, as soone as we have any intelligence of there redynes to saile.

All o^r freinds in England, I heare, are in health. My wife still at Deall, and stayes to accomp^a Aunt Morgan to London; my unkle now being in the Downes, and conseave may saile very sodainely, the wind presenting faire at present. Sir, please at yor arrival at Ven^a to present my service and respects to my Mr. and Mrs. Hobson, with Mr. Jno. Hobson, jun^r. my saluts; as also to Mr. Jones and his wife.

Sir, I have not else at present worth yor advice. With my earnest prayers to Almighty God to preserve you out of the hands of yor mercyles enemyes, and send yo^u a safe returne to the injoym^t of yor

---

[a] By the treaty (23 Mar. 1657) with France against Spain, Cromwell agreed to find 6000 men, with a sufficient fleet, to operate against Gravelines, Mardike, and Dunkirk; the two latter towns, when reduced, to be delivered to the English. Mardike was captured in September of this year, and Dunkirk in June 1658; and both towns were duly handed over to the English forces.

relations, for the happy accomplishm^t whereof itt shall be the earnest request of,
>Sir, yor most affetionate and obedient sonne till death,
>>RICHARD HADDOCK.

To his hon^d freind Capt. Wm Haddock, Comander of the
ship Hanniball, these present, at Livorno.

THE SAME TO THE SAME.

>Dragon frig^t in Dunkirke Road, this 26 Aprill, 1658; Monday.

HON^d FATHER,

S^r, my most humble duty presented unto yo^u wth my deare Mother, Grandfather, and Grandm^o, wth my loveing saluts to my wife, bro^s, sisters, and freinds. My last, of 18 instant, I sent by my Bro^r Wm., whome I gave leave to goe to London; W^{ch} hope is safely arrived with you. Since w^{ch}, litle of acction here in these parts. The 21 instant, about midnight, heere escaped out a small pickeron of 4 or 6 guns out this habo^r, notwthstanding our vigilancy and indeavors for his surprizall, haveing o^r boates in wth the shore and a small frig^t, who gave him chase and fired seavrall guns at him; but the darknes of the night prevented there long keepeing sight of him, and, notwthstanding they made after him to the best of there understanding, yet he got away and noe sight of him at day light. Last Saturday heere went from Mardike Marshall d'Aumon, Duke of Bouligne,[a] wth 13 hundred French souldiers, imbarqued in seavrall vessells, and gone to Oastend, before wch place they arrived that night wth the Vice Admirall.[b]

[a] Antoine, Marshal d'Aumont, Governor of Boulogne. Negotiations had been opened with traitors within Ostend; but the matter was kept no secret, and the garrison was prepared. When therefore D'Aumont attempted a surprise, the tables were turned; he was caught in a trap and had to surrender.—Sismondi, *Hist. des Français*, vol. xxiv. (1840), p. 564.

[b] Edward Montague, afterwards Earl of Sandwich, who had command of the English fleet.

If the intelligence given me be true, we shall see a sodaine alteration in Flaunders. Its said y^t, for a considerable summe of mony, the towne of Ostend is to be delivered up to ye King of Fraunce by the Governor and inhabitants of s^d place, they being in such a sad condition by reasone of the extreame burden y^t lyes upon them.

For security of performance there is a considerable man, who hath confirmed the accord wth the K. of Fraunce, now wth Marshall d'Aumon, that belongs to Ostend, who hath ingaged his life for performance. I pray God they faile not in there undertakeings; and, although treachery be hateful and odious throughout the world, yet doubtles 'twill prove hapye for our poore traders when such a considerable place as y^t is, a neast of roages, shall be routed. If it proves efectuall, farwell most p^{ts} of Flaunders this sumer.

S^r, please to keepe this intelligence to yor selfe, least it should come from me, being privately advized me. I hope, when our victualling is out, we shall come over to tallow; wch God graunt, that I may not fayle of my earnest desire of seeing you before you goe forth. I intend sodaynly to send to the Vice Admirall to know where we shall be disposed by him or otherwise from the Comiss^{rs} of Admiralty. S^r, I have not other at present. Wth my humble request to ye Allmighty for yor preservation, I remayne

Yo^r most loveing and obedient son till death,

RICHARD HADDOCK.

To his hon^d freind Capt. Wm. Haddock, at his howse nere the Newstaires in Wapping, these present, in London.

THE SAME TO THE SAME.

Dragon frig^t in Dunkirke Road, this prim^o May, 1658; Satuarday.

HON^d FATHER,

S^r, my last from this place was of 26th past, since wch not anything hath ofered. The great Monsr with the soldiers I gave yo^u acct of are yet before Oastend with the Vice Admirall have efected nothing, not haveing had opertunity, these out winds preventing there landing. God sending us shore winds, we shall quicklie see the result of the action in hand.

I sent to the Vice Admirall to desire he would order us into the river to tallow and revictuall; but he wrights me, in regard he hath noe ship with him to place in our roome, he will not wthout order from the Adm^{ty}. Soe this day I have wrote to them, advizeing the neere expiration of our victualling, also makeing it my humble request that we may come to Chatham to tallow and revictuall; wch I hope they will graunt, but am dubious of my desired hapynesse of seeing yo^u before yo^u goe forth. My humble duty presented to my deare Mother, Grandfather, and Grandm^o, Father and Mother Steevens, wth my loveing saluts to my wife, brothers, sisters, and freinds in gen^{ll}; and, wth my most humble duty to yor selfe, wth prayers to the Allmighty for yor continued preservation, I remaine,

S^r, your most loveing and dutyfull sonne till death,

RICHARD HADDOCK.

Being hast, ye frig^t under saile with a lee tyde, my wife must excuse my not wrighting her at present.

THE SAME TO SIR WILLIAM COVENTRY.[a]

Portland frig^{tt} in Oasely Bay,[b] 11th Sept. 1666; Tuesday, 8 at night.

RIGHT HON^{ble},

Yours of 8th instant, wth his R. Highnesse order inclosed, I received this afternoone; wch shall put in execution to morrow morning, wind and weather permiting. Sonday last, in comp^a wth the Adventure and a fire ship, we sayled out of Oasely bay through the Slade Way,[c] intending for the North Forland, and soe unto the

---

[a] Sir William Coventry was at this time one of the Commissioners of the Navy.
[b] Hollesley Bay, or Haven, on the Suffolk coast, between Orford Ness and the River Deben.
[c] The channel leading south from Hollesley Bay.

Downes, in search of our fleet. About noone we gote sight of the Forland, and within one hower after we espied a fleet of shipps on the back of the Goodwin sand, wch we deemed to be our fleet; but, standing wth them, we found them to be the Dutch fleet, consisting of 70 in 75 sayle. Two ships of the fleet makeing us bore downe wth us, and presantly after two more followed them. We stood away from them to the eastwards, towards a ship then to leewards, wch we suposed to be a Hollander, but proved a Sweed bound for Burdaix Light; and, finding two of the men of warr spring there luffs againe and only 2 bore downe wth us, we clapt upon a wind and stood towards them, haveing gote them about 5 or 6 miles to leewards of ye body of there fleet. But, when they came w^{t}hin neere shote of us, they keept there wind, would not come neere to fight us, but kept fireing guns to windwards and makeing a waft wth there ensignes for more assistance; whereupon 7 or 8 sayle more bore away wth us. Night comeing on, we thought it not convenient to lye by for them, but stood away for our owne coast, not being able to keep our lower tire of guns out to windwards, and but 32 br^{lls} powder on bord. Yesterday we got into Alborough bay, when I gave acc^t to the Comiss^r at Harw^{ch} by an expresse from Alborough of our proceedings, desireing him to send the said letter to yor Hon^r, if he thought it convenient. I have now rec^d from Harw^{ch} an aditionall suply of sixty barills of powder. The Adventure intends alongst wth us. The Litle Mary, I understand, will not be ready in 3 or 4 dayes. To conclud, Sonday night proved such a hard galle of wind y^t I iudge the Dutch fleet either drove or bore away towards there owne coast, for we saw them all under sayle before twas dark. I shall not be wanting to give yor Hon^r an acc^t of our proceedings, wch is w^t ofers at present from,

R^t Hou^{ble}, y^r humble serv^t att Com^d,

RICHARD HADDOCK.

Endorsed: " Copie of lett^r to S^r Wm. Coventry, from Sr R^d Haddock."

Declaration of Captain Richard Haddock.

A° 1657,
Novemb^r.   Dragon frig^t, Novemb^r, 1657.

18. The 18th November I rec^d orders from Sr Richard Stainer[a] to sayle out ye Downes, and in company wth the Colchester frig^{tt} to plye of of Ostend.

26. The 26 day, Thursday, we sailed out ye Downes, ye wind at west. We went out at ye North Sand Head, twixt ye Brake and Goodwin. This noone we spake wth the Pembrooke frig^{tt}, come from Harwich cleane tallowed; N.E. from ye north Forland, in 15 fadoms watter, we clapt by under a maine course, intending to drive all night; but, upon sight of 6 sayle of Holland men of warr, 3 wth there flaggs abroad, to say Adm^{ll} Vice and Rear Admirall, we stood with them. Y^e Pembrooke haveing espied them before us, though bound into ye Downes, bore away on the back of the Goodwin towards them; comeing up with them, first fired at ye Adm^{ls} flagg, but was not struck. Upon wch ye Comand^r of the Pembrooke sent his boats on bord to know ye reason of itt. Whilst they were in dispute, we, comeing in shote, fired at ye Adm^{lls} flagg alsoe, and presantly after they sent up a man to topmasthead and struck the flagg, wch his Vice and Reare Adm^{ll} did the like. Then we bore under his lee ahead of him, and hayld him and stood asterne, and, after, tackt and came and lay on his weather quarters. There flaggs hang as a waft for about $\frac{1}{2}$ an hower, and afterwards furld them; the Adm^{ll} fired a gun to lewards, filld, and stood away to y^e e^{t}wards. We answerd him with another; lay by and drove all night. These men of warr came there from y^e coast of Portugall, y^e Ld Updam Adm^{ll}, as I was informed by Sr Richard Stayner at my returne into y^e Downes. This I can testifie upon oath, if calld thereunto.

Given under my hand this primo January, 167$\frac{1}{2}$.

RICHARD HADDOCK.

---

[a] Admiral Sir Richard Stayner was knighted for his gallantry in Blake's attack on Santa Cruz. (See above, p. 3.)

Captain Richard Haddock to his Wife.[a]

On bord y^e R. James, at anchor 4 miles wthout St. Hellens, this 5th May, 1672; Sonday night.

My deare Betty,

This afternoone we arrived this place wth our noble fleet. W^{t}hin, at Spitthead, we see ye French fleet gote heere before us wilbe good company. Tomorrow I doubt not but we shall joyne wth them. A few daies will prepare us to goe to seeke ye Hollanders, who are out. We saw some of there scouts that day we sailed out ye river. I have no other news to write thee at present.

I hope these will find y^e at London, where I advize thee to stay that I may the more certainly direct my letters to the. I shall not be wanting to give the advice by all opertunities how itt fares with us. God Almighty preserve and keepe the and us in good health, and in His good tyme send us a ioyfull meeteing. My deere love to all myne and thy loveing relations. Wth intire saluts to thy selfe and my daughter, I remayne thyne, whilst I am

RICHARD HADDOCK.

My love to my deare Coz Goodlad at Wapping. Pray venture a letter or two to Portsm^o to me.   R. H.

The same to the same.

On bord the Royall James, this 14th May, 1672; Tuesday evening, at anchor neere Dungenesse.

My dearest Love,

These are to give the an acc^t of my wellfare and good health, wch I blesse God I doe injoy. We are now at anchor neere Dungenesse wth our whole fleet, consisting of 80 men of warr, English and French, about 20 or 22 fireships, and many small vessells besides. We have bine tydeing it up from the Isle of Wind (*sic*). Ever since

[a] His second wife, Elizabeth; maiden name unknown.

Wedensday last the winds have hung easterly. The Dutch fleet, we heard yesterday, were at ye North Forland. We doe our utmost endeavor to get to them, if they have a mind to fight us. To ye westwards of ye Downes they may easely be wth us; but we judge there designe is to ingage us amongst the sands, wch posibly they may be deceaved in there expectation. God Almighty goe along wth us and give us victory over our enemyes. I know I shall not want thy prayers and the well wishes of all my deare relations for my preservation. We have a brave fleet and, in the maine, well mand. For our parts we doe not complayn, haveing neere 900 men on bord us; ye Duke 1000, I beleive, and upwards. It is probable, before we ingage, we may have ye ships in the river ioyne wth us, wch are 10 or 11 men of warr and 4 fire ships. I desire we may put our strength in God Almighty; but soe noble a brave fleet have not bine seene together in our dayes.

My deare, speake to my bro^r Joseph for the ballence of the mony I desired him to rec^e for me of Mr. Forth and Mr. Beare, and to pay out of it severall debts wch at present I doe not remember the perticulars. I know not how to direct the to answer these, nor where you may send to meet us. If this arrive yo^u on Thursday, you may venture a lyne or two to Dover Road, where posibly we may stop 24 houres to watter, and next I supose for Sowle Bay or the coast of Holland. Desire my Coz Goodlad, the draper, to rec^e three pounds for the of Cozen Boys, wch is due April last; and pray, when the bond is due of Mr. Welsted and Temple, goe to them and rec^e the interest £9, and desire them to lett me have £100 or more, if posible, to suply my occasions. Thou knowest the imploym^t I am in is very expencive, and therfore let me not faile of haveing £100 at least of them. Twas Mr. Welsted's promise in a month, but I have stayd neere 10 weeks. Pray let me know w^t is done wth the mony in bro^r Hurleston's hands and brother Thornburgh. I know they will be very kind. I have heere inclosed sent the my will, wch have made for all good respects. I desire the to keepe it by the, sealed as it is. If God Almighty in His providence should take me out this life, you will find I have not failed of my promise to thee, though I have some reason to lament the kindnes done me by thy freinds; but that shall not trouble me at this tyme. God Almighty, I doubt not, will preserve me, that I may live to see the againe wth ioy and comfort. Pray lett me know by some meanes or other of the receipt of these. My deare love to my sister Jessen, bro^r and sister Thornburgh, bro^r Hurlestone. My respects to my Unckle Moyer; all of them. My kind saluts to my dear Coz Goodlad at Wapping. To all my loveing freinds comend me. My deare, I have only to add my prayers to God for thy wellfare. Wth my intire love and saluts to thee and my daughter, I remaine

Thyne, till death us p^t,
RICHARD HADDOCK.

These I send to Dover by our kitch, who is goeing to watter for us, but doe beleive we may get thither ourselves as soone.

THE SAME TO THE SAME.

R. James, neare Sowle Bay, this 21 May, 1672;
Tuesday evening.

MY DEARE BETTY,

The 18th instant, wch was Satuarday last, I wrote the by one of the yachts, and as thou advised. Y^e next day we saw the Dutch fleet. We drew ours into a lyne of bataile, the French leading, we in the reare, all prepared to fight, haveing stav'd and heft over bord all ours, and I think all the cabins of the whole fleet. The Hollanders stood over for ye Flaunders Banks and ye Weelings. About 7 at night we were up wth them in a lyne, as they lay in the same posture very orderly to rec^e us; but, finding it would have bine darke before we could have well began with them, being about 4 or 5 miles to leewards of us, ye wind at W.S.W., we thought it not convenient to ingage them. Y^e night following, upon there tacking of, we tackt in ye reare, ye whole fleet following to keep them to leewards of us, as we did y^t night by our twice tacking againe. Yesterday morning it proved a very thick fogge. We wth our division anchored, standing in wth the Banks of Flaunders of Oostend. About 10 in ye morning, upon cleareing up, we wayed anchor, ye Dutch fleet 3 miles to leewards of us. We stood of and mett our fleet standing in. Y^e Dutch stood of wth us. This day it proved much wind, that we could not fight them; whereupon we stood in to our shore N.W., and about ½ seas over we anchored all night. This morneing we saw ye fleet again. We stood of towards them, expecting they would have stood wth us; but they stood of intending to draw us over amongst those shoulds, to fight them there. We keeping our wind, and they bearing away, as we suposed, from ye wind, we lost sight of them. It blowing hard we tackt, and now come neare to Sowle Bay, where I supose we may stay a day or two to watter our fleet.

This day came into us the Katherine, Princes, and Advice, wth 2 fire ships more; soe y^t I supose we are neerer 90 then fowerscore men of warr, upwards 25 fireships, amongst wch my unckle R. H. is come. The Dutch fleet not soe many men of warr as we, I beleive, by 8 or 10 saile, many small vessells and fire ships. Had it pleased God yesterday to have given us faire weather, God assisting, we had given a good acct of o^r actions; our men briske and brave and very ready and willing to fight. The Earle of Bristow[a] on bord wth us. I thinke a fourth part the nobles of England in the fleett. This I send on shore to Sowle, to take its fortune towards thee. Being in hast, have not tyme to wright any body else. If my bro^r Bradenham be in towne, shew him this letter. I two dayes since rec^d a letter from Mr. Clarke, ye apothecary, wth a case of spiritts, come very opertunely (as he wrights me) to raise my courage, but I have not yet tasted them. Pray returne him my kind thanks. I hope shall survive this warr to make him amends. My deare, I should be glad to heare from the, but I know not how. I shall not be wanting to give the a constant advice, as opertunity presents, of my

[a] George Digby, 2nd Earl of Bristol.

wellfare and our actions. Youl excuse me to my loveing relations y^t I wright none of them. At present it is fowle weather. Am glad we gote hither, for stormy weather may shatter us and disable us more then a bataile. God Almighty be our guard and defence, and give us victory over our enemyes. His providence hath hitherto prevented our ingageing twice. My deare and loveing saluts to all my loveing relations at Rederif,[a] and to my lo: Coz. Goodlad at Wapping and London, &c. W^th intire love and saluts to thyselfe wth my daughter, I remaine

    Thy loveing husband till death us part,
        RICHARD HADDOCK.

His Royal Highness the Duke of Yorke is very zeolus to ingage ye Dutch, God sending a good opertunity and watter enough under our keels.

I had almost forgot to desire the to returne my thanks to Capt. Grantham for ye barill of Muscadine he brought me from Mr. Wilkinson, of Messina, and for a chest of Florence he sent me from himselfe, wth seavrall other things, all wch I rec^ed, wth a chest of Florence for my Lord Sandw^ch. Pray pay him three pound for itt. I shall rec^e it heere of Mr. Lowe, my Lord's serv^t. Thyne,

        R. HADDOCK.

THE SAME TO THE SAME.

  R. James, in Southold Bay, this 25th May, 1672; Saturday evening.

MY DEAREST LOVE,

These I send by Capt. Poole,[b] who, wth the Garland frig^tt in comp^a, hath leave to goe his former intended voaidge for Barbados. Pray advize my bro^r Bradenham of itt. They will be good convoy for Mr. Naufan's ship wth masts, &c., wch lyes at Gravesend, to goe thorough the Channell wth them.

[a] Rotherhithe.
[b] Sir William Poole, distinguished by his share in the reduction of Tobago, this year.

This day I gote two protections from the Duke, one for Mr. Naufan's ship at Lancaster for 50 men, ye other for ye ship wth stores for 20 men, wch is speciall protections, y^t the men will not be molested. Tell my Bro^r Bradenham I have given them to Mr. Sam. Hawkes, who is comeing wth them.

I am sory to heare poore Sam Lane was prest into ye French Victory, and since caryed into Holland. I pitty the losse of the men in her, but ye Capt. will have his reward for looseing her soe basely. The Dutch fleet lye now neare the Gallaper in expectation of us; we are very neere, ready to waite on them. 2 or 3 days must not breake square wth us; but they are deceaved to think we intend to fight them amongst the sands. I supose our martch wilbe over for ye coast of Holland into sea roome and deepe watter. We are, notwithstanding Capt. Poole and his consarts leaveing us, 90 men of warr, 26 fire ships, many small vessels. I supose the Dutch daylie add to ther strength as well as wee. God Allmighty be our defence.

My deare, I am sory that my first letter from Southold, wch went by land, advized the of our 2 days stay, whereas we have bine heere 4 days, and shall stay 3 or 4 longer. Then we shall have wattered our whole fleet for one month, and victualld compleat for 2 months, and mand I beleive thoroughout ye fleet, not 500 wanting. I rather think, in a day or two longer, we may have 1000 supernumeraryes. A very worthy brave fleet, I think, as ever were together. God give us couragious hearts, and then I beleive they may be ventured.

I hope all my loveing relations at Rederif and Wapping are in health, to whome present my love and saluts. I expect to heare from the by the yacht wch I sent my last letter by, Captain Burstow, Comander.[a] I blesse God I am now in good health, though 5 or 6 days since, and when we were going to fight the Dutch, I had such a paine in my right arme that could not use it but very litle; but now, thanke God, am very well. My deare Betty, I have only to

---

[a] William Bustow or Burstow, commanding the Mary yacht.

add my saluts to thyselfe wth my daughter; doe remaine thyne till death us part,
RICHARD HADDOCK.

This I intended thee by Capt. Poole, but was gone ere I could put it on bord him; therfore doe send it by the post. I rec^d last night bro^r Thornbrugh's letter, 23 instant, by ye Dreadnought's Leiveten^t. He wrights me of thy health, and y^t I shall rec^e a letter from the by ye Hatton ketch. I am thyne,

26 May, '72.
R. HADDOCK.

COPY OF CAPTAIN RICHARD HADDOCK'S[a] ACCOUNT, GIVEN HIS ROYAL HIGHNESS THE DUKE OF YORK, OF THEIR ENGAGEMENT, MAY 28TH, 1672, IN THE ROYAL JAMES.

In obedience to your Royal Highness's commands, I here humbly present to your view a brief narrative of our actions on board the Royal James, the 28th May last past, as followeth:

Upon signal from our scouts of the Dutch fleet's approach (betwixt 3 and 4, the wind E. by S.), we put our ships immediately into a fighting posture, brought our cable to the capston, and heaft a peak of our anchor, which, upon firing a gun and loosing foretopsail of your Royal Highness's ship, we presently weighed, and afterwards lay kedging with our headsails at the mast till our anchor was up; which done (steered N.E. by N.), we made sail and stood off, with our signal abroad for the squadron[b] to draw into their line of battle, which was done as well as the short time we had would permit. But, finding myself one of the weathermost ships, I bore to leeward till I had brought ourselves in a line; the Vice Admiral and part of his division right a head, the Rear Adm^l and his right astern; only two or three frigates to leeward, and so near, one of

---

[a] The MS., which is a modern transcript, has "Sir Richard Haddock;" but he was not knighted until 1675, and therefore, for uniformity, the title is suppressed.

[b] The blue squadron.

them within call. The Dutch squadron, Van Ghent, attacked us in the body and rear very smartly, and let the van go ahead sometime without engaging them, so far as I could perceive. We engaged about an hour and an half very smartly. When the Dutch found that they could do no good on us with their men of war, they attacked us with two fire ships, the first of which we fired with our shott, the second disabled by shooting down his yards. Before which time I had sent our barge, by my Lord's[a] command, ahead to Sir Joseph Jordaine,[b] to tack, and with his division to weather the Dutch that were upon us and beat them down to leeward of us, and come to our assistance. Our pinnace I sent likewise astern (both coxswains living) to command our ships to come to our assistance; which never returned, but were on board several who endeavoured it but could not effect it.

About two hours after we engaged we were boarded athwart hawse by one of their men of war, notwithstanding our endeavours to prevent him by wearing our ship two or three points from the wind to have taken him alongside. When he had been athwart our hawse some short time, my Lord would have had me boarded him with our men and taken him, which I refused to do by giving him my reason that it would be very disadvantageous to us: first, that I must have commanded our men from our guns, having then I believe 300 men killed and wounded, and could not expect but to lose 100 in taking him; secondly, had we so done, we could not have cut him loose from us, by reason the tide of flood bound him fast; and, thirdly, had we plyed our guns slowly by taking away our men, we had given cause to the enemy to believe we had been disabled, and consequently more of them would have boarded us, which might possibly have overpressed us, and would have been more dishonour to have lost her by that means than being at last burnt;—so that my Lord was satisfied with my reasons, and

[a] Earl of Sandwich.
[b] Sir Joseph Jordan, Vice-Admiral of the Blue. See a defence of his conduct, as described in this letter, in Charnock's *Biographia Navalis*.

resolved we should cuff it out to the last man, still in expectation of assistance

About 10 o'clock Van Ghent himself, finding those his other flags could do no good upon us, nor the party with them, came up with us himself, we having lost the conduct of our ship. He ranged along our side, gave us a smart volley of small shot and his broadside, which we returned to him with our middle and lower tier, our upper guns almost all disabled, the men killed at them. He passed ahead of us and brought his ship too to leeward, and there lay till I was gone off the deck.

Some short time after, Sir Joseph Jordaine (our barge having been with him and given him my Lord's commands) passed by us very unkindly to windward, with how many followers of his division I remember not, and took no notice at all of us; which made me call to mind his saying to your Royal Highness, when he received his commission, that he would stand betwixt you and danger; which I gave my Lord account of, and did beleive by his acting yourself might be, in his view, in greater danger than we, which made my Lord answer me: "We must do our best to defend ourselves alone."

About 12 o'clock I was shot in the foot with a small shot, I supposed out of Van Ghent's main top, which pressed me after a small time to go down to be dressed. I gave my Lord account of it, and resolved to go up again as soon as was dressed. In the mean time, when I went off the deck, sent up both Sir Charles[a] and Lieutenant Mayo[b] to stand by my Lord; and, as soon as I came down, remembring the flood was done, sent up to my Lord to desire him to command the ship to anchor by the stern, which was immediately done; and, after we had brought up, the ship athwart our hawse fell away, and being entangled with our rigging our men boarded and took her, cut her loose from us, and, at my Lord's command, returned all aboard again. Upon which I, hearing the ship was loose, sent up to my Lord that the cable might be cut and the ship

---

[a] Sir Charles Harbord, who served as a volunteer and perished.
[b] Thomas Mayo. He was one of the few who escaped from the Royal James.

brought to sail before the wind, and loose our mainsail; which was presently done. Then my Lord sent me his thanks for my advice, and withall doubted not but to save the ship. At that time the surgeon was cutting off the shattered flesh and tendons of my toe; and immediately after we were boarded by the fatal fire ship that burnt us.

Captain Richard Haddock to his Wife.

My dearest Love,

On bord the R. Charles, this 29th May, 1673;
7 leagues of Oostend.

These are to give the an acct of God's goodnes to me. I am very well and in health, praised be His name therfore. Yesterday, the 28th instant (ye same day twelve month they atacqued us in Sowle bay), we atacqued the Dutch fleet, consisting of 74 or 76 men of warr and 20 fire ships, as the Dutch prisoners informe us. We set upon them in the Schoon Velt, the wind at W.N.W^t., but changed to ye N.N.E. in the bataile towards evening. We buoyed the outward banks wth our smacks and ketches, and had a smart brush with them from 12 at noone as long as day light lasted. The damage we have done them we certainly know not. Severall of ther ships we disabled, wch we forced into leewards. Trump, whose squadron we ingaged wth ours, shifted his ship once, if not twice. What number of men we have lost in the fleet not yet know; I believe not 500. In our ship not above 20, as I can learne; some mortality wounded, others dismembred. Amongst our dead men is poore Capt. Wasey, who first lost his arme close to his shoulder, and about 6 howers after dyed of his wounds. My brother Joseph very well; was wth me last night after ye bataile. My unckle Richard very well: he hath burnt his ship; was faire to burne De Rutter within his length, when they shote his masts about his eares; for wch indeavoured service ye Prince[a] hath given him one hundred pounds, and gratified

[a] Rupert.

also his oficers, &c. I supose we shall not atacque them in that place againe. Our greatest care was to keepe cleere of the sands in that narrow hole. Our ship, so tender with a saile that we fought wth the watter some tymes comeing into our lower tire of ports, wch was very disadvantagious, could not do that service intended by us.

There is severall Capt^s killed that we have already an account of; I hope no more. Capt. Finch in the Yorke, Capt. Tempest in the Sweepestakes, Capt. Fowles in the Lyon; and Capt. Werden, in the Heneretta, mortality wounded.[a] We have severall of our ships shattered, not above two disabled, and none, as I heare of, lost, but 2 or 2 fire ships burnt.

We ride now wthin 3 leagues of the Dutch fleete; they ride in the place we atacqued them in, and we in our former birth, only about 2 leagues further of the shore. How soone we shall fight them againe cannot resolve, but in ye place they now ride I iudge we shall not atacque them a second tyme. I beleive the Prince may shift his ship and goe into some other; but of y^t in my next.

I desire that thanks and prayes may be returned to Almighty God for his preservation of me. My humble duty to my deare mother; loving saluts to my brothers and sisters, and all my deare relations. God in mercy blesse and preserve them all, and send us a joyfull meeteing. Wth my intire love and saluts to thee wth my daughter and litle Dickee, I remaine

Thine, till death us part,
RICHARD HADDOCK.

We have a rumor that Capt. Trevanion[b] is killed, comd^g the Dreadnought; but I hope it is not true.

---

[a] William Finch, third son of Thomas, first Earl of Winchilsea; John Tempest, Thomas Foules, and Robert Werden. The last was not killed in this action, according to Charnock, *Biogr. Navalis.*

[b] Richard Trevanion. He was not killed. He followed James II. into exile.

THE SAME TO THE SAME.

Yet on bord ye R. Charles, this 31 May, 1673.

MY DEARE BETTY,

I wrote the two dayes since of God's goodnes to mee in o^r late bataile. I gave the acct of Capt. Trevanions suposed to be killed, but he is well; and allso Capt. Courtney,[a] wch was reported to be killed, is alive and well. Capt. Worden is since dead of his wounds.[b] We are now shifting ships, goeing on bord the London; the reason I gave in my last. Sr Jno Harman[c] goes from the London into the Sovraigne, and Capt. Hayward[d] out ye Sovraigne into this ship. It is no smal trouble to me to part from this brave ship; her only fault is she is tender sided, in all respects otherwayes the best ship in the world.

My deare, I am very well; My bro^r Joseph and unckle Richard likewise. The Prince in good health, and our fleet prepareing for another incounter, if the Dutch comes out. My deare, I am thyne till death, RICHARD HADDOCK.

Pray, if Com^r Deane[e] be not in towne, send forward the inclosed to Portsm^o

---

THE SAME TO THE SAME.

R. Charles, rideing N^o, 7 leagues from Oostend, this 1st June, 1673; Sonday.

MY DEARE BETTY,

Wee ride in sight of our neighbours the Dutch, not above 3 in 4 leagues distant. This morning they were under saile; we thought

[a] Francis Courtney. He fell in the action with the Dutch on the 11th August of this year.

[b] This is denied. (See above, p. 20, note ª.)

[c] Became Vice-Admiral of the Red, on the death of Sir Edward Spragge, this year.

[d] John Hayward. He fell in the action of 11th August, this year.

[e] Anthony Deane, Commissioner of the Navy at Portsmouth.

they would have come of to us. We put ourselves in a posture to rec^e them. They have now the wind of us, being easterly; and may come out if they please. This morning we have acct from a good hand from Oostend y^t they sent in 6 or 7 disabled ships to Flushing, two whereof sunck in going in. They likewise sent on shore 400 or 500 wounded men, and, as they advize from Oostend, com^d was given not to speake of the fight at Flushing. So doe beleive, till they recrute ther strength, we shall not heare of them; however, we are not wanting to prepare ourselves ag^t they come. The Swiftsure is this day come to us; had like to have bine snapt Tuesday last by the Amsterdam squadron y^t came into the Schoon Velt tyme enough to fight.

I have but little else to write to thee. Sr Roger Strickland sends his hoy to Deptford for watter; and these goe by S^r Ed. Spragg's yacht, who caryes up one Coll. Hambliton into the River, who lost his legg on bord us. Pray lett me heare from thee by one or both of them. My humble duty to my deare mother; love and saluts to all freinds in gen^{ll}. Wth my deare love to thy selfe, my daughter, and little Richard, I remayne

Thyne, till death us part,

RICHARD HADDOCK.

JOURNAL [OF CAPTAIN RICHARD HADDOCK] IN HIS MAJ^{tys} SHIP R. CHARLES, MAY, 1673.

A°. 1673.

May 11. This Sonday morneing, about 7 aclock, we anchored in the Prince's fleet, to the westwards of them, about 2 leagues to the westwards of Dongenesse, in 1 fadom watter, ye lighthouse beareing N.E. by E. This day I went on bord the St. Michell to waite on ye Prince, who comanded me to weigh and plye up to his ship; but, bloweing so hard, could not.

12. This Monday morneing wind at N.E. and N.E. by N.; blew very hard, and raine some part of the forenoone; could not weigh.

13. This Tuesday morneing, ye wind at north, we wayed and gote up to the Prince's ship, the St. Michel; anchored alongst her side without her. This forenoone his Highnes Prince Rupert came on bord us, but went of at noone; dyned on bord the R. Prince; after diner returned on bord us. This day we tooke on bord all the Prince's retenue and goods, &c.; struck downe some of our gunns into hold, to rec^e new ones in ther roomes. All this afternoone ye wind at north; constant rain.

14. This Wednesday we tooke on bord seaverall of the new gunns and mounted them. The wind this day came round from the N.W. to S.W^t., S.E. and E. by N^o. This day the French fleet apeared in sight about noone; being litle wind, they anchored short of us about 3 leagues.

15. This Thursday we mounted all the rest of the new gunns; the wind at N.E^t. to E.N.E. Y^e French fleet wayed and plyed towards us; anchored about 4 miles short of us.

16. This Fryday morneing the French fleet weighed and plyed up to us. About 9 a clock this morneing Monsr Conte d'Estrees,[a] ther Adm^{ll}, who wore his flagg at ye foretopmast head, being V. Adm^{ll} of Fraunce, past by us about musket shote or somew^t more asterne of us; struck his flagg, lored his topsailes and saluted us, I meane ye Prince, wth 13 peece of ordnance; we returned him eleven in answer. Presantly after Monsr Conte d'Estrees came on bord us, to waite on his Highnes ye Prince. This evening came of from Rye his Maj^{ty} and R. Highnes in there yachts; came on bord us; stayed about one hower and a halfe, and then returned to the yachts againe after 8 at night.

17. This Satuarday morneing, the wind at N. by E., blowing very fresh, the Prince went on bord the Cleeveland yacht to waite upon his Maj^{ty}; and about $\frac{1}{2}$ an hower after the King, Duke, and Prince came on bord this ship. This forenoone we spread a standard in the mizen shrowds, fired a gunn to call on bord us the flagg oficers. This day the King and Duke dyned on bord us. The wind hath blowne very hard at N.N.E. and N.E. by N. all day.

[a] Jean, Comte d'Estrées.

18. This Sonday the wind vered to the east and by north, and back to ye N.N.E^t. at night; blew very fresh all day. This day the King dyned on bord Conte d'Estrees; the standard at maine topmast head; his flagg struck wch he wore at the foretopmast head. This evening the King and Duke supt on bord us, and at 9 aclock tooke ther leaves of us and went on shore to Rye. This day the noble Lord Ossory[a] hoysted the Reare Adm^ll blew flagg on bord the St. Michael.

19. This Monday morning, about 3 aclock, being at anchor still, the wind at E.N.E^t., we designed to weigh, but, bloweing fresh, we rode fast all this day.

20. This Tuesday, at 3 in the morneing, being alaramed by seavrall gunns from the eastwards, we fired a gunn and put out a light in the mainetopmast shrowds, our signall of weighing, but did not weigh by reason of the ebb tyde, the wind being at S.E^t. We had intelligence, by a sloop, of 70 saile of Hollanders seene on the back of ye Goodwin, and w^thout the S^o Sands Head; but proved to be, by our 2d intelligence by the litle Greyhound, a fleet of Hamburghers of 26 saile only. This forenoone we weighed with all the fleet; stood to the southwards; at noone tackt; litle wind. We anchored about 2 aclock, ye Nesse light howse N. by E., in 21 fadoms, 7 miles distance. This day his Highnes the Prince dyned on bord the Conte d'Estrees, who struck his flagg as soone as the Prince was on bord him, and the Prince's Jack flagg hoysted up at mainetopmast head; and, whilst the Prince remain on bord him, his flagg (I meane ye Conte d'Estrees) was kept furld. Towards evening the Hamburg^rs fleet plyed by us to the w^twards; gave us many gunns in saluts. Y^e wind, since 4 in the afternoone, at W.S.W. and W^t. This night we rode fast.

21. This 21 day, Wednesday morneing, at 4 aclock, we wayed wth the whole fleet; wind at W. by N^o., a fine fresh gale. By 10 aclock the wind came to ye S.W^t. We steered away on the back of the Goodwin. About 4, afternoone, we anchored in 10 fadom watter,

[a] Thomas Butler, Earl of Ossory.

on the flatts of the N° Forland, the lighthouse beareing W by S. southerly, about 6 miles distant.

22. This Thursday morneing we wayed by 5 aclock; steered away E. by N°. and E.N.E^t. to goe cleare of the showld of the Falls;[a] the wind at S.W., a fine gale. After we had gote without ye Falls, we hauled up E. b. S. and E.S.E.; a fresh gale at S.W. About 4 in the afternoone we made the coast of Flaunders. At 6, evening, we anchored in 15 fadoms watter, Oostend spire steeples beareing S.E. by S°, 5 leagues distant. This evening we saw the Dutch fleet, part of them; they rode in Schonvelt. Our scout gave us acct they were but 86 saile, the outside, small and great. They wayed and turned up amongst ye bancks towards the Weelings.

23. This Fryday morneing, by 6 aclock, ye flood being done, we wayed; wind at S.S.W., litle wind. We stood in; drew our ships into a lyne of batayle. Our squadron ledd the van, the French in the midle, and ye blew squadron in the reare. We sayled and drove soe farr to the N.E.wards that we brought Oostend steeples south easterly, about 5 leagues or six leagues of. Anchored in 11 fadom watter, within the oyster bancks. Y^e Dutch fleet, ye n°most, bore E.N.E.; and ye southmost E^t, southerly from us, about 3 leagues. This night have had but litle wind at S.S.W. and S.W^t.

24. This Satuarday morneing we intended, if the should watter hindred not, to goe in wth our fleet and set upon the Dutch; sending a party of 35 men of warr, 13 fire ships, and 24 tendors ahead of us, to make the onsett, and we wth the whole fleet to have seconded them. But this our intention was this day prevented by God Almighty's providence, the wind bloweing very hard at S.W. and W^t.S.W^t. This morneing came in to the fleet the Soveraigne, Victory, and Dyamond, out of the river of Thames. Yesterday our scouts gave us acct that ye Dutch fleet, of all sorts that could be told, did not exceed 84. All this day the wind hath blowne very hard at S.W. and W.S.W.; forct us strick our yard, and some ships both topmast and yard.

[a] A long narrow shoal off the North Foreland.

25. This Sonday the wind hath blowne very hard at W.S.W^t.; forct us in ye afternoone to strick our topmasts and get our spritsaile yard under the boltsprit. This day severall of the French ships broke from ther ground tackle, but brought up againe wth other anchors and rode fast.

26. This Monday, in the forenoon, the wind continued bloweing hard at W.S.W., as did also the night past, but not so violently as the day formerly. In the afternoone the wind dullered. We sett our topmasts and got up o^r yards; our neighbours the Dutch did the like also. Toward evening indiferent faire weather.

27. This Tuesday the wind hath bine from the S.W^t. back to ye S.E^t., wth very thick weather, and then veered to the N.W^t., wth some tymes very thick [weather] and raine and wind; all this day very unconstant weather. This afternoone we spread our red flagg for the severall divissions drawne out of the fleet to get themselves into a body for the first onsett upon the enemy; but did not weigh ourselves. Our party out of our squadron anchored to leewards of us, and neere half way betweene ye Dutch fleet and ours. This day ye standard was spread for the flagg oficers. When come on bord, twas resolved that tomorrow, about 10 in the morning, the flood being done and faire weather, that we weigh and atacque the Dutch fleet now rideing in the Schoonvelt, steereing with an easey saile upon them; and, in case they go in to Flushing, then to anchor in their places; and, that they stand of into sea, to stand out with them.

28. This Wedensday morneing, being indiferent faire weather, we prepared our ship; gote upp our sheat anchor, slung our yards, &c. The wind at west, a fresh gale. By 10 aclock we gote up our anchor, and made sayle. Brave weather; wind at W. b. N. and W.N.W^t. We wth our squadron steered N.E. b. E. wth the north end of the Dutch fleet, ye French wth the body, and ye blew squadron wth the south part of them. To 11 aclock thay rode most of them fast at anchor, not so much as ther fore topsailes loose. About 12 at noone we bore downe upon the Dutch and ingaged ther van, and the French in the body, our blew squadron in the reare. We fought

till twas darke, tacking to and againe in the Schoon Velt. What certaine damage we did the enemy we cannot tell. This night we sailed and drove out againe; came into 6 fadom watter on ye oyster banck. By day light we were gote 3 leagues without the Schoon Velt.

29. This Thursday morneing we anchored in 13 fadom watter by our judgement, S. b. E^t. from Oostend, 6 or 7 leagues of. This day y^e Prince called a councill of flagg oficers. Ordered, that y^e respective flaggs call ther divisions on bord and take acct of what damages rec^d yesterday in the bataile. This day the wind blew very hard at S.W^t.; forct us to strick our topmasts and yards and veere out our shot of cable $2\frac{1}{2}$ without bord. This afternoone, about 3 aclock, the Prince sent away a packet for Whitehall, by whome I wrote for London.

30. This Fryday the wind blew very hard, most part of the day, at S.W^t. and W.S.W^t. Towards evening lesse wind. We got up our topmasts.

31. This Satuarday forenoone, foggy weather; afternoone, very faire weather; the wind at N.E^t. This day the Prince tooke resolution to shift shipps, ours being so tender that we could not beare out our lower tire of gunns in the late bataile.

June 1. This Sonday, ye first day of June, the Dutch fleet many of them were under saile, but came not out to us. We gote up our anchor and came to saile wth all the fleet, but anchored againe and birth't our selves in our anchoring posture agreed on, to say: the flaggs to ride N. and south of each other, 4 cables length distant; and the ships of the severall divisions to ride N.W. and S.E. from there flaggs, 2 cable length distant of one side and the other; the flagg ships as they are ranged in ther line of bataile. This day we struck some broken gunns down into hold, and some whole, to the number of tenn, to stiffen our ship if posible.

2. This Monday the wind blowes very fresh at N.E., and did so all the last night and the day before. This day the Prince resolved to shift his ship and goe on bord the R. Soveraigne.

3. This Tuesday evening his Highnes the Prince went on bord the Soveraigne. I and Capt. Young[a] followed him, and this night lay on bord her.

4. This Wedensday morneing, very early, I went on bord the R. Charles to shift the men. Chose out 250 men to come on bord the Soveraigne.

Journall in the R. Soveraigne, June, 1673.

This 4th day of June, Wedensday, before noone, the Dutch fleet, then rideing in Schoonvelt, all wayed and came to saile and came out to us. We wayed with our fleet; put ourselves in the best posture we could; but, makeing saile, we gote ahead next the blew squadron, leaving most of the French in the reare, with our Vice Admirall. Betwixt 4 and 5 aclock the Dutch fleet—Trump in the van, De Rutter in the body—bore downe towards us (the wind at N.E^t., a very fresh gale). We ingaged till twas darke, more then $\frac{1}{2}$ range of our shot distant. We kept our lufe; they did likewise the same; would not come close to us. What damage we did them we know not. On our parts we lost 2 fire ships; shatterd our ships, many of them, in hull, masts, yards, and rigging. Comd^{rs} killed were: Capt. White of the Warspight, and Capt. Sadleton of the Crowne.[b] What number of men slaine in the fleet, know not. This night we stood to the northwards with our foresaile and mainetopsailes only. Most of the Dutch fleet, at 12 aclock at night, tackt away from us; the remainder tackt after them at 2 aclock.

5. Betwixt 4 and 5 we tackt of after them; stood of wth 2 topsailes; put out our Jack flagg. Called a council of warr to know the condition of our fleet; found our ships to be shatred in our masts and rigging, not to be repaired in the sea; our powder and shot the greatest part spent in two batailes. Haveing no shot in the fleet for

[a] Henry Young.
[b] Richard White and Richard Sadlington.

recrute, twas resolved by the Prince, for the more expedition (*sic*) fitting the fleet out againe, to saile for the buoy of the Nore. We tackt; stood in for the shore, seeing Laistoforland.[a] Stood away alongst the shore, wthout the sands called Alborough knapes. The wind at N.E., we steered away S.W. by S., haveing an ebb tyde to goe without the Shipwash.[b] The flood comeing upon us sett us in so neare ye Sheepewash, that we were within a mile and a halfe of itt. We hauld of south, and, after we were about that sand, we steered up the Swine.[c] After 8 at night we anchored in 13 fadom watter, above the Gunflit at least 2 miles. All the fleet likewise anchored.

6. This Fryday morneing the wind came to the S.W.; litle wind. We wayed to plye up, and plyed the tyde to an end. Anchored about 2 miles belowe the Midle Ground buoy,[d] in 8 fadom watter.

7. This Satuarday, 8 in the morning, we wayed; wind at W^t. and W. b. N. We turned up as high as the Oase Edge buoy;[e] there anchored and rode all night.

8. This Sonday, wind at east, we wayed and ran up to the buoy of the Nore. There anchored, about a mile below the buoy.

9. This Monday the wind blew very hard at E^t and E.S.E^t, with raine; forct us to strick our topmasts and yards. The wind hath blowne very hard all this day, and vered back to the E.N.E^t.

10. This Tuesday, wind came to tho north. Slaby weather and cold; bloweing a fresh gale.

11. This Wednesday wind at N.W^t. and north. This day the King and Duke came on bord us. At night, after they had supt, went on bord ther yachts.

12. This Thursday the wind at E^t to S.E^t. The King came

[a] Lowestoft Ness.

[b] The Shipwash sand-bank off the mouth of the Deben.

[c] The King's Channel or East Swin, running down east of the Gunfleet sands, off the Essex shore.

[d] The Middle Ground shoal lies at the mouth of the Thames, some miles below the Nore, on the Kentish side of the river.

[e] The Oaze Edge shoal near the Middle Ground, but on the Essex side.

out Sheerenes about noone and dyned on bord us. This evening his Maj^{ty} and Duke of Yorke tooke there leave of us and went in ther yachts to London.

13. This Fryday the wind blew hard at E.N.E^t. This day we were falcely allarum'd by the Holmes frig^{tt} comeing up from the Gunflet wth topgalant sails flying and fired gunns, uppon a certaine, or rather uncertaine, intelligence that 19 or 20 saile of Dutch men of warr were seene w^{t}hout the Gallaper. All this day it hath blowne very hard, wth some raine.

14. This Satuarday morneing, about 5 aclock, his Highnes Prince Rupert went up the river in our barge for Black Heath. The wind at S.E^t. This day Sr John Harman, upon the receipt of a packet from Whitehall, called a councill of warr. There ordered to send downe 7 or 8 frig^{tts} and as many fireships, to ride twixt the Oase Edge and Redd Sand,[a] and the rest to birth themselves N.N.E. and S.S.W. one of each other, at ye Nore.

15. This Sonday the wind hath bine from north to W.S.W.; little wind till evening. It then blew hard, westerly. This day we had intelligence, by a Hellicar land[b] dogger, that 17 saile of Dutch men of warr were rideing without the Gonflitt. Yesterday he was on bord them.

16. This Monday the wind hath bine at W^t. bloweing fresh. Towards evening the wind came to the S.S.W^t. This day I sent up the Barbabella wth our empty caske to London. Tookeing (*sic*) aship of beere about 60 ts.

17. This Tuesday wind at S.E.; faire weather; I sent Bassets hoy up to Chatham againe for stores.

18. This Wednesday morning wind at south and S.E^t. I went into ye Swale, to setle our muster booke of the R. Charles.

19. This Thursday wind at north and N.W^t.; some tyme badd weather.

20. This Fryday we tooke on bord 16 ts. of watter. The wind

---

[a] The Red Sand lies between the Ooze Edge and the Middle Ground.
[b] Heligoland.

hath bine at north and back to W.S.W^t.; sometymes badd weather.

21. This Satuarday the wind at S.W. In the afternoone the Prince returned on bord againe.

22. This Sonday wind southerly. The Prince went into Sheerenes.

23. This Monday wind at S.S.W. to W.N.W^t.; sometymes bad weather. This day ye Prince went on shore on Essex side; came on bord againe at noone. This day severall of our fleet came out Sheerenes.

29. To this Sonday we have had the winds southerly to the west; some 3 days badd weather. Have bine dispatching our ships out Sheerenes, and takeing in our provisions. The Dutch fleet rideing in the Slade Way and at the Gonflitt since Wedensday. This night his Highnes ye Prince lay on bord the Monmouth yacht.

NAVAL OPERATIONS, 1652—1673; WITH OBSERVATIONS BY CAPTAIN RICHARD HADDOCK.

Year.	Mo.	D.		Observations.
1652	June[a]	19	Fight in Downes between English and Dutch.	Genl Blake comanded. Fight to the w^{t}ward off Dover.
	Sept.	5	French fleet beat by English.	Genl Blake comanded.
	Nov.	15[b]	Blake worsted by Dutch.	True; and retired to the Buoy of the Nore over the Flats.
	Feb.	18, 19, 20	Fight near Portland. Dutch beaten.	True. Blake, Deane, and Monck. Genl Blake and Deane in the Tryumph; Monk in the Vanguard. Blake wounded.
			English worsted in Levant by Dutch.	True. Capt R^d Balilo comanded.

[a] A mistake for May.
[b] On the 29th November. It was after this action that Van Tromp hoisted the broom at his mast-head.

NAVAL OPERATIONS, 1652-1673—*continued*.

Year.	Mo.	D.		Observations.
1652	June	——[a]	Dutch beaten.	Deane and Monk Gen[ls]. Deane killed.
'53	July	29, 30	Fight between English and Dutch.[b]	True. Dutch beaten. Gen[l] Monk only comanded. Trump killed, and his flag shot down.
'64	Dec.	30[c]	Fleet off Portsmouth took 112 Dutch prizes,	True. Brought into Portsm° and afterwards made prizes.
'65	Apr[l]	20	De Ruyter attempted Berbadoes; and beaten.	True.
	May	30	Hamburgh fleet taken by Dutch.	True. Were taken with their convoy.
	June	3	Dutch beaten by y[e] Duke, and 30 capit[l] ships taken and destroyed.	True. Opdam then blown up; the rest taken and burnt.
	Aug.	16	Dutch Smerna Streights East India ships attacqu'd by R[r] Adm[l] Tiddiman[d] in Bergen.	True; and was forced away by the Danes and Dutch, who landed ther gnns, contrary to the concert between the two Crowns of England and Denmark.[e]
	Sept.	1	2 East India and sev[l] merch[t] ships taken by E. of Sandwich.	True ; and two men-of-war then taken by Sprag in the R[l] James, formerly called the Richard.
	,,	9	18 s[l] of Dutch beaten, and greatest part taken	True.
	Feb.	8	Dutch chas'd into Weilings by Myngs[f]	True.
'66	June	1	Duke Albem[a] engaged 90 s[l] of Dutch on coast of Flanders.	Fought 3 days. Then came Prince Rupert in the R[l] James, wth the squadron w[ch] had been to the westw[d] to look out for Beaufort from Toulon. Were sent for back. Y[e] 3[d] day, Sonday, on our retreat, the R[l] Prince was lost on the Galliper; set on

    [a] On the 2nd and 3rd June, off the North Foreland.
    [b] Off the Dutch coast.
    [c] Before declaration of war, in retaliation for attacks by the Dutch on the colonies.
    [d] Sir Thomas Tiddiman, or Teddiman.
    [e] The Governor of Bergen not having yet received the instructions from his Government and refusing to admit the English fleet.
    [f] Sir Christopher Mings ; died of wounds received in the action of 1st June.

NAVAL OPERATIONS, 1652-1673—*continued*.

Year.	Mo.	D.		O^bservations.
1666	June	4, 5, 6	Dutch beaten.	fire. The Swiftsure taken by the Dutch. The 4th day both fleets retird : Prince Rupert and Duke of Albemarle to the Nore, the Dutch to their own coast.
,,	July	25, 26	Dutch beaten by Prince Rupert and D^k Albemarle.	The Dutch run home to their harbours.
,,	Aug^t	7	Sr R^t Holmes burnt 150 Dutch in ye Fly.	True. .Sr R^t Holmes went in the Tyger wth the Dragon and some fireships and ketches. Burnt 3 men of war that were in the Fly amongst the number. Afterwards burnt the town of Brandros^a before he went out.
,,	Dec.	25	Robinson^b took and destroyed 3 Dutch men of warr near ye Texell.	True. It was in his return from Gottenburgh, whither he was sent to convoy home a great fleet laden with naval stores.
1667	April	30	Dutch attempted Burnt Isleand in Scotland and beaten of.	True, I beleive.
,,	June	11^c	12 Dutch taken and 2 sunck near Norway.	True.
,,	June	20	Rich Dutch East India ship, 74 guns, taken.	True. Taken by Sr Jeremy Smyth in his sayling about Scotland to Ireland.
,.	June	25	Sr Jno. Harman wth 16 Engl. men of warr engaged 30 French near Martinego ; burnt and destroyed most of them.	True.
,,		26	8 Dutch prizes with masts and deals taken.	True, I beleive.
,,	July	19	Dutch attempt^d Torbay, but beaten off.	True.
,,		23	23 Dutch make up ye Thames.	

^a Bandaris in the island of Schelling.
^b Sir Robert Robinson.
^c The day that the Dutch were in the Medway.

Naval Operations, 1652-1673—*continued.*

Year.	Mo.	D.		Observations.
1667	July	24	Fought by Spragg near ye Hope and retire.	True. He forc't 'em out of the River, after having burnt and taken 12 sayle of their fireships; and we lost but one of our 12. So forct them down the King's channel below the Middle,^a having but 6 men of war and 12 fireships. Sr Joseph Jordain came from Harwich in a smal man of war with sev^l colliers made fireships. We rode then at Lee Road.^b Dutch at the Nore. Wind blew hard easterly. Did no execution on the Dutch.
,,	Aug^t	3	De Ruyter attempts ye Virginia fleet.	True, bnt did no execution on y^m.
,,		24	Six Engl., cruiseing northw^d, fought a squadron of Dutch and took 3.	I beleive it true, but know not of it.
'71	May	10	10 Algerines burnt at Bugia by S^r Ed. Spragg.	True. The boom was first cut by Capt. Harman,^c that comanded the boats
,,	July	5	St Christoph^r restor'd by the French.	
'72	Mar.	14	Sr R^t Holmes fought ye Dutch refusing to strike.	True; but 'twas not for refusing to strike.
,,	May	28	Fight wth ye whole Dutch Fleet off Southwold bay.	True. In that fight the R^l James was burnt, after she had quitted herself of Brackel,^d a Dutch 70 gun ship, that lay athwort her hawse, which she took; and being disabled gave opportunity of a fireship clapping her aboard.
,,	Dec.	20	Tobago Island taken from ye Dutch.	True.

^a The Middle, a shoal off Foulness, between the West Swin and the East Swin or King's Channel.

^b Near the mouth of the Thames, off the village of Lee on the Essex side.

^c Thomas Harman.

^d Adrian Brackell, the captain of the Dutch man-of-war.

NAVAL OPERATIONS, 1652-1673—*continued*.

Year.	Mo.	D.		Observations.
'72	Dec.	31	St Hellena taken by ye Dutch.	True.
'73	May	6	St Hellena retaken by Capt. Monday.	True.
,,	May	28	Engl. Fleet engage ye Dutch and force them to retreat.	True. Fought in ye Schonvelt.
,,	June	4	2^d engagem^t wth ye Dutch on ye coast.	True. Fought ye Dutch on y^r coast, but stood over to our own all that battle. The next morn we tackt on the Dutch; but they stood away for their own coast; and we stood back and came to the Nore after 2 battles in eight days.
,,	Aug.	11	3^d victory against ye Dutch by Pr Rupert.	Fought the Dutch; but no great victory. The French declined fighting, and fleet retired to the Nore some time after. Sr Edwd Sprag then drownd. R^l Prince's mainm^t shot down; had like to have been burnt.

WILLIAM BRANDON TO SIR RICHARD HADDOCK.

Portsm^o Victuall^s Office,
July 24th, 1688.

Honble S^r,

The last post brought a news letter to this place, wherein are these words: It is reported that Sr Richd Haddock, Capt. Pennyman, and severall other seamen, are gone for Holland; wch are lookt upon heere as a verry greate reflection upon your Hon^r, that cannott without ingratitude and breach of duty omit acquainting you with itt and the author's name, wch is Edmond Sawkell, att the Generall Post Office. I have and shall vindicate your Hon{r} to my outmost power; and begg leave to subscribe myself

Yor Hon{rs}
Most humble and obedient servt,
Wm BRANDON.

To the Honble Sr Richd Haddock, Kn{t}, one of the Comm{rs} for Victualling his Maj{ty} Navy, att the office on Tower Hill, London, These.

SIR RICHARD HADDOCK TO PHILIP FROWD.[a]

Tower Hill, London, this 29th July, 1688.

Sr,

The last weeke, in a news lett{r} wrote by a servt of yours, one Mr. Edm{d} Sawkell, there is a scandallous reflection on my hon{r} and reputation, by his writeing that Sr R{d} Haddock wth seuerall other seamen were gone into Holland, wch I have recd a{cct} of sd letter from 3 or 4 countys, and must beleive it hath flowne all the kingdome over.

Sr, I was this day to waite on you at yr post ofice; but, haveing acct given me that you were in the country, thought fitt, before I spake wth Mr. Sawkill, to give you notice hereof, and yt you will readylie conclude I shall expect satisfaction from him for this scandall, at least yt he finds out his author or else must conclud him to be the inventor himselfe. I do presume you know me so well as to beleive, however the King may please to deale wth me (wch hetherto hath bine extra kind), I shall never forsake my loyalty and duty to him, even to my last breath. Praying a lyne or two in answer, with great respect, I remaine

Your very afect{e} servant,
R{d} H.

To JN. (*sic*) FROWD, ESQ.

---

[a] Postmaster-General.

CAPTAIN JOSEPH HADDOCK TO HIS BROTHER,
SIR RICHARD HADDOCK.

Abord the Ship Princess of Denmark,
17th Xher, 1688. Balasore Roade.

Sr RICH^d HADDOCK.

MY EVER HON^d BROTHER,

My last, of the 7th Augt from Visagapatam, gave yor Hon^r acct of our arrivall Madras and of our affaires to that tyme. The 10th Augt we saild thence for Balasore, wher we arriv'd the 15th; in wch bay we have cont^d and rid out the monsoone, wch has prov'd favourabler then expected (beinge leape yeare).

The 15th 7ber Capt Heath arriv'd this place, who, by virtue of the President and Counsell of Madras order requir'd my goeinge up wth hime to Chuttynutte^a in the river of Hugly (the place where our Agent and factorie resided), myselfe wth the rest of the comand^{rs} of the Europe Shipps then in the river to assist hime in the R^t Honble Comp^s affairs.^{b} In fews days after our getting up to Chuttynutte, a letter was writ to the Nabob of Dacca (the cheife goven^r of that citty), who had formerly requested our Agent that if we would assist hime wth ships to transport soulders and horss from Chottagam to Arraccan (they beinge in warrs wth that Kinge), he would give us his Pharwanna^c of a settlem^t of trade, wth prevaledges as formerly accordinge to the 12 articles formerly sent hime from our agent &c. Capt. Heath, in the letter sent, condesended to

^{a} Chuttanuttee, now Calcutta.

^{b} Early in 1686 the Company fitted out an expedition to retaliate on the Nawab of Bengal for past injuries, and to attempt to seize Chittagong. But before the arrival of the forces a premature quarrel with the natives forced the English to abandon Hoogly and retire to Chuttanuttee. In Sept. 1687, a truce was patched up, but the Company was not satisfied. An armament was despatched under command of Heath. The result was the attack on Balasore, as told in this letter, an abortive attempt on Chittagong, and the abandonment of the Company's factories in Bengal.—See Mill's *Hist. of British India*, book i. chap. v.

^{c} Farwana, the licence granted by a viceroy; as distinguished from a firman, granted by a sovereign.

the Nabob's request, in suplyinge hime wth 10 ships and vessells for the Mogull's occations, to transport ther soulders and horss, provided they would allow of the buildinge of a fortyfiction w^thin the river of Hugly, for the better security of the R^t Honble Comp^s estate and ser^ts; w^thout wch grant of a fortyfied place the Comp^s ord^rs possitive are, to w^thdraw off all our factory from this place.

We continued heere 5 weeks for the Nabob's answer to the proposall: but not comeing, we, haveinge taken off all the Honble Comp^s concernes from the shoare, saild from Chuttyn^ty the 8th 9ber, and passed by ther fortts peaceably. At our arrival Balasore found that the goven^r of the towne had (some tyme before our comeinge) detaind the R^t Honble Comp^s goods, beinge this yeares investm^ts, alsoe partic. mens goods; and would not permit none of the factors, nor our people that were ashoure buying provit[ions], to come off. Capt Heath sent 2 of our factors wth a letter to the goven^r (who was come downe to the bancksall, or point of sand goeinge into the river, wher he was makeinge a fortyfication), to demand the R^t Honb^e Comp^s goods wth all our men. His answer was, what he did was by order from the Nabob; and, if he did dilliver our goods and men, should loose his head. 3 days after, 2 of the factors were againe sent to aquaint the goven^r that our intention was to depart out these parts peaceable, we haveinge come away out Hugly river w^thout doeinge any act of hostillity to any of the Mogull's subjects; therfore requir'd hime to send off our goods and people by faire meanes; if not, we would have them by force of armes. W^ch hee not permitting them too goe off, the next day all our soulders, about 320, and upwards 240 seamen were put into the small vessels and all our boates; and early next morninge they landed a mile to the W.ward of the fort (wch the govn^r had rais'd); against wch landinge place they had planted 5 small guns on a sandhill, wch they discharg'd at our men, and killd 2 and wounded 2 more; soe fled from the guns. And soone after, the cheife capt of our soulders had drawne all the soulders and seamen in order of battalia, marcht up to the fort, w^ch, at ther aproach, fired all ther guns they had planted to the land; but, soone after, the goven^r and all his men fleed out the fort w^thout doeing much harme to our men; the wch we possest w^thout any farther opposition. In and about this fort they had upwards 40 guns mounted and a good wall made wth timber and clay; might have bine sufficient (if manag'd by Europeans) to [have] wth stood a great armie of men, or at least done much more mischief then they did.

The goven^r, after deserted his fort, made all hast possable up to Balasore towne, and orderd the factory house (in wch were confind all our people, thirteene in number) to be sett on fire. Our people in the house defended themselves bravely, killinge sev^l of the Moors; but by the firsness of the fire were forct to surrender themselves on tearmes to have ther lives and good useage. The next day Capt. Heath (who went ashoare wth the soulders—Capt Sharpe comanded the small vessells and boates that were to goe over the barr, leaveinge mee in comand of the ships in the roade) went up with all the soulders and seamen to Balasore towne by watter and landed short of old Balasore fort, the wch they soone tooke; soe marcht into the towne, few or noe people beinge left to oppose them; the goven^r disertinge it at ther comeinge, caryinge wth hime all our English, amongst wch are 3 of our ships comp^a, vizt. Mr. Davenant (beinge ashoare buyinge provit[ions]),Charles Scarlet, midshipman, and Sam Harbin, gun^r, sert of Cap^n Heath's, his pursur, and 3 more, Mr. Stanly, cheife of the factory, the rest free men that trades in the country. As yet we cannot gett the goven^r to give ther releasem^t. We have sent sev^l messingers to hime, that we have not burnt ther towne nor ships, expecting he would dilliver up our men; but, if not, we will returne and doe both. Our soulders (but seamen more espetially) have comitted many inhuemane actions in the towne, plundringe not only Moors but sev^l Portugeese houses, and killed sev^l innocent people. We have had the greatest loss in this axtion, vizt. 4 men killd and 3 wcunded. Ther names are: Mr. Starland, 3d mate, Henry Grove, cheife trumpetter, Christopher Hogg, and Jn° Hinton, who very indiscreetly went out wth sev[l] more seamen to a garden house, expectinge great plunder, were cut off, sev[l] of them, by a party of horss. The 3 wounded are Hen[ry] Roxby, Fran[s] Johnson, and Jn[o] Smart

I have, by the Williamson (by whom this is alsoe intended you), sent S[r] Hen[ry] Johnson and S[r] Tho. Rawlinson, and alsoe to my wife, a list of our dead &c[a] men, in all 44. Our supernumery men w[ch] I brought out of. England, beinge 27, at my arivall Madras, I aquaintd the President therw[th], who offred them to Cap. Bromwell, the Rotchester haveinge lost most of ther men. But he refuseinge to pay the charge the Hon[ble] Comp[a] were at sendinge them out, they were not taken out ther; and what of them that are alive doe still remaine in our ship, not beinge demanded here by the agent. I supose our owners will be alowed for them at 50[s] per m[o], noe longer then our departure Madras, to w[ch] tyme we had lost 30 men. I doe not repent ther continueinge abord, haveinge had soe great mortolaty and most of them the best of our seamen.

I supose our next enterprize will be towards Chottagam, a place neere the coast of Arraccan. The R[t] Hon[ble] Comp[a] possative orders are for endeavouringe the takinge it; but I feare we shall not have strength sufficient to effect it, the Nabob haveinge sent many thousand of [men] this yeare ther to over run and take the kingdome of Arracan. The king of that country beinge some tyme since dead, part of the people are in rebelion against the present goverm[t]; by wh[ch] its supos'd the Mogullers will goe farr in takeinge that country this yeare, and we frustrated of our designe.

Hon[ble] Sir, I have not writt to any of owners (except the 2 in charty party), beleivinge we shall returne to Madras before the Williamson sailes for England. Our ship is in a very good condition and very thite. I beleive our stay in India will be the extreme of our tyme, for at present noe prospect of a freight for Europe; and I feare the brave trade of Bengall will be lost, at wh[ch] the Dutch and French rejoyce, that this trade may wholy fall to them.

I have not elce to add; only please to present my duty, respects,

and love to all our deere relations and freinds. Thus, wth my due respects to yor selfe and my good lady sister, doe remaine,
    Honble S^r, yor affectionate bro. and
      Sert, whilst
            Jo^s Haddock.

S^r I rec^d yor letter, alsoe one from my wife sent per the Defence; and returne my humble thancks for it.

For the Honble Sr Richd Haddock, at his house on
  Tower Hill. Present. London.

P^r the Williamson,
  Capt. Ashby, Comand^r, D.G.

Richard Haddock[a] to his Father, Sir Richard Haddock.

         Aprill[b] ye 23^d [1692]; Munday, in ye Hooke.[c]

Honourd S^r,

This is to acquaint of our ingaging wth ye French and of our haveing gott ye victory. Wee mett y^m of sea, May 19. There was about 60 saile. Wee fought y^m from 11 to 9 att night; since w^{ch}, have been in pursuit of y^m. There is run ashoare, in Sherbrook bay, Torveil[d] wth 3 more capitall ships, wch are now burned. Cozen Tom Heath[e] burnt Torveil; and have chased 14 saile more in ye Hooke, where wee now are. Sr Cloudsly Shovel is goeing in wth ye 3^d rates and fire-ships to destroy y^m. Wee have been soe un-

---

 [a] Afterwards Comptroller of the Navy. See Preface.
 [b] A slip of the pen for *May*.
 [c] "The Hooke" and "Sherbrook," nautical English for La Hogue and Cherbourg.
 [d] Tourville fought in the great three-decker "Royal Sun," the largest vessel afloat.
 [e] Afterwards captain of the Chester. Died in the West Indies in 1693.

CAMD. SOC.   G

fortunate as [to] lose Rear Adm^ll Carter^a in ye fight. I am very well and have received no wound; only a small splinter hitt mee on ye thigh, but did no damage, only made itt black and blew. I would write more particularly, but ye vessell I heare is goeing away presently; soe, haveing no more att present, butt duty to your self and my mother,

I remain your dutyfull Son,

RICH^d HADDOCK.

Cozen Ruffin is alive and very well. I will write ye particulars of our fight as soon as wee come into any port.

R^d H.

For Sr Richd Haddock, att ye Navy Office, in
Crutched Fryers, London.

ISABELLA CHICHELEY [b] TO SIR RICHARD HADDOCK.

Wedensday night, the 4 July, [16]94.

Your good nature, S^r, hath drawne upon you the gossupin of a company of women. My sisters desire we may drinke our punch with you to-morrow in the evening, about six aclocke, if it is not inconvenient to you. I should have sent to you to day, but was prevented. However, S^r, it may yett be ajorned for longer time, if you are othere wise disposed. The docters are sending me to Tunbridge ere long, soe that a warm foundation before drinking those cold waters will not [be] amisse for, S^r,

Your oblidged, humble servant,

ISABELLA CHICHELEY.

For Sr Rich. Haddocke, These.

---

[a] " Carter was the first who broke the French line. He was struck by a splinter of one of his own yard-arms, and fell dying on the deck. He would not let go his sword. 'Fight the ship,' were his last words; 'fight the ship as long as she can swim.' "—Macaulay, *Hist. of England*, chap. xviii.

[b] Probably related to Admiral Sir John Chicheley.

SIR RICHARD HADDOCK TO HIS SON RICHARD.

Navy Office, this 27th Nov^r, 1702.

DEARE SON,

I have yo^{rs} of yesterday's date, from the Downes, wch brings us the joyfull tydeings of yor safe arrivall there. Yo^r long passage from Newfoundland put us in great feare of your wellfare, and perticularly your mo^r hath bine for a month or 5 weekes crying for you and yor brother Nic^s safety; but blessed be God you are both come well home. Your bro^r now with us came up from the Downes by leave from his Captn, and hath behaved himself with so much bravery and couradge that he hath gained the good report of the Duke of Ormond, his Captn, &c., both in the action at Rotta and St. Mary Port,[a] and Vigo, and was the first man that borded one of the gallions at Vigo,[b] wch is come home. I do not find by yor letter that you were wth your Comodore at the takeing and destroying the French shipps to the southwards of Trepassa,[c] and consequently you will not come in for your share of that capture. The news papers tells us yor prize is got into Plym^o, and for your boate wth 5 men you say you left behind at Plym^o we never heard anything of it, wch gives you trouble; and because you write not of my Coz W$^{m's}$ [d] wellfare, I am conscernd for feare he might be in that boate. To morrow morning I intend to go to y^e Adm^{ty} and endeavor you may come into the River, if his R. Highness orders your cleaneing.

God Allmighty hath blest y^e forces of her Maj^{ty} and her Allies,

---

[a] In the expedition against Cadiz, the Duke of Ormond effected a landing at Rota at the north end of the Bay of Cadiz, on the 15th August, and occupied Puerto de Santa Maria, on the east of the Bay, six days afterwards.

[b] The attack on the shipping in Vigo took place on the 12th October.

[c] Trepassey, in Newfoundland.

[d] This is probably the William Haddock noticed by Charnock, *Biographia Navalis*, iv. 44, who died in 1726. He may have been the son of Richard Haddock, Sir Richard's uncle.

both by land and sea, in a wonderfull manner; for wch we lately had a publick day of thanksgiveing in this citty. The Queene, House of Lords and Comons, wth the Bishops, Judges, &c. came to St Paul's Church, where, after sermon, Te Deum was sung.

Since your leaveing England, two of our bord are dead, vizt. Mr. Sotherne and my good freind Com^r Willshaw,[a] who dyed ye 23^d Sepr last. My Coz Anna Babb, that was in one of our almes houses at Stepny, is likewise dead, and my poore Coz^n Lockwood's son in law, Coz^n Hodges, dyed lately at Gosport, since his arrivall from Cadix and Vigo, who waited a tender on ye Duke of Ormond's shipp. We are all in good health, praised be God, and do kindly salut you. I am your most afection^t father,

R^d HADDOCK.

Pray let me know how yor shipp proves. I have concernd my selfe to get one of ye 4th rates building at Deptford for you, and this day spake to Sr Geo. Rooke about it, and formerly to ye other 3 Councill of ye Lord High Adm^ll. I know she is tender by your reifeing your courses; and twas well hinted in yours to ye Adm^ty. I am glad you past by Plym^o. Orders went thither some tyme since to cleane you and severall of yor consarts. R^d H.

On Her Majesty's Service. To Captn Richard Haddock, Comand^r of her Maj^ty Shipp the Reserve, these present, In ye Downes.

THE SAME TO THE SAME.

Navy Office, this 10th Decemb^r, 1703.

MY DEARE SON,

Your letter of the 17th Novr past, giveing me acct of the unhapy disaster of your ship being run ashore by a Dutch pilot and of your happy getting off againe, I rec^d 3 or 4 ds. after its date; but, hope-

[a] Thomas Willshaw, Commissioner of the Navy and Master of the Trinity House.

ing you might have gote away before an answer could arrive you, I forbore answering it to you to Helvoet Sluce. I have just now rec^d yours of the 7th instant, Tuesday, and, to our great joy, the acc^t of God Almighty's wonderfull preservation of you in the late most dreadfull storm,^{a} wch no man liveing can remember the like. I perseave you have had an acct of the most sad and lamentable efects of it heere in England, not only in the losse of our shipp[ing], but about 1500 men in the Queen's shipps. I shall not eneumerate ye perticulars of the losse, only that Capt. Emes,^{b} wth his wife and son and all ye men in ye Restauration, lost on ye Goodwin, and poore Tom Blake drowned at Bristoll in ye Canterbury store ship cast away. The Dorcetshire we have acct of her being on ye back of Yarm^o Sands, cruseing, I supose for want of anchors and cables, and hope ye Association is cruseing in the sea on the like occasion. My deare son Nic^o hapend to be sick on bord her, as Sr S. Fairebone^b wrote me from the Downes. I sent Tom Apleby imediatly to Deale to bring him up; but the ship sailed ye morning before he gote downe. I hope he will come well home to us. Pray God the Russell may be got of ye sands and into Helvoet Sluce.

Wee haue 7 or 8 vessells wth anchors and cables in Harw^{ch} or Oasely bay, ready to put to sea when we heare where Sr Stafford is. Sr Cloud. Shovell I hope now safe at the Nore; his mainemast cut downe after he had drove 3 leag^s from ye Longs^d, very neare the Galloper. Y^e St Geo. and R. Oake, now at Blackstakes, rode out ye storme wthout damage; and the Cambridge I beleive the same. The 4 ships that broke from their ground takle was the Association, Russell, Revenge, and Dorcetshire. The Revenge was in Solebay some tyme since, and furnish wth anchors and cables from ye Nottingham and another man of warr y^t went out Yarm^o roads to looke for our shipps. Capt. Kerr^d in ye Revenge gave acct that he saw

---

^{a} On the 26th November.　　　　　^{b} Fleetwood Emms.
^{c} Sir Stafford Fairborne, Vice-Admiral of the Red.
^{d} William Kerr. Dismissed the service, in 1708, for joining in a contraband trade with the enemy.

ye Association, Monday last was sevenight; so that we are in hope she is very well. I shall not inlarge, only to give you our kind saluts. Pray God send you wth ye King of Spaine well out that place and over to us. My harty and humble service to Sr Geo: Rooke.

I am your most afec^t father,
R. H.

Captain Edward Whitaker[a] to Sir Richard Haddock.

Dated on board her Maj^{ties} ship Dorsetshire,
in Gibralter Bay, July ye 29th [1704].

S^r,

I heare give you an accot of our good success, especially what has related to my own particular part. July 21st we anchor'd here in ye Bay, and about 4 in the afternoon landed about 2000 marrines, Dutch and all. I commanded ye landing with three captaines more; all which was don wth little opposition. About 40 horse came downe from ye towne, wch was all; and they run away soe soon as our guns began to play upon them. We landed about 2 miles from the towne, in ye Bay, and march'd directly to the foot of the hill, were they posted themselves within muskett shott of the gates; so cutt of all manner of communication from ye land. We hove into ye towne this evening about 17 shells. The Prince of Hess[b] landed with us and immediatly sent a summons to the Governer, wch did not returne any answer tell the next morning, and then the Governer said he would defend the towne to the very last. Then Admirall Byng, who commanded the cannonading, began to draw up all his ships in a line before the towne; but, it proving little wind, could not gett in with them all, so

---

[a] Afterwards knighted and Rear-Admiral. This letter has been printed by Charnock in his *Biographia Navalis;* but it is worth re-printing.

[b] George, Prince of Hesse-Darmstadt.

that we did little this day. There was three small ships in the old mold, one of which annoy'd our camp by fireing amongst them, having about 10 guns lying close in the mold and just under a great bastion at ye north corner of the towne. I proposed to Sr George [a] the burning her in the night. He liked itt; accordingly ordered what boats I would have to my assistance; and about 12 at night I did it effectually, wth the loss of but one man and 5 or 6 wounded.

July 23rd. At 4 this morning, Adm^l Byng began with his ships to cannonade, a Dutch Rear Adm^l with 5 or 6 ships of theirs along with him; which made a noble noise, being within half shot of the towne. My ship not being upon service, I desired Sr George to make me his aducon to carry his comands from tyme to tyme to admirall Byng, which he did accordingly; and after about 2 hours continuall fireing sent me with orders to forbare. Upon this I went to every ship in the line wth this orders, and coming on board Capt. Jumper,[b] in ye Lenox, found him extraordinary well posted within muskett shott of the new mold head, and had beat them all out of ye battery and of the mold, so that I beleived we might attack it with our boats. I went immediatly and acquainted Adm^l Byng wth it, who ordered all the boats to be man'd and arm'd. From him I went to Sr George and gave him my oppinion that the mold might be attack'd. He immediatly made the signall for all the boates in ye fleet, and gave me the command of ye attack, wth 3 or 4 captaines along wth me. I made all the hast I could with orders to Admirall Byng to send me accordingly; but some of the boats got ashore before I could reach them, wth little or no opposition. Severall of our men gott into ye Castle; upon which it blew up. We had kill'd between 40 and 50 men. Most of all the boates that landed first were sunk; about 100 or two wounded; upon which, all y^t remain'd came running downe and leap'd into the water, being so mightyly surprized. I landed within a minute

---

[a] Rooke.
[b] Afterwards Sir William Jumper, Commissioner of the Navy.

after the accident, and rallied our men. We went over a breach in the wall but one at a time, and took possesstion of the hill. I immediatly sent Capt. Roffy[a] and Capt. Acton,[b] wth between 40 and 50 men, and took possesstion of a bastion of 8 guns within less then half muskett shott of the towne wall; and there we pitch'd our collours. Soon after, Adm^l Byng came ashore to me and sent in a drumer wth a sommons, who returnd in about 2 hours wth a letter in answer that they would surrender the next day; wch they accordingly did. I beleive I had wth me, at the first onsett, between 2 and 300 men; but we grew in a very little time to neare 1000. This was the manner we took Gibralter, which I hope we shall maintaine.

I hope, S^r, youle excuse this trouble I give, butt, beleiving that every boddy here rights att this tyme uppon this occation, I could not forbeare giveing my very good friend Sr Ric^d this perticuler acc^{tt} of ye whole matter; which I dont doubt butt Capt. Haddock will give ye much ye same acco^{tt}. Pray please to favour my spouse with a line or two, feareing mine should miscarry. My most humble servis to my good lady and all y^r good family. I beg youle make use of this as farre as you shall think fitt, itt being a trew acco^{tt} of ye whole matter. I am

      Y^r most harty humble Ser^t and
       kinsman to serve, whilst
          Edwd Whitaker.

P.S. This is rite all in a hurry, so y^t I hope youle excuse me.

---

[a] Kerril or Kerrit Roffey.   [b] Edward Acton, killed in action in 1706.

NICHOLAS HADDOCK[a] TO HIS FATHER SIR RICHARD HADDOCK.

St George in Barcelona Road, this 1st of May, 1706, O.S.

Hon^d S^r,

This comes to you by the Faulcon pink, which is sent home express wth the good news of our releiving Barcelona in the greatest extremity. The French had made preparations for a generall assault that very day we came; and it must have been infallibly taken, had we not had the luckiest passage imaginable (being but five days from Lisbon to Cape Martin, where we joynd Sr Jno. Leake).

Saturday last in the morning, when were about 5 leagues to the w^{t}ward of Barcelona, my Lord Peterborow came of to the fleet wth twleve hund^d soldiers embarqued in felucas and boats, and in the afternoon got in and landed them, wth all the soldiers out of the transports and most of the marines of the fleet. We have now about nine thousand soldiers in the towne. The French army consisted at first of twenty thousand; four of w^{ch}, horse under the command of the Duke of Anjou.[b] Their loss during this seige is computed to be five [thousand] including a thousand sick and wounded they have left behind, when they raised the seige, wch was at twelve aclock last night. They have left 50 peices of brass cannon mounted and 15 mortars, and are now bound to Roussilion. They will find great difficultys on their march. The Miquelets,[c] being very numerous and all in arms, will destroy a great many of 'em before they get out of Catalonia, it being a close country. The French squadron before this place consisted of 26 saile, line of battle ships. They sailed the night before we came, having intelligence of us by their scouts. They were all the supply the army had for provisions, for the Catalans have not given them the least; nor could a man of 'em stirr from his tent a musquet shot out of the Camp but they killed him. We are now sending four ships with

---

[a] Afterwards Admiral.
[b] Philip V. of Spain.
[c] Irregulars of the militia of Catalonia.

6 hundred soldiers for Girone, to reinforce that garrison, lest the French should make any attempt on it, it lying in their way.

I hear there is an express come to Barcelona from my Lord Gallaway, giving an account of his being got to Toledo and on his march for Madrid. The lucky turn Providence has given to our affairs in these parts I suppose will be joyfull news in England; and this being the first certain acct you'l have, this long letter wont seem tedious.

I can expect no letters from you till Sr Clowdsly joyne us, and then do hope shall hear of your welfare and some good news in return of all this, which, with my duty to y^r self and mother and love to all friends, is from,

Hon^d Sir,
Y^r dutifull Son,
N^s HADDOCK.

P.S.—We have had an eclipse of the sun to-day; lasted above two hours, and for a quarter 'twas total and as dark as night. W^t it may portend, I leave to the learned. Our fleet consists of 50 saile in the line; 13 of w^{ch}, Dutch.

THE SAME TO THE SAME.

Alicant, this 31st of July, 1706.

HON^d S^r,

I have both y^r letters by Captn Delevall,[a] as also the butter and cheeses, for wch I returne you thanks. I'm glad to hear both my sisters are so well recovered by the Bath. Pray God continue their healths. Sunday last we took this place, attacking it by land and sea; and almost all the people of it are run up to the castle, wth the garrison, for protection. We assisted our army with 500 seamen. I have been ashore with 50 of our ship's company during

---

[a] George Delaval, of the Tilbury.

the seige; am very heartily fateigued, but very well in health. After we have got the castle, I hear the fleet will go for the Islands of Minorca and Majorca, and, after that, I hope home. If the St George should not do, intend asking Sr Jno Leake leave for my self.

I'm glad to hear the ship at Sheernes will be launcht so soon as March. I hope I'm pretty secure of her. I desire your excuse for this bad scrawle and blotted paper, but I write wth a pen made wth an old razor that I find in the house I'm quartered in. I have no more to say but my duty to y^r self and mother and love to all freinds in London and Mile end, and remaine,

Hon^d S^r,
Y^r dutifull Son,
N. HADDOCK.

P.S. This lett^r goes by the Rye.

To Sr Richd Haddock, at the Navy Office in
Crutched Fryars, London, these.

SIR RICHARD HADDOCK TO THE COMMISSIONERS OF THE ADMIRALTY.

25th July, 1709.

GENTLEMEN,

In the yeare 1672 I comanded as Captn of the Royall James, under the R^t Honble the Earle of Sandw^{ch}, in the Sowle Bay fight. The said shipp, after a vigorous defence, was burnt by the Dutch; in wch action I was wounded, the cure of wch cost me, in surgeons, apothicary, nurses, &c., betwext fower score and a hundred pounds. I have bine so remise and negligent as not to demaund satisfaction for my reimbursem^t. Do pray the favor of the bord I may have a bill made out, what you shall think convenient, haveing bine out of my mony now 36 ys. I likewise, in the yeare 1690 (being then one of the Com^{rs} for Victualling), was taken into custody at Portsm^o, and brought up a prisoner from thence by order of the then House of Comons, and remained as such a considerable tyme in ye hands of Mr. Topham, then sergant at armes to s^d house, under pretence of our poisoning the fleet then at sea (under com^d of Adm^ll Herbert, now Earle of Torrington), with gutts in our beere and gaules in our beefe;[a] and with great dificulty obtained to be bailed. I must not call it injustice in that august assembly, what they did to me; but it cost me about a hundred pounds to Mr. Topham for his fees, and to lawyers soliciting the House of Comons, wth expences of entertainment whilst in custody; for satisfaction of wch I presume the bord will not think fitt to allow me, except directed soe to doe by order of the Lord High Adm^ll, for wch shall make my aplication to him; but for my cure, I doubt not the favor and justice of the bord in ordering a bill to be made out.

I remain, Gent^n, yor very humble serv^t,

R^d. HADDOCK.

SIR RICHARD HADDOCK TO HIS GRANDSON.[b]

Clapham, 28th May, 1712, Wednesday.

DEARE GRANDSON,

I came yesterday to this place, and, according to my promise, do answer yours of 18th instant from Christ Colledge in Oxford.

It happens to be this day 40 years that I was burnt out of the Royall James in the Sole Bay fight against the Dutch. Am well pleased to find the efforts you intend to make yourselfe famous in Westminster Hall. It is like the saying of your Unckle Nich^s, who doubted not but to be as great as Sr Cloudesly Shovell was; and he pushes very faire for it. Your father and family went to Wakehurst

[a] Macaulay's "casks of meat which dogs would not touch, and barrels of beer which smelt worse than bilge water."—*Hist. of England*, ch. xiv.

[b] This must be a son of Sir Richard's daughter, who married a Mr. Lydell.

Satuarday last; tooke Betty and Fanny Clark[a] downe wth them; gote well thither. Yo^r Unckle Richard, the weeke past, hath bine very ill wth a feavor and ague, wch kept me from hence longer then I designed; is under the advice of Doctor Ratclif,[b] who gave me leave to come downe hither, promiseing his care of him; and was downe staires when came away.

With my harty prayers for yor health and wellfare, I am

Yo^r most afec^t grandfather,
R^d. H.

Captain Nicholas Haddock to his Wife.

Grafton at sea, about 10 leagues from Cape Passaro,
Aug. the 4th, 1718.

My Dr Fanny,

The Superbe being orderd from the fleet wth the Admirall's letters, I send this to tell you I am well.

Five days ago we had a battle wth the Spanish fleet off of Cape Passaro,[c] on the Island of Sicily, in wch severall of their ships were taken and some destroyd. The Grafton had her share in that action, and the Admirall has been pleased to make me great compliments on my behaviour that day. I shall soon be orderd to be refitted at Port Mahon, the ship requiring it. I had fifty men killd and wounded. Among the former was Lt Bramble, who was appointed by the intrest of Sir Cha. Wager. I'm sorry for him, he being a

---

[a] Children of another of Sir Richard's daughters, who married John Clarke, of Blake Hall, in Bobbingworth, co. Essex.

[b] No doubt Dr. John Radcliffe.

[c] On the 31st July, when Sir George Byng almost destroyed the Spanish fleet.

good officer. My Cousin Haddock[a] chased towards the shoar after part of the Spanish fleet, when they separated, wth 4 or 5 other ships whose signalls were made for that purpose, and they are not yet come into the fleet. However, I doubt not but he is well, the ships that they were sent after being of the smaller sort.

My d^r, pray send to Mrs. Harris to tell her her spouse is well.[b] He dined aboard me the day after the action; he was one of the ships engaged.

Just before we saild from Naples I received y^r letter, and am glad to hear y^{r}self and the little boy are well. I give my love to all freinds, and remaine, my d^r Fanny,

Y^r most affect husband,

N^s. HADDOCK.

THE SAME TO THE SAME.

Grafton, at Regio, Jan^{ry} the 19th, O.S., 171$\frac{8}{9}$.

MY DEAR SPOUSE,

I send this to tell you I am well. I believe, before this come to you, you will have heard of my having forced ashoar on Sicily a Spanish man of war of 70 guns, wch is overset and sunk. I rec^d some shot from her, but without much damage. My d^r, we are here at an anchor, in company wth the Kent, Roy^l Oake, and Rochester to block up Camock,[c] who is at Messina and will not venture out,

---

[a] Probably William Haddock. See above, p. 43, note [d]

[b] Captain Barrow Harris, of the Breda.

[c] George Cammock, the Spanish Rear-Admiral, who had taken refuge in Messina. He slipped out in a frigate, which however he had to abandon, and escaped by boat to land. He was an Irishman who had served with distinction in the English navy under Queen Anne, but had been dismissed on account of his Jacobite tendencies. He then entered the Spanish service; and it is said that, if the Spanish Admiral had followed his advice, the battle off Cape Passaro might have had a different result.

his squadron being much inferiour to us. By the news we receive from England, I conjecture Spain will soon be oblidgd to accept the terms proposed to 'em; after w[ch] I suppose the bigger ships will be orderd home, where I shall always be glad to be, whenever it consists wth my honour; for, indeed, my dear Fanny, I heartily love you.

Pray give my love to all freinds, and I remaine, my d[r],

Y[r] most affect. husband,

N[s]. HADDOCK.

P.S. This goes for Naples wth an express that Capt. Mathews[a] sends to the Adm[l], and from thence it will be forwarded to you.

N[s]. H.

[a] Thomas Mathews, afterwards Admiral, who commanded the blockading force.

INDEX

Acton, Edward, Captain: at the capture of Gibraltar, 48
Aumont, Antoine d', Marshal: attempt on Ostend, 5, 6

Babb, Anna: 44
Balasore: attacked by the English, 37-39
Barcelona: relief of, 49
Blake, Robert, Admiral: his last victory, 3
Blake, Thomas: 45
Bramble, Lieutenant: 53
Brandon, William: letter, 35
Bristol, George Digby, Earl of: 13
Burstow, William, Captain: 15
Byng, Sir George, Admiral: at the capture of Gibraltar, 46-48

Cammock, George, Spanish admiral: 54
Carter, Richard, Admiral: killed at La Hogue, 42
Charles II. of England: visits the fleet, 23, 24, 29
Chicheley, Isabella: letter, 42
Clarke, Elizabeth: 53
Clarke, Fanny: 53
Courtney, Francis, Captain: 21
Coventry, Sir William: 7
Cromwell, Oliver, Lord Protector: 2

Davenant, ——: 39
Deane, Anthony, Navy Commissioner: 21
Delaval, George, Captain: 50

Emms, Fleetwood, Captain: 45
Estrees, Jean d', Comte, Admiral: 23, 24

Fairborne, Sir Stafford, Admiral: 45
Finch, William, Captain: 20
Foules, Thomas, Captain: 20
Frowd, Philip, Postmaster: 36

Galway, Henry de Massue de Ruvigny, Earl of: 50

Gibraltar: its capture, 46-48
Goodlad, ——: 10, 11, 12, 14
Grove, Henry: 39

Haddock, Andrew: 2
Haddock, Elizabeth: letters to, 10, 12, 14, 19, 21
Haddock, Fanny or Frances: letters to, 53, 54
Haddock, Joseph, Captain: 11, 19, 21; letter from India, 37; at attack on Balasore, 37-39
Haddock, Lydia: 3
Haddock, Nicholas, Captain: at Vigo, 43; 45; letters, 49, 50, 53, 54; at Barcelona, 49; at Cape Passaro, 53; at Messina, 54
Haddock, Richard: 4, 13, 21; his gallantry, 19
Haddock, Sir Richard, Admiral: letters, 1, 3, 5, 6, 7, 10, 12, 14, 19, 21, 36, 43, 44, 51, 52; with squadron off Dunkirk, 3-7; declaration on the Dutch striking their flag, 9; serves against the Dutch, 10-31; account of the battle of Southwold Bay, 16-19; wounded, 18; journal, 22-31; observations on naval engagements, 31-35; reported desertion, 35, 36; claim for compensation, 51, 52
Haddock, Richard, Captain: 43, 44, 53; letter on the battle of La Hogue, 41-42
Haddock, William, Captain: letters to, 1, 3, 5, 6
Haddock, William: 3, 5, 43; at battle of Cape Passaro, 54
Hambliton [Hamilton?] Colonel: 22
Harbin, Samuel: 39
Harbord, Sir Charles, 18
Harman, Sir John, Admiral: 21, 30
Harris, Barrow, Captain: 54
Hayward, John, Captain: 21
Heath, Captain: attacks Balasore, 37-39
Heath, Thomas: gallantry at La Hogue, 41

CAMD. SOC. I

Hesse-Darmstadt, George, Prince of: at the capture of Gibraltar, 46
Hinton, John: 39
Hodges, Captain: 44
Hogg, Christopher: 39
Hogue, La: battle of, 41-42

Johnson, Francis: 40
Jordan, Sir Joseph, Admiral: his conduct at Southwold Bay, 17, 18
Jumper, William, Captain: at the capture of Gibraltar, 47

Kelsey, Thomas, Major-General: 1
Kerr, William, Captain: 45

Lane, Samuel: 15
Lydell, ——: 52

Mathews, Thomas, Captain: 55
Mayo, Thomas, Lieutenant: 18

Ossory, Thomas Butler, Earl of: 24
Ostend: attempt on, 5, 6

Passaro, Cape: battle of, 53
Pennyman, Captain: 35
Peterborough, Charles Mordaunt, Earl of: relieves Barcelona, 49
Philip V. of Spain: 49
Poole, Sir William, Captain: 14, 15, 16

Roffey, Kerril, Captain: 48
Rooke, Sir George, Admiral: 44, 45; at the capture of Gibraltar, 47
Roxby, Henry: 40
Rupert, Prince: 23, 24, 28, 30, 31; his actions with the Dutch, 19, 20, 26-28

Sadlington, Richard, Captain: 28
Sandwich, Edward Montague, Earl of, Admiral: commanding off Dunkirk, 5; at Southwold Bay, 16-19
Sawkell, Edmond: 35
Scarlet, Charles: 39
Sharpe, Captain: 39
Shovel, Sir Cloudesley, Admiral: at La Hogue, 41, 45
Smart, John: 40
Sotherne, ——: 44
Southwold, or Sole, Bay: battle of, 16-19
Stanier, Sir Richard, Admiral: 9
Stanley, ——, Factor at Balasore: 39
Starland, ——: 39
Storm of 1703: 45
Strickland, Sir Roger, Admiral: 22

Tempest, John, Captain: 20
Thanksgiving-day: 44
Topham, ——, Serjeant-at-Arms: 52
Trepassey, in Newfoundland: action off, 43
Trevanion, Richard, Captain: 20, 21

Wasey, ——, Captain: 19
Werden, Robert, Captain: 20, 21
Whitaker, Edward, Captain: account of the capture of Gibraltar, 46-48
White, Richard, Captain: 28
Willshaw, Thomas, Navy Commissioner: 44

York, James, Duke of: account of battle of Southwold Bay addressed to, 16-19; visits the fleet, 23, 24, 29
Young, Henry, Captain: 28

LETTERS

OF

RICHARD THOMPSON

TO

HENRY THOMPSON,

OF ESCRICK, CO. YORK.

EDITED BY

JAMES J. CARTWRIGHT M.A.,

TREASURER OF THE SOCIETY.

PRINTED FOR THE CAMDEN SOCIETY.

M.DCCC.LXXXIII.

PREFACE.

The few letters which follow came quite recently into the possession of the British Museum. But little introduction is needed to them. The Thompson family was a very prominent one in York in the seventeenth century, and some account of it is given by the late Mr. Robert Davies in his *Life of Marmaduke Rawdon*, printed by the Camden Society in 1863. Sir John Reresby, who must have known most members of it very well, speaks of some of them as " very anti-monarchical persons." Henry Thompson was elected for York city in the Parliament which met in March 1690, and was dissolved in October 1695. He was an ancestor of the present Lord Wenlock, whose seat is at Escrick.

LETTERS

OF

RICHARD THOMPSON TO HIS BROTHER HENRY

[Egerton MSS. 2429A.]

DEAREST BRO. [1684.]

Tho I have no business nor news to send you, yet write I must, if it be only to plague you for y^r silence; but (to confess a truth) I myself take a vast pleasure in this sort of entertainment; and this way of enjoying you by ye strength of imagination is ye only consolation left me, for ye want of ye reall enjoyment. And since my fancy runs low I shall supply ye defect of it by telling you 2 or 3 idle stories which fly about town. T'other day (then to fall upon ye matter) one Mr. Evelyn, son to ye virtuoso Evelyn, and Mr. Foster with another gentleman, were all in a certain musick club room, after having drunk to a great pitch, and it happen'd that one of 'em, finding himself dispos'd to be musicall, took up a violin and began to fumble upon it. Mr. Evelyn, having likewise an harmonious soul, was resolv'd to bear some part in ye musick, and, being able to do nothing else, kept time with a great heavy case knife y^t laid very conveniently for ye purpose upon ye table; ye other gentleman, Mr. Foster, while his camarades were in ye heat of action, chanc'd by ill luck to lay his finger on y^t part of ye table upon which his neighbour beat time, and whether it was y^t ye man's ill genius guided his hand or how it came about, adhuc sub judice est, but he cut ye poor finger of, with ye greatest dexterity imaginable, insomuch y^t ye surgeons do all admire ye man's address in nicking ye joint so critically. However its a bad wind y^t blows no body profitt, and this ill accident is likely to make work for ye lawyers, ye man y^t is maim'd designing to bring his action of assault and battery against his companion. We have every day actions of scandalum magnatum brought against some honest fellow or other; not long since there was one brought against Mr. Gelstrop, an apothecary, for speaking scandalous words agst ye Duke. Dick Nelthorp[a] had a false allarum given him, and was inform'd y^t ye action was against him, ye nearness of ye names raising ye mistake; but it put him in a horrible sweat and spoyl'd his sleep for one night, so y^t ye next morning he was for decamping and packing up his tools and away beyond sea; but ye next day, to his unspeakable joy, he was undeceiv'd, and so his voyage stopt. The report too of ye scandalum against Williams, ye quondam Speaker,[b] was founded upon a like mistake, for it is really agst Sr Trever Williams. Not long since a clergy-man came into a coffee house with some of his acquaintance, amongst whom was Poet Flatman.[c] Ye Levite told his friends of a design y^t he had to take a spouse, and desir'd each of 'em to give him somthing towards housekeeping, which their generosity made no scruple to doe; but knowing Mr. Flatman to be in a poeticall condition and y^t he had but very little of ye bona fortunae, as ye philosophers call it (quoth Mr. Slip), he only beg'd of him a motto for his wedding ring. Mr. Flatman cou'd not

---

[a] Richard Nelthorpe, a barrister, was implicated in the Rye House Plot, and afterwards in the Monmouth Rebellion.

[b] William Williams, recorder of Chester and member for that city, was elected Speaker in October 1680; and filled the same office during the short parliament which sat at Oxford in March 1681. He conducted the prosecution of the Seven Bishops. Sir Trevor Williams sat many years for Monmouthshire.

[c] Thomas Flatman, born about 1633, was educated at Winchester and New College, Oxford. His poems were printed in 1682. He died in 1688.

deny so reasonable a suit, and, knowing ye size of ye parson's abilities and being acquainted with ye dimensions of his spouse in future, he told ye pedagogue gentleman he wou'd supply him out of his friend Lilly, and so presented him with ye motto of Sus atque Sacerdos. Tom Rymer[a] is writing ye history of ye Barons' warrs; to this end he has rummag'd all ye libraries in town and ferreted all ye old manuscripts he cou'd lay his hands on. He is now gone to my Ld Stamford's in Leicestershire, who desired ye favour of his company, and promis'd him ye use of his own library (which is an excellent one) for ye carrying on his laudable design. I suppose you have seen ye lives of Plutarch, *i.e.* ye first volume of ye translation, to which is prefix'd an epistle to ye D. of Ormond by J. Dryden, which is ye most nauseous satyr y^t was ever penn'd, and they say ye Duke himself is extreamly offended with it, because he makes him an Irishman, whereas he was born in London; this nettles ye Duke devilishly, and I hope he may have ye grace to bring an action of scandalum ag^st him for't. We may expect ye next volume to be much better done than this. Dr. Sprat and T. Rymer have each of 'em a life in't. Sed quousque tandem, say you. Well, I'll abuse y^r patience no longer, and only add my sincere protestations of being all my life,

                Dear bro.
                Your most affect. bro. and humble serv^t,
                        R. THOMPSON.

My service pray to Philip.

Prince and Monsieur Gibson, Mun Waller, and ye rest, often remember you. I add nothing to my Ld Mayor, because I hope you are so kind as always to assure him of my respects whenever you see him.

---

[a] Thomas Rymer, afterwards the well-known historiographer royal, and editor of the *Fœdera*, was probably born at Yafforth, in the North Riding; he was educated at Northallerton and Sidney College, Cambridge. The most complete account of him is to be found in the preface to the first volume of the late Sir T. Duffus Hardy's *Syllabus* of the *Fœdera*, published in 1869.

If you please you may tell my Ld Mayor y^t Mr. Sacheverill talks of him in ye London coffee houses as of ye greatest heroe of ye age. It is no small thing to merit ye praises of a person who, tho' all people commended him to ye world's end, yet can never be commended enough. So vous avez[a] my Lord Mayor.

Twenty kisses to little Harry de ma part.

Pray write me word how my father do's, it is long since I heard of him.

For Henry Thompson, Esq.
    in Escrick, near York.

CARO MIO, [February, 1688-9.]

I did not write to you ye last post, because I had not then seen Tom Rym^r nor any man able to inform me tolerably of ye present state of affairs. I thought by this post to receiv light enough to give you som smal acount of afairs, but truly after having talk'd with several of my friends, I do not find my self in any condition to satisfie you. I do not send you ye adress nor ye K.'s answer, becaus you will certainly have 'em at ye Caffé houses. You will find ye K.'s speech to be extreamly gracious and not less handsom, and to my thinking ther is something in it, of ye manner of Dr. Burnet. You may suppose y^t upon so extraordinary a turn, all people can not be satisfied, ye Church of Engl: seem rather to comply outwardly then from ye heart, tho tis thought ther wil not be above two or three Bps. who wil refuse ye oaths. Ken and Ely are guess'd to be two of ye obstinate refusers. You know their characters.[b] Danby and Hallif: seem to be in great favour, tho' ther is an honest party y^t peck at 'em. It is not known who are of y^e

---

[a] *Sic.*

[b] Ken, Bishop of Bath and Wells, and Turner, Bishop of Ely, were both deprived of their bishoprics for declining the oath of allegiance.

K.'s Cabinet—Benting[a] is ye premier favourite, tho' his parts seem to be rather solid than fine. I believe ye K. himself has ye best head; he is close, says little, hears all, and whether you tell him things agreable, or disagreable, preservs ye same meen. Matters are carried with deep secrecy, and in al apearance they can not miscarry under so great a King. My Lord Churchil, and Kirk, were not look'd upon with a very good eye, so ye first is to be sent a cõmander into Holland, ye 2^d into Ireland. The parliam^t seems to proceed slowly. Dr. Burnet is Bp. of Salisbury, and perhaps wil be remov'd to Durham. Bob Sawyer[b] has retir'd himself upon ye enquiry's made by ye Committee of grievances. Tom Rymer and I drank y^r health this afternoon. Y^e little burgess has sent for me, so I am forc't to cut short. My service to my sister, &c., to Ned, and al ye fox-hunters.

For Henry Thompson, Esqre,
    at Escrick, near York.

CARO MIO, [March or April, 1689.]

* * * * * *

Y^e Parliam^t men know nothing, and our brave esprits—T. Rymer, Dr. Blackmore,[c] &c.—with whom last night I drank y^r health, are al in ye dark. The K. seems to be complaisant to al parties, espouses no faction, which is ye reason why no one sett of men admire him. He has reason. The Bp. of Lond. [Compton] has som stroak; he has put in, in one county, several Tory justices of ye peace, for

---

[a] William Bentinck, afterwards Earl and Duke of Portland.

[b] Sir Robert Sawyer, Knt. was member for Cambridge University. He had been Attorney-General, and at this time was attacked by the Whigs for his part in the trial and condemnation of Sir Thomas Armstrong. He died in 1692.

[c] Richard Blackmore, poet and physician, knighted by King William. He was a favourite butt of the satirists of that age, otherwise his writings would have been forgotten.

which ye Whigs let fly at him, but there may be a trick in't. It is a general complaint, y^t he and his family govern my Ld. Chamberlain (my Ld. Dorset). I am pleas'd with it. Thus much for publick news; I must now beg leave to talk with you of private. My Lady Calverley, who says she can't endure to see a person of my rank shut up in such a lowsy apartment, as I am at present confin'd to, has generously offer'd to lend me 200*l*. in order to buy me a chamber in ye Inn. There has accordingly fal'n out a convenience of one just under L. Agar, which I might be able to compass provided I cou'd find credit in ye world for ye borowing 150*l*. It wou'd be a fine establishment for my life, and ye chambers are always worth ye mony y^t is demanded for 'em.

For Henry Thompson, Esqr,
    At Escrick, near York.

CARO MIO, [April, 1689.]

I wonder I have not heard from you since I came to town, you are two letters in arrear to me. Our proceedings of parliam^t seem to be very slow. I don't send you ye votes of ye houses, becaus they are comõn, and you can not miss 'em at ye public houses. Ther are two or 3 of ye Bps. y^t stil hold out ag^st reason, and ye oaths, 'tis a wonder there are no more; Canterbury, Ely, Bath and Wels. The Bp. of Rochester [Sprat] has writ a handsom letter to justifie or excuse ye part he had in ye ecclesiactical comĩssion; he addresses ye letter to my Ld Dorset, it is printed, and I supose you may have it at York. Watson is likewise a dissenting Bp. A propos of him, I met last night ye University Oratour Billers,[a] with whom I had two hours conversation. I perceiv by him ye Cantabs are for ye most part disafected, they do not so much as pray for ye K. and Q.

[a] J. Billers, LL.B. of St. John's College, was elected public orator of Cambridge in 1681.

at St. Marie's. It is impossible this shou'd not be resented ill, so they are contriving an oath for al Clergymen to take, all ye refusers of which are to be turn'd out of their livings. A bill is brought down to reverse ye attainder of my Ld Russel. Soll. Finch made a speech in ye house, to satisfie y^{em} concerning ye part he acted in y^t tragedy, but ye harangue was ill relish'd. My L^d De la Mere has writ observations upon my Ld Russels tryal, but I fear they are of no great force; however 'tis sure he is full of indignation agst ye family of ye Notingham's. 'Tis thought Notingham is in to gain ye Churchmen, but I doubt they will neither lead nor drive. For ye rest, matters go on calmly, and by consequence wisely, ye hot men speak ill of Benting, and for y^t reason I guess him a man of prudence. We have nothing to fear but too much eagernes. I find by Harry Trenchard, who is himself warm, y^t they are apt to overdo, they are for removing in an instant al ye old instruments to that purpose. Jack How[a] told em in ye hons y^t if in ye cobler's shop, ye same lasts, ye same tools were found, it was ye old cobler's shop stil; thus violent are they, they wou'd not leave so much as one last in ye shop. I have run my self out of breath, and wish you heartily a good night.

Y^{rs}

My service to al at home; Mr. Tailour, &c.
Tuesday.

For Henry Thompson, Esq.
    at Escrick, near York.

CARO MIO, [Dec. 1693?]

Quid cum illis agas, qui neque jus, neque aequum sciunt? said ye comœdian, before Deans and Chapters were instituted indeed, but having an eye without doubt upon their deanships in futurity. In

---

[a] M.P. for Cirencester, and vice-chamberlain to Queen Mary at this time, the "quick-witted, restless, and malignant politician," celebrated by Macaulay.

effect they are odd things to deal with. In answer to y^r letter, I think it proper enough to send you one I received from Mr. Rob: Squire, formerly by which you wil find ye Dean's demands run somthing higher then they did, and y^t there seems to be a change in ye church-measurs. Methinks when they talk of rents, or clear yearly value, they shou'd have som regard to what Tenants will, and do pay, as well as to what they ought to pay . . . . . .

My Lord Colchester,[a] who was thought to be taken by ye French, is safely arriv'd. T. Rymer is going to pursue his critique upon som mor of ye old celebrated plays, and to lay down further instructions for ye reformation of ye stage. Y^r Diocesan is preparing for his journey into Yorkshire. They say in town, ye poll-mony fals short of what was expected, ye tradesmen all swearing them selves off. I want to hear wh^t becoms of Scarb: elect. it makes a great noise here.[b] My service to every body.

Thursday.

For Henry Thompson, Esq.
    Member of Parliam^t,
        at Escrick, near York.

---

[a] Richard Savage, who succeeded his father in the Earldom of Rivers in 1694; father of the poet Savage.

[b] On 11 Dec. 1693, Viscount Irwin was returned for Scarborough in the place of Francis Thompson, deceased.

Agar, L. 6
Bentinck, afterwards Duke of Portland, 5, 7
Billers, J. public orator, 6
Blackmore, Dr. afterwards Sir Richard, 5
Burnet, Dr. 4, 5

Calverley, Lady, 6
Cambridge, feeling against William III. in, 6
Churchill, Lord, 5
Colchester, Lord, afterwards Earl Rivers, 8
Compton, Bishop, 5

Danby, Earl of, 4
Dorset, Lord Chamberlain, 6
Dryden, John, his epistle to Ormonde, 3
Delamere, Lord, 7

Evelyn, John, his son, anecdote of, 1

Finch, Solicitor-General, 7
Flatman, Thomas, the poet, 2; motto by, 3
Foster, Mr. accident to, 1

Gelstrop, Mr. an apothecary, 2
Gibson, Monsieur, 3

Halifax, Marquis of, Savile, 4
Howe, John, 7

Irwin, Viscount, 8, note

Ken, Bishop, 4, 6
Kirk, General, 5

Nelthorpe, Richard, the plotter, 2
Nottingham, Lord, 7

Ormonde, Duke of, and Dryden, 3

Rochester, Bishop of, Sprat, 6
Russell, Lord William, his trial, 7
Rymer, Thomas, his History of the Barons' Wars, 3; his dramatic criticisms, 8; other references to, 4, 5

Sacheverill, Mr. 4
Sprat, Dr. 3
Squire, Robert, 8
Stamford, Lord, his library, 3

Trenchard, Harry, 7
Turner, Bishop, 4, 6

Waller, Mun, 3
Watson, Bishop, 6
William III. his conduct and character, 4, 5
Williams, William, late Speaker, 2
Williams, Sir Trevor, 2

REPORT OF THE COUNCIL

OF

THE CAMDEN SOCIETY,

READ AT THE GENERAL MEETING

ON THE 2ND MAY, 1883.

The Council of the Camden Society has to regret the loss of two its Members—

EVELYN PHILIP SHIRLEY, Esq. M.A.

J. R. DANIEL-TYSSEN, Esq. F.S.A.

who have died during the past year, and of

HENRY HILL, Esq. F.S.A.

who had for many years acted in the most efficient manner as one of th Auditors to the Society, and who was at all times most helpful in givir advice on financial questions.

The Council has also to regret the loss by death of the followir Members:—

DECIMUS BURTON, Esq. F.S.A.
CHARLES CLARKE, Esq.
CHARLES HOPKINSON, Esq.
Rev. T. F. KNOX, D.D.
C. R. SCOTT MURRAY, Esq.

REPORT OF THE COUNCIL, 1883.

The following have been elected Members of the Society during th past year:—

SOUTH AUSTRALIAN INSTITUTE.
BALLIOL COLLEGE, OXFORD.
EDMUND BOYLE, Esq. F.S.A.
F. A. BROCKHAUS, Esq.
CHARLES HARDING FIRTH, Esq. M.A.
E. LEIGH GRANGE, Esq.
WM. H. HATTON, Esq.
WILLIAM KELLY, Esq. F.S.A., F.R.H.S.
R. BOWNAS MACKIE, Esq. M.P., F.S.A.
W. T. MARRIOTT, Esq.
Mr. S. J. MULLEN.
F. YORK POWELL, Esq.
SCHOOL LIBRARY, RUGBY.
ST. LOUIS MERCANTILE LIBRARY.
EDWARD SIMPSON, Esq.
Miss L. TOULMIN SMITH.
F. E. WHEELER, Esq.

In the last Report, the Council expressed a fear that, in consequence o financial pressure, it would be unable to issue to the subscribers of th years 1882-3 more than one book, the CATHOLICON ANGLICUM. For tunately, the financial situation cleared up as the year proceeded, and, i not before the Annual Meeting, the Members will very soon afterward have in their hands the eighth volume of the CAMDEN MISCELLANY These publications have always been favourably regarded, and the Counci trusts that, on this occasion, the matter furnished will be thought of a least equal interest to that given in any of the preceding volumes of thi Miscellany.

REPORT OF THE COUNCIL, 1883.

In the forthcoming year, unless unforeseen accidents occur, thre volumes will be published:—

1. The Official Narrative of the Cadiz Voyage in 1625. Edited by the Rev. A B. GROSART, D.D.
2. Gabriel Hervey's Note Book. Edited by E. SCOTT, Esq.
3. Selections from the Lauderdale Papers, Vol. I. Edited by OSMUND AIRY Esq.

Of these, the first gives a full account of an expedition in the reign o Charles I. the failure of which was attended with important politica results; the second throws light upon life in the University of Cambridg in the age of Elizabeth; whilst the third will illustrate the Restoration i Scotland, and clear up what has hitherto been a dark page of history Amongst other valuable information it will, it is hoped, set at rest con troversy on the character of Archbishop Sharpe.

The Council, in conclusion, would express a hope that the publication o these three volumes will be taken as evidence of their anxiety to throw light upon the history of the country, and will thereby induce some o those who take an interest in that history, and who are not yet subscribers to support them in the efforts which they are making.

By order of the Council,

SAMUEL RAWSON GARDINER, *Director.*
ALFRED KINGSTON, *Hon. Secretary.*

REPORT OF THE AUDITORS.

WE, the Auditors appointed to audit the Accounts of the Camden to the Society, that the Treasurer has exhibited to us an Account of t Expenditure from the 1st of April 1882 to the 31st of March 18 have examined the said accounts, with vouchers relating thereto, an to be correct and satisfactory.

And we further report that the following is an Abstract of th Expenditure during the period we have mentioned:—

RECEIPTS.	£	s.	d.	EXPENDITURE.
To Balance of last years' account...	119	15	11	Paid for Binding.............................
Received on account of Members whose Subscriptions were in arrear at last Audit, and on account of new Members' Subscriptions for preceding years......	67	0	0	Paid for Transcripts .... Paid for Miscellaneous Printing .... Paid for delivery and transmission of Bo paper for wrappers, warehousing expen cluding Insurance)..............................
The like on account of Subscriptions due on the 1st of May, 1882......	193	1	3	Paid for postages, collecting, country expense Paid for Advertising ....
The like on account of one Composition in lieu of Annual Subscription	10	0	0	
The like on account of Subscriptions due on the 1st of May, 1883......	13	1	0	
One year's dividend on £466 3 1 3 per Cent. Consols, standing in the names of the Trustees of the Society, deducting Income Tax..	13	12	3	
To Sale of Publications of past years..................................	22	4	0	
To Sale of the Medieval English-Latin Dictionary Promptorium Parvulorum (3 vols. in 1)	4	15	0	By Balance.—Bank Current A On Deposit......
	£443	9	5	

And we, the Auditors, further state, that the Treasurer has repo over and above the present balance of £382 16s. 6d. there are out subscriptions of Foreign Members, and of Members resident at London, which the Treasurer sees no reason to doubt will shortly be re

JAMES RA
WYNNE E.

DA   Camden Society, London
20   ₍Publications₎
C17
n.s.
no.31

PLEASE DO NOT REMOVE
CARDS OR SLIPS FROM THIS POCKET

UNIVERSITY OF TORONTO LIBRARY